TED STRONG IN
MONTANA

Or, With Lariat and Spur

EDWARD C. TAYLOR

1st WORLD
LIBRARY
Literary Society

Ted Strong in Montana

Edward C. Taylor

© 1st World Library, 2009
PO Box 2211
Fairfield, IA 52556
www.1stworldlibrary.com
First Edition

LCCN: 2009923388

Softcover ISBN: 978-1-4218-8826-2
Hardcover ISBN: 978-1-4218-8925-2
eBook ISBN: 978-1-4218-8727-2

Purchase *"Ted Strong in Montana"*
as a traditional bound book at:
www.1stWorldLibrary.com/purchase.asp?ISBN=978-1-4218-8826-2

1st World Library is a literary, educational organization
dedicated to:

- Creating a free internet library of downloadable ebooks

- Hosting writing competitions and offering book publishing scholarships.

Interested in more 1st World Library books? contact:
literacy@1stworldlibrary.com
Check us out at: www.1stworldlibrary.com

1ˢᵗ World Library Literary Society

Giving Back to the World

"If you want to work on the core problem, it's early school literacy."

- James Barksdale, former CEO of Netscape

"No skill is more crucial to the future of a child, or to a democratic and prosperous society, than literacy."

- Los Angeles Times

"Literacy... means far more than learning how to read and write... The aim is to transmit... knowledge and promote social participation."

- UNESCO

"Literacy is not a luxury, it is a right and a responsibility. If our world is to meet the challenges of the twenty-first century we must harness the energy and creativity of all our citizens."

- President Bill Clinton

"Parents should be encouraged to read to their children, and teachers should be equipped with all available techniques for teaching literacy, so the varying needs and capacities of individual kids can be taken into account."

- Hugh Mackay

CONTENTS

CHAPTER I

THE BIG SNOW

"We're going to have snow to-night!"

Ted Strong, leader of the broncho boys, was sitting on the back of Sultan, his noble little black stallion, on the ridge of a prairie swell, looking at a lowering sky.

Out of the northwest a chilling wind, damp and raw, was sweeping dull-gray clouds before it.

Ted had addressed his remark to Bud Morgan, his chum and able lieutenant, who threw a glance at the clouds and grunted.

"I reckon we be," he muttered, "an' I'm free ter say I'm dern sorry ter hear it."

"It's hard luck," resumed Ted. "If we had got away a week earlier, or hadn't been held up by the high water at Poplar Fork, we would have been at the ranch now, and settled for the winter."

"Thar's no telling whar an 'if' won't land yer sometimes. If we hadn't started we wouldn't hev been here at all. But here we aire, an' we'll hev ter git out o' it."

"Think we better push on, or make camp?" asked Ted.

"Got ter make camp fer ther night somewhere," answered Bud. "But I wisht ther storm hed held off till ter-morrer this time; we'd hev been within hootin' distance o' ther Long Tom Ranch."

"Suppose we push on a few hours more. We can camp down in the dark if we must. If the snow gets deep before ye reach the high ground you know what it means."

"I shore do. I wuz all through a big snow in this yere man's country a few years back, an' it wuz some fierce."

"All right. Ride back and drive them up. I'll point. We'll drive until it gets too dark. Tell the wagons to move up."

Bud wheeled his pony and dashed to the rear of the great herd of cattle that was coming on at a snail's pace.

The cattle were lowing uneasily. They knew even better than the men that a storm was coming, and they dreaded it.

This was the big Circle S herd which the broncho boys had bought in Texas in the spring of that year, and which they had herded and driven northward throughout the summer to winter on the Montana plateau, later to be driven to Moon Valley, and there put into condition for the market.

Various things had delayed the arrival of the herd on their winter grounds. A detention of several days at a time by flood, by a stampede, and by fights with rustlers, had brought the cattle several weeks late to their winter grounds.

Ted Strong had determined to try the experiment of wintering Southern cattle in the Montana country in order to harden them and improve the quality of the beef.

The broncho boys had a large order to fill for the government the following summer, and it was to accomplish their contract that they had bought the Texas cattle and driven them north to the Long Tom Ranch in northern Montana.

Now that they were within a few miles of it, and still on the low ground, it appeared that a big snow was inevitable, which might frustrate all their plans and cause them great loss.

But Ted Strong did not complain. It was a condition which he could not have foreseen, and, being close at hand, there was nothing for them to do but meet it with all the fortitude at their command.

Soon the herd began to move forward, being crowded by the broncho boys and the force of cow-punchers whom they had employed to assist them.

Stella Fosdick, who, with her aunt, Mrs. Walter Graham, had accompanied the boys on their drive, now came galloping up to Ted. She had been riding beside the carriage in which her aunt had been comfortably traveling.

"Going to keep on, Ted?" she asked.

"Yes. Got to do it. Those clouds are full of snow. If it catches us down here we're likely to be snowed in, and if we do it's all up with the Circle S," he replied.

"That's bad."

"Oh, I guess we'll pull through all right, if we can keep the cows moving; but it is not going to be very comfortable for your aunt or you. We'll have to drive until the cattle refuse to move farther."

"I can stand it, and aunt will have to. She's getting a little anxious, though, and asked me to ride ahead to learn when we're going to stop. Poor auntie likes her comfort. I often wonder why she became the wife of a ranchman."

"Or why she consents to traipse all over the country with you," laughed Ted.

"Ted, she absolutely cannot refuse me a thing."

"So I see. You've got her hypnotized—as, indeed, you have all the rest of us. But ride back and cheer her up all you can. I told McCall, the cook, to make some good, strong coffee and to serve it to any of the boys who wanted it, as it will be some time before we can have supper. Have Mac take her a cup of good, strong coffee and something to eat. That may make her a little more cheerful."

"I'll do it. But don't you want some coffee, too?"

"Not for me. I've got something else to do right here. This is going to be a race between the herd and the snow clouds, and it means a whole lot to us."

"Afraid of being snowed in?"

"You bet. If this bunch of cattle gets snowed in I see our finish. We'll lose half of them before we get to the grass."

"I don't know a thing about the Northern range, and I can't see how you're going to bring that herd through to spring. It would take thousands of tons of hay, and I don't know how much corn to feed them."

Ted laughed.

"I see you don't know much about the North," he said. "But what should a girl brought up in Texas know of wintering cattle in the snow? You see, it's this way: Montana is the best winter cattle range in the United States.

"The winds from the mountains sweep the snow, which is dry and loose, from the high, level ground, exposing the grass which has been cured on the ground, and which makes the best kind of feed. Then there is plenty of water, and the deep coulees, with which the country is cut up, afford ample protection for the cattle during storms.

"Occasionally there comes warm winds from the northwest. These are called chinook winds, because they come from the direction of the country of the Chinook Indians. They are warm and balmy, and melt the snow as if by magic. Their warmth is caused by having come in contact with the Japanese stream, which crosses the Pacific Ocean, after being warmed in the sunny East, and which strikes the shores of North America along about south Alaska. This stream is called by the Japanese, Kuro Siwo. It is the equivalent of the Gulf Stream, which leaves the Gulf of Mexico to cross the Atlantic and warm the shores of Great Britain."

"Quite a lecture," said Stella, laughing.

"I didn't mean to lecture," replied Ted, laughing also, "but I wanted you to know why it is that it is a good thing to winter cattle in this north country. In the first place it puts strength and stamina into the cattle, and makes the beef better, and all the conditions of which I have spoken make it possible to keep cattle on the open range out here, where one would think they would perish of cold and starvation. But it is no picnic to run a winter range, as we will all learn before spring comes again."

"I understand now, and I'm sure I shall enjoy the experience. But I must go back to aunt and jolly her up, for she is easily discouraged, and she is no more used to rough winters than I."

"She'll be all right when we get to Long Tom, for there is a bully ranch house there, and she'll be as snug as a bug in a rug when we get settled."

The cattle were going forward over the gentle, rising ground, being pushed by the punchers in the rear and the fellows on the side lines, while Ted and Kit were pointing them in the direction of a tall butte, which they could see in the distance, rising needlelike and black against the gray sky.

This was Long Tom Butte, after which the ranch, which Ted had leased, had been named.

Suddenly, Ted felt something wet on his cheek, and looked up. A snowflake, big and floating lazily down, had struck him.

Others followed it, and soon there were myriads of big, wet snowflakes falling slowly through the air.

The cattle began to hurry, and were lowing in a distressing way. Their instinct told them to seek shelter, and they were telling their drovers as much in their own fashion.

For a half hour the snow continued to come down, wet and soft.

Edward C. Taylor

But suddenly the wind changed in temperature. Before it had been raw and damp. Now it became sharp and frosty.

The snow changed quickly from heavy, wet flakes, to small, dry, sharp particles, which, driven by a strong wind, which had veered around into the north, stung the faces of the boys like needles, and worried the cattle, which seemed to want to lag in their pace.

"Kit, go back and tell the boys to keep pushing harder. The cattle want to stop, and if they quit now it's all up. There's a blizzard coming. If we can keep them at it an hour longer, we will be in the lee of the buttes, and there's a deep coulee into which we can drive and hold them until morning."

At Ted's command Kit dashed toward the rear, and repeated the order, and the cow-punchers rode into the herd with shouts and with active lashing of their quirts, and the beasts picked up their pace again and hurried forward through the snow, which had begun to whiten the ground.

Kit returned to Ted's side.

"What do you think of it?" he asked.

"If we had an hour more of daylight, I think we could make it," said Ted.

"Any doubt of it?"

"Well, when it becomes dark we'll lose sight of Long Tom, and we're likely to drift, because, unless the cattle are driven into the storm, they'll turn tail to it and go the other way."

"I can't see Long Tom now."

"I can, although the snow almost blots it out. There it is right in the northwest. I can just make it out. The herd is drifting south of it now. Better get over on your point, and head them up this way a bit."

Soon the herd was driving forward in the right direction again.

But suddenly the darkness came down like of pall of black smoke, shutting out everything, and the wind increased in violence, rising with a howl and a shriek like some enormous and terrible animal in rage.

"It's all off," said Ted to himself, with a sigh.

The cattle came to a stop.

"Keep them going!" shouted Ted, riding back frantically along the line.

The cow-punchers dashed among the animals, shouting and beating them with their quirts, and managed to get them started again, but it was only for a short time, for again they stopped, bellowing, the leaders milling and throwing everything into confusion.

"That settles it," shouted Ted to Bud. "They're going to drift all night if we don't stop them."

"Dern ther luck, I says," growled Bud. "How fur aire we from ther ranch?"

"The worst of it is we're right on it. The ranch house isn't more than three miles from here, and if we could have got there we would have been all right. By morning we may be ten miles away, if we let the herd drift, and we'll have a dickens of a time getting the brutes back through the snow."

"What aire we goin' ter do with the wimminfolks?"

"I'm going to try to get them to the ranch house. You boys will have to make a snow camp, and hold the herd from drifting at all odds. Don't let them sneak on you. Keep pushing them from the south. You see, they're all turned that way now with their tails to the wind. As soon as they get cold they will begin to move. Don't let 'em do it."

"All right, Ted. We'll do the best we can. You take care o' ther wimminfolks. So long, an' good luck."

Ted rode back to where Mrs. Graham was shivering in the closed wagon the boys had provided for her, and Stella was sitting her pony by her side, trying to encourage her.

Carl Schwartz was the jehu of the outfit, and sat on the driver's seat, a fair imitation of a snow man.

"Carl, get a move on you. We're going to try to make the Long Tom ranch house," said Ted. "I'll lead, and you follow. If you lose sight of me, yell to me and I'll come back. I've got my pocket searchlight, and will send you back a flash now and then."

Carl was half frozen and would have been pleased to get down and walk the rest of the distance, but he knew the danger that surrounded them, and simply yelled back "Yah!" and gathered up the reins for a start.

"Come on, Stella," said Ted. "We're going to try to make the ranch house."

Without a word Stella followed him, and the little caravan

struck into the teeth of the snow-laden wind, which was now blowing half a gale.

The wagon moved slowly through the snow, which was getting deeper every minute, and was like heavy sand.

Every few minutes Carl's voice could be heard, and Ted called back to him.

Ted was traveling entirely by instinct, for it was so dark that he could not see a foot in front of them.

So they struggled on for an hour, halting occasionally to give the horses a breathing spell, then drove obstinately forward again.

"We should have been at the ranch house long ago," shouted Ted at last, pulling in his panting horse.

"Then we're lost, I suppose," shouted Stella in return.

"Looks that way."

"What are you going to do?"

"Stop for the rest of the night."

"I wouldn't. Keep on until the horses won't go any farther."

"All right, if you think best."

On they went again for a half hour more, and Ted was beginning to believe it was folly to go any farther when his pony stumbled and almost fell.

In front of them loomed a darkness more intense than before.

Edward C. Taylor

Ted scrambled from the back of his pony and led it forward. The pony had stumbled over the horse block at the very door of the Long Tom ranch house.

CHAPTER II

THE LONG TOM RANCH

Ted and Stella raised such a shout that Carl pulled his horses up just in time to keep them from trying to climb upon the veranda.

With the aid of his searchlight Ted had found the door and entered the house, followed by Stella.

In the big, front living room they found a lamp, which they lighted and looked around.

The house had been left ready for occupancy, and in the great, wide fireplace logs were piled high ready to be burned.

In a moment Ted had a fire leaping high up the chimney, then hastened out to the carriage.

Carl had scrambled down from the seat of the carriage, and was so cold and numb that he couldn't walk, while Mrs. Graham had to be carried into the house by Ted and placed before the fire to thaw out.

Soon the room was comfortable, and Ted, who had set out on a tour of inspection, found that the kitchen was well stored with food.

He started a fire, and soon had coffee and bacon cooking.

Outside the storm continued to rage through the night, but all within was tight and warm, and Stella and her aunt retired to their comfortable bedrooms. But Ted sat up through the night.

He had considered starting back through the storm to the herd, but thought better of it, for Bud was perfectly capable of doing all that could be done with the cattle until daylight came to their rescue.

While daylight was struggling up through the leaden eastern sky the wind died down as suddenly as it had risen, and the snow ceased falling.

Ted had fallen into a doze in a chair in front of the fire, but a stray sunbeam coming through a window fell upon his closed eyelids, and he awoke with a start. For a minute he could not think where he was. Then the cheery voice of Stella fell upon his ears. Somewhere in the distance she was singing, and he sprang to his feet and looked about him.

It came to him that he was at the Long Tom, and he remembered having left the Circle S herd out in the blizzard.

This stirred him to action, and he went back to the kitchen with the intention of lighting the fire and getting breakfast.

He stopped in the doorway in astonishment. Stella, with her sleeves rolled to the elbows, was busily engaged at the stove, singing as she worked.

"Good morning," said Ted. "You beat me to it. Why didn't

you wake me up and put me to work?"

"Hello!" said Stella cheerily. "You looked so tired sitting in that chair that I thought I'd let you sleep. At any rate, cooking breakfast is no work for a boy in a house. Get ready. Breakfast will be on the table in a minute. What do you think I found in the shed behind the house? A mountain sheep already dressed, and hung up for us. The fellow who left this house for us certainly was a good one. He knew we'd come in hungry, and left everything ready for us."

"That was just like Fred Sturgis. He's one of the best fellows in the world. He's the owner of the ranch. Young New York fellow. Wanted to spend the winter in the East. That's how I was able to get the ranch. But I'll bet he'll be back here before the snow melts. You couldn't keep him off the range for any length of time."

"He certainly has good taste. The house is almost as nice as the Moon Valley house, but nothing is quite as nice as that."

Mrs. Graham and Carl were roused, and they were soon sitting down to chops from a mountain sheep and corn bread which Stella had made; and they all voted that winter life in Montana promised to be a very jolly thing.

When Ted went outdoors the whole world was simply a glittering waste where the sun shone on, and was reflected back from the vast field of snow.

Sultan was in the sheltered corral, and as Ted threw the saddle on his back he reared and jumped about like a playful kitten.

"Quit your cavorting about, you rascal," said Ted, as Sultan wheeled away from the saddle with a playful snort, at the same time reaching around and trying to nip Ted's shoulder with his teeth.

"My, but you're feeling gay this morning," said Ted. "Here, hold still, won't you? How do you suppose I'm ever going to get this saddle on you if you don't stand still?"

But the cold weather and the bright sunshine had filled Sultan with ginger, and he was as full of play as a small boy when he wakes up some early winter morning and sees the ground covered with the first snow, and remembers the sled that has lain in the woodshed all summer.

But at last the saddle was on, and then Ted had his hands full getting into it.

"Gee, but you're skittish this morning," said Ted, giving Sultan a vigorous slap on the haunch. "But just you wait a few minutes until I get on you. I'll take some of that out of you."

But when he tried to find the stirrup with his toe, Sultan wheeled away from him with a little kick that was as dainty as that of a professional dancer.

But at last Ted made a leap and landed safely upon Sultan's back, and gave him a slap with the loose end of his rein. The little horse gave a leap like a kangaroo, and dashed through the gateway of the corral and across the white prairie, running like a quarter horse.

The herd was nowhere in sight, but in the far distance Ted saw a thin blue stream of smoke rising in the still, frosty air.

He knew it to be the camp fire of McCall, and that breakfast was going forward at the cow camp in the snow.

Heading Sultan toward it, Ted rushed on through the stimulating air of a Northern winter, and soon came in sight of the chuck wagon, and several of the boys standing around a fire.

As he dashed forward he raised the long yell, which was gleefully answered, and soon he was at the camp.

This was where he and Stella had started from the night before.

Turning his eyes back in the direction he had come, Ted could see the smoke rising from the chimney of the ranch house, although the house itself was hidden behind a swell in the surface of the prairie.

Had he only known it, he might have driven the herd right up to the ranch house during the night. As it was, he saw now that he and Stella, with the carriage, had ridden for almost two hours in the night, traveling in a circle, and by the merest chance had stumbled upon the ranch house.

"Hello, fellows!" he shouted as he rode up. "Where are the dogies?"

"Oh, to blazes and gone!" exclaimed big Ben, who was trying to thaw out his boots at the fire.

"Where?" asked Ted anxiously.

"Away off yonder." Ben pointed disconsolately toward the south.

"Are they all right?"

"All right, nothing. They're up to their bellies in snow in a

Edward C. Taylor

coulee, and won't stir. They're the sickest-looking lot of beef critters you ever saw. We've been working with them ever since daylight, then Bud sent us along to thaw out and get some chuck into us, and hurry back so that the other fellows could get limbered up some. Find the house?"

"Yes, accidentally stumbled on to it. Bully place, and the womenfolks are comfortably settled."

"Looks like it," grunted Ben, pointing to the north.

Ted looked in that direction and saw a spotted pony leaping toward them, and above it a dash of scarlet. It was Stella, riding like the wind on Magpie.

"Have any trouble with the critters in the night?" asked Ted.

"Did we? Well, I should howl. After you got under way they began to drift before the wind. We fought them all night, and if we'd let them go they'd been plumb into Colorado by this time. I don't want any more such nights in mine."

"That was only a starter, my friend. That was a picnic compared to what you may have to go up against before the daisies bloom again."

"Chuck!" yelled McCall, beating on the bottom of a griddle with a big iron spoon.

The fellows left the fire in a hurry and, squatting in the snow with a tin cup full of steaming coffee and a plate heaped with fried bacon and griddle cakes, were soon too busy to remember their weariness.

Stella had ridden up, her cheeks glowing, and her eyes sparkling with the frost and the exercise.

"Why didn't you wait for me?" she cried to Ted. "You're a mean thing. Thought you'd leave me behind, but here I am." She made a little face at Ted.

"I thought you'd rather stay indoors to-day on account of the cold," stammered Ted.

"Well, change your line of thought. There's going to be nothing to keep me indoors in this country, and don't you forget it. If I've got to stay indoors, I'll go South."

As soon as the boys had finished breakfast they were ready for another day's work.

"Come on, fellows," shouted Ted. "Let's hurry to where the critters are, and send the other boys back. Mac, cook up another breakfast for them."

They were in the saddle in a jiffy, and scurrying toward the south as fast as their ponies could carry them.

Ted found the herd bogged in a shallow coulee that was filled to the top with snow, in which they stood up to their bellies, lowing from fright, hunger, and thirst.

They were packed in a solid mass, and could not get out on the other side because the wall of the coulee was too steep for them to clamber up, as they might have done had it not been for the deep snow with which it was drifted full.

As a matter of fact, though, the coulee had saved the herd from drifting many miles in the night.

But how to get them out was the question that perplexed Bud, and with the arrival of Ted he thankfully turned the task over to him.

"Hike for the chuck wagon, boys," shouted Ted, as he came up.

"Well, I should smile to ejaculate," said Bud, "we're as hollow an' cold as a rifle bar'l. I'll turn this leetle summer matinee over ter you, my friend, not wishin' you any harm."

"Go ahead and enjoy yourselves," said Ted. "But as soon as you have filled up and warmed up come back. As soon as we get the bunch out of this hole it will be a snap to get them near the ranch house. If we'd only known it, we could have made it in half an hour more last night."

When Bud had ridden away Ted took stock of the situation, and found that he had a difficult problem to solve.

Under ordinary circumstances it would have been easy to snake the cattle out of the coulee by roping them around the horns and dragging them out with the ponies, but it was utterly impossible to do that with a couple of thousand of them.

While he was looking things over he became aware that Stella had ridden away. He looked anxiously after her, for he knew her propensity for getting into trouble when she rode alone. Soon she dropped out of sight behind a swell in the prairie with a flash in the sunlight of her scarlet jacket.

Ted was still studying the situation, riding up and down the edge of the coulee, trying to figure out some plan of rescue, and noting the cattle that were down, and which were rapidly being trampled to death by the other beasts, or being smothered by the snow.

The prospect was not a pleasing one to the young cow boss, for he saw the profits of the venture fading away hourly.

Suddenly a faint, shrill yell reached his ears, and he wheeled his pony in the direction from which it came.

Stella's scarlet jacket was coming toward him in a whirlwind of flying snow, and he rushed toward her.

What could have happened to her? He looked in vain for whatever was pursuing her, and saw that she was not being followed, but was swinging her arm above her head with a triumphant gesture.

He slowed his pony down, and soon she dashed to his side.

"You fellows are certainly a bright lot of cow-punchers," she exclaimed.

"What's the matter now?" asked Ted gloomily.

"Didn't any of you think of scouting down the coulee?"

"I confess I didn't."

"You ought to be laid off the job for a week."

"Why?"

"You can get those cattle out of that hole in an hour."

"We can! How do you know?"

"The coulee runs out about a mile to the west, and straight to the north, up a wide swale, lies the ranch house in full view."

"Stella, you're all right. But the cattle are bogged, and they can't move even down the coulee."

"I believe they can."

"How?"

"When the other boys come back from breakfast all of you jump into the coulee and tramp the snow down as much as you can ahead of the leaders. Then start them up."

"Bully for you, Stella; you're a better cow-puncher than any of us."

"No, I'm not, but because I don't know as much about it I go at it in a woman's way, which is a roundabout way, and nearly always foolish to look at, but sometimes does the work."

This suggestion had the effect of taking a great load from Ted's shoulders, for if he did not succeed in getting the herd out before night they would freeze solid in their molds of snow, and then he would never get half of them out alive.

Presently Bud and the other boys came winging back from breakfast, and Ted told them of the plan for releasing the cattle, at the same time praising Stella and giving her all the credit for the idea.

"Peevish peppers, but I'm a tenderfoot," grunted Bud. "Why in Sam Hill didn't I think o' that myself? I reckon I'm gettin' too old fer ther cow business. I ought ter be milkin' cows at some dairy farm."

The boys followed Stella's suggestion, and, leaping into the coulee, wheeled their ponies about until they had a well-beaten road for several hundred feet toward the west.

Then, cutting out a bunch of about fifty steers, led by a wise old fellow, the herd leader, whom they called Baldy on account of the spot of white hair between his horns, drove them along the path. After getting the bunch going well, the boys drove them with yells and the lashing of quirts into the deep snow ahead, and would not let them stop.

Another bunch was driven up, and soon there was a smooth road along the bottom of the coulee to the open ground, over which the cattle passed to safety.

Stella's good common sense had saved the herd.

CHAPTER III

THE SIGN-CAMP GHOST

As the last of the herd came out of the coulee to the open ground, a cheer went up for Stella, who blushed rosy-red, and told the boys to hush.

Then the drive to the big pasture began, word having been sent to McCall to follow with the chuck wagon.

The big pasture ran north from the home pasture, which was near the ranch house.

It comprised thousands of acres, and was so high that nearly always it was free of snow, which the strong winds coming down from the mountains swept as clear as if a gigantic broom had been used.

Back of the pasture lay a range of low mountains, the Sweet Grass they were called, in which several high buttes towered like sentinels.

The Sweet Grass Mountains had the reputation of harboring a great many "bad men," both whites and Indians, who had forsaken the Blackfeet Indian reservation to the west.

The mountain valleys afforded a splendid protection for the cattle, as did the numerous coulees with which the country was seamed.

The big pasture of the Long Tom was reputed to be the best winter feeding ground in Montana. The grass was high and nutritious, and there were plenty of water holes.

Once on the pasture the cattle scattered into smaller herds, each under the leadership of a bull, while the steers drifted off by themselves.

All that was necessary to care for the herd was to ride the lines of the pasture, and keep the cattle on their own feeding grounds, prevent them from straying, and hunt down the packs of wolves which preyed upon the weak cows and young cattle.

At stated intervals along the lines of the pasture were cabins, known as "sign camps," in which the line riders lived.

The first sign camp out of the home pasture was eight miles distant, and the next was under the lee of the mountains, on the west line.

As Ted directed the drive of the herd to the big pasture, on the south and west line of which the first sign camp was situated, he cut out part of the herd and held it back, while the remainder of the cattle went forward.

At the first sign camp Bud and Carl were dropped, for they were to ride the line to the north and east from that point.

Bud was glad to get some rest, and with a wave of the hand went on his way to the camp to await the arrival of Carl, who had ridden back to the ranch house for his blankets and other supplies.

During the day the chuck wagon, following the instructions of Ted, stopped at the sign camp, and left a supply of provisions and Bud's blankets.

Bud looked out the window of the cabin, and saw that the herd was grazing quietly, for the cattle were very hungry, and as they were safe for the time being, he rolled himself in his blankets and was soon sleeping soundly.

He awoke on hearing a fumbling at the door, and sat up.

It was pitch dark, and he had slept nearly all day.

Unlimbering his six-shooter, he called, "Who's thar?"

"Ach, Pud, it's me alretty," came the muffled reply.

"So it's you, Carl. Why don't you come in?"

"Der door open, Pud, please. I my arrums full mit dings have."

Bud sprang from his blankets and threw the door open, admitting a cold blast and a flurry of snow.

"Ugh!" he ejaculated, with a shudder. "Come in, yer fat wad o' Dutch. What yer waitin' fer?"

"Someding has my hat stolen off mit my head." Carl's voice expressed both perplexity and awe.

Evidently something unusual had happened, and Bud put on his hat and stepped outside.

He had no sooner passed through the doorway than his own hat was snatched from his head.

He drew his revolver, leaped into the open, and looked about him.

There was no one in sight except Carl, who was standing near him with his arms full of blankets and bundles.

Carl could not have played the trick on him, and there was not wind enough to have blown the hat away. Anyhow, it had been snatched from his head by a hand and not by the wind.

There was something uncanny about this.

It was still light enough to see out in the open, and the snow-covered ground reflected light enough to have discovered an intruder had one been there.

Bud ran around the house, but could find no person, and there were no tracks of a man's foot in the snow.

"Jumpin' sand hills, but that's queer," said Bud, coming back to where Carl was still standing in the snow before the door, staring about in a bewildered way. "Gosh ding yer, Carl, I believe yer swiped my hat, an' if yer don't give it up I'll plant my toe whar it'll be felt onpleasantly."

"Honest, Pud, I ain't your hat taking," said Carl distressfully. "Vhy, I my hat losing too, yet."

"That's so, an' yer loaded down with truck. Throw them things inter ther house an' help me hunt ther thief. Don' be standin' thar like a sausage."

"Don'd you calling me a sissage," said Carl wrathfully. "I ain't feeling mooch as having fun mit you now. I bring all dese dings mit der saddle on, und I lose two or three every dime der pony makes his jumpings, und get down kvick to pick dem up maype as fifty dimes."

"Oh, all right. Quit yer bellyachin', an' come an' help. We can't get along without hats. That's a cinch."

Carl retired into the house with his bundles.

"Wow! Stop it, cuss ye," yelled Bud, as Carl came out of the cabin.

"I ain't didding noding," said Carl, backing away as Bud rushed upon him.

"Yer did, yer fat galoot. Yer pulled my hair 'most out by ther roots."

"I ain't pulling no hairs," Carl persisted.

"Then who done it? Yer ther only person what I can see. It's a cinch some one pulled my hair."

"Say, Pud."

"What?"

"Let us camp outside."

"What, an' freeze ter death before mornin'? Nixy. Not fer me."

"Ain't you heard about der shack?"

"No, I ain't, an' I don't want ter. What I'm after now is ther galoot what got our hats an' pulled my hair."

"Ain't you heard about der ghost?"

"Ghost!"

Bud was staring at Carl with his jaw dropped.

"Yah. Dis is a ghost haus, filled mit ghostesses."

"Don't you go making any monkey talks at me. There ain't no sich things as ghosts. That'll do fer ter frighten kids with, but not fer me."

"Den who tooken our hats, und who your golden locks pulled?"

"That's so. Who took them? Tell me, who put all thet dope about this bein' a haunted house in ther shell what yer calls yer head?"

"Bill Simms, der cow-puncher vot we picked up on der drive, informationed me about it. He says a man was kilt in dis shack, und dot he valks aroundt mit it ven der night cooms."

"That Bill Simms is ther worst liar in forty States. He tried ter fill me with wild dreams about a feller what rides ther line on this yere ranch what can stand havin' ther contents o' a six-shooter pumped inter him, an' it don't feaze him none."

"Yah. Dot's der ghostes vot runs dis shack. I don'd vant ter stay here, Pud. Please let us camp out in der snow."

"Why, yer doodle, can't ther ghost come out yere jest ez easy ez he kin' go inter ther house—that is, if he's a sure-enough ghost?"

"Yah, I guess he can. Vat vill ve didding?"

"I don't care what you do, but I'm goin' inter ther shack ter start up ther fire an' get warm. I don't care what you do, but I'm 'most froze."

"Don't leaf me alone, dear Pud. Please, I imploring you."

"Come on, then."

Bud stepped inside, and, as he did so, he uttered an exclamation of surprise.

Both the purloined hats lay in the middle of the floor.

"There, didn't I told you?" exclaimed Carl, in an awed voice.

Bud simply stared at the hats.

"Nopody but a ghostes could haf did dat."

Bud looked around the room, and then up at the ceiling.

Then he burst into a roar of laughter.

"Thar's ther ghost," he shouted, grasping Carl by the arm and twisting him around so that he could see.

In the corner just below the ceiling were two sharp, green points of light that glowed in the faint radiance cast by the fire, which had sunk to embers.

"Ach, mutter, save your liddle Carl. It vor der ghostes."

"That ain't no ghost," said Bud scornfully. "Ain't you never hear tell how ghosts look? They're all white an' long an' skinny, an' when they walk they carry chains what clanks, an'—"

"Oh, Pud, stop. Don't say it some more. My plood vas chilling now so I ain't aple to svallow in my troat alretty. I vas so scared as nefer vas I."

"Yer a cheerful roommate, I must say. See, ther ghost is gone."

"I ain't nefer goin' ter be happy some more. I haf seen a ghost. I vill die, I am sure."

"Yer kin bet on that ez a shore thing, an' I reckon I will, too."

"Listen!" Carl grasped Bud by the arm with the clutch of despair.

There was a faint and stealthy noise on the roof.

Both stood for a few moments listening breathlessly.

Then they heard a faint, far-away wail, like that of a banshee.

Carl threw his arms around Bud in an agony of fear.

"Dere it iss. Ve are gone. All iss lost."

Again the gruesome wail came to them, this time louder and clearer, and in a moment or two a hand was at the door. The latch clicked softly, and the door swung slowly open.

CHAPTER IV

THE BIG COON TREE

"Hello, what's the matter with you fellows? Are you going to have a waltz, or is it going to be a two-step, or a catch-as-catch-can wrestling match? Perhaps you've suddenly grown very fond of one another."

It was Ted who spoke, standing in the doorway, laughing as if he would burst his buttons off, at the strange tableau in the middle of the floor, Carl clinging to Bud, who was trying to shake him off.

"Let loose o' me," shouted Bud. "Why, ther feller's plumb daffy on ghosts. He says as how this shack is haunted, an' he's plumb loco."

"Yah. Didn't we just hear der ghostes yell mit der outside?" said Carl, who had been thrust away from his clutch on Bud, and was standing in the middle of the floor, trembling like one with the ague.

"Ha, ha!" laughed Ted. "Ghost, eh? It was me calling to the cattle, and sending them back from the line."

"Yah, aber I seen mit mine own eyes der green ones oof der

ghost up in dot corner, und heart him on der roof."

"Come outside, and I'll show you the footprints of the ghost," said Ted, leading the way.

Out in the snow by the side of the cabin Ted showed them several tracks, something like a small hand, which ended at the wall of the cabin.

"That's where the ghost went up," said Ted. "Let's climb the wall, and see what is on the roof."

It was easy climbing up the log wall, for there were plenty of footholds.

When they were high enough to look over the edge of the roof, Bud gave an exclamation of surprise, and then burst out laughing, in which Ted joined.

But Carl could not see the joke.

"It's a vild cat," he shouted, scrambling to the ground.

"It ain't, neither," asseverated Bud. "It's a bully little ole pet coon. That's what it is."

He held out his hand, and the coon, making a queer little chuckling noise, came slowly toward him as he held out his finger, which the sharp-eyed little beast clasped in its fingerlike paw and pulled.

Bud reached out, tucked it under his arm, and climbed down with it.

"This yere coon was a pet ter ther fellers what rid line yere before," said Bud, when they were in the cabin again. "He's been hangin' eround ever since, an' when he saw us he thought it wuz his ole pardners come back. He's been taught ter swipe hats an' drop 'em down inter ther house through ther chimbley hole. That accounts fer it, an' I reckon he's ther whole ghost."

"Yah, mebbe I dinks so," said Carl, who looked rather sheepish at his exhibition of fear.

"He's a smart little piece," said Ted. "By the way, Carl, get busy with the pots and pans. I'm going to stay to supper and sleep here to-night. I've got the cattle and the boys planted, and it is too far to go on to the ranch house to-night. Stella and Kit went back an hour ago."

Carl went to work to cook supper, while Bud played with the coon, which was as full of tricks as a monkey, and kept the boys laughing all the time.

"A coon is a mighty smart animile," said Bud as they sat down to supper.

"So I've heard," said Ted. "But I've never seen many of them."

"Dere is no such beast in Chermany," Carl put in proudly.

"That's so," said Bud. "Ameriky is the land o' ther free, an' ther home o' ther coon. Never went coon huntin', did yer, Ted?"

"I never did."

"Well, ye've missed some mighty good fun. Down in Missouri is whar ther coon grows wild an' independent, an' ther ain't one o' them what's come o' age what ain't as smart as ary congressman you ever see."

"I've heard something about coon hunting," said Ted.

"It's great down in Missouri. Thar's whar ther coon trees grow."

"Vat such foolishment for?" said Carl, with a sneer. "Coons don't grow mit trees on."

"Nobody said they could, but they live in trees, yer loony. A ole gum tree what's holler is ther home o' ther coon. Thar's whar ther best coon dogs come from, too. Ever hunt coons with a dog?" continued Bud.

"Never did," said Ted. "It seems too picayunish fer me. I like bigger game than that. Besides, I don't care much fer hunting in the nighttime."

"Do they hunt mit der coons in der nighttime?" asked Carl, who was beginning to be interested.

"Shore! That's ther time ter tree 'em. My Uncle Fletcher out in ole Missou, we ust ter call him ole Unc' Fletch, had four or five coon dogs that was ther cream o' the coon-huntin' canines in several counties, an' Unc' Fletch was out near every night chasin' coons."

"Many of them there?" asked Ted.

"Ther country was overrun with 'em. They ust ter eat all ther roastin' ears o' corn in ther bottom lands, an' git away with more chickens than ever those that raised 'em did, until it got so that ther farmers said they was only raisin' corn an' chickens ter keep ther coons fat."

"No money in that."

"Not much. But I wuz goin' ter tell yer what happened ter Unc' Fletch one night ter show how plenty coons wuz in his section.

"One night he starts out with his best coon dog, Ballyhoo, so called because he made sech a noise when he treed a coon.

"Bally runs acrost ther scent o' a coon an' takes after it. Unc' Fletch trails along, an' Ballyhoo stops at a big sycamore tree. But there don't seem ter be no hole, an' after unc' looks around, an' can't find nothin', he calls Ballyhoo off, an' they start through ther woods ag'in.

"Pretty soon Ballyhoo scents another coon, an', by jing, it leads them ter ther same sycamore. About twenty times that night they strikes ther scent, an' every time it stops at the same tree.

"Now, Unc' Fletch wuz some o' a woodman, an' he says it ain't nat'ral fer ther dog ter tree so many coons at ther same place, an' wonders if thar is somethin' wrong with ther dog, if he's gone daffy, er whether it's jest an onusual smart coon what has gone out jest ter have a joke by runnin' them ter ther same tree every time.

"While he is contemplatin' thus he is leanin' with his back ter ther tree. Pritty soon he thinks he'll go home, an' he starts away sorter disgustedlike with ther night's sport, an', by gee, he finds he's caught by ther tail o' his coat an' can't break loose.

"He tries ter get away, but he's shore fast. He reaches around, an' ther tree hez got hold o' him all right, an' bein' some superstitious, Unc' Fletch begins ter git some scared. Then he ricollects about hearin' the colored folks talk about the haunted coon tree."

"Coons is ghostes, not?" asked Carl.

"Wait an' you'll hear," continued Bud. "Long about this time, Ballyhoo begins ter howl in ther most sad an' lonesome way, an' that don't make Unc' Fletch feel any better. Jest as he's thinkin' about hollerin' fer help—"

"Why didn't he skin out of his coat, and leave it sticking to the tree?" asked Ted.

"I ast him ther same question, an' he says as how he was too plumb scared ter do sich a thing. But jest as he was goin' ter holler he finds that he's loose, an' all his spunk comes back again.

"Then he begun ter be curious ter find out what it was that held him fast. He lights a fire an' gets a torch ter examine ther tree, but can't find nothin' that would hev cotched him thataway.

"But as he's lookin' ther strangest thing happens. Ther tree opens a crack runnin' all ther way from ther roots up as far as Unc' Fletch kin see. Ther crack is big ernuff ter put yer finger in, but Unc' Fletch doesn't do no such fool trick ez that.

"In less than a minnit ther crack closes up ag'in, an' thar ain't no sign o' it. Now this is some puzzlin' ter Unc' Fletch, an' he hez some more o' them funny feelin's erbout ghosts, an' them things.

"While he's still watchin' ther tree, ther crack opens again, then closes an' opens an' closes, same as if it wuz breathin'. This makes Unc' Fletch some riled, fer he wa'n't never a feller what can stand bein' made a joke of, an' he thinks ther ghost in ther tree is havin' fun with him."

"What did he do?" asked Ted, when Bud stopped and looked reflectively into the fire.

"Well, he starts out ter make a fool out o' ther ghost, if it is a ghost, er outer ther tree, if it is jest a tree what is triflin' with him.

"He has his ax with him, fer every real coon hunter always carries an ax ter chop down ther tree when he finds a coon in it. But he wa'n't goin' ter chop down this tree none."

"What did he want with the ax, then?"

"I'll soon tell yer. First he chops down a small tree, an' he makes a wedge with an edge erbout ther size o' yer little finger, an' he waits until ther tree breathes ergin. Then he slips ther wedge in, an' hammers it home.

"'Ha, ha!' says he ter ther tree, 'ye'll make monkey-shines with me, holdin' me by ther coat tails, will yer?' An' all ther time he is choppin' out another wedge, bigger than ther first.

"As he keeps choppin' out, an' shovin' bigger an' bigger wedges inter ther crack, he hears noises comin' from ther tree like what he ain't never heard before. But ther tree is beginnin' ter give out crackin' noises, too, like as if it was splittin'.

"While this is goin' on Ballyhoo is makin' a terrible fuss, an' jest tryin' ter tear ther tree down with his claws. At last ther tree busts plumb open, an' what d'yer think Unc' Fletch sees?"

Neither Ted nor Carl replied. What the tree contained was a thing unguessable, but Carl's eyes were as big as saucers as he stared at Bud, awaiting the solution of the mystery.

"What did it contain?" asked Ted at last.

"It was plumb full o' coons," said Bud solemnly. "Thar must 'a' been two hundred coons in that tree. It was a regular coon hotel. They made it a sort o' winter colony. Every coon fer miles eround made it home."

"But that doesn't explain the crack in the tree and the strange way in which it opened and closed."

"That's easy now that yer knows that the tree was holler an' plumb full o' coons."

"I don't see it yet."

"Why, it wuz like this: Every time them coons drew a long breath it expanded ther tree so that it opened a crack, an' when their lungs filled the crack opened wide. Then, when they let out thar breath ag'in, ther crack closed tight ag'in. Unc' Fletch happened ter lean up ag'in ther tree jest ez ther crack closed, an' that's how his coat tails got caught."

"And what became of all those coons?" asked Ted.

"Yer see they got inter ther tree through a hole in ther top. Unc' Fletch didn't dare leave ther tree alone, so he tied a note ter Ballyhoo an' sent him back ter ther village fer a carpenter. When ther carpenter come they put a roof on ther tree an' made a door at ther bottom, an' let ther coons out one at a time. By this means they got every dodgasted coon in them woods, an' Unc' Fletch's bounties was enough ter enable him ter lift ther mortgage on ther farm."

Edward C. Taylor

"I guess that will do for to-night," said Ted, laughing. "I'm going to hit the blankets, for it's up at daylight for all of us. I only hope your pet coon does not attract so many others as to turn this sign camp into a coon hotel."

CHAPTER V

THE PHANTOM LINE RIDER

For several days the weather remained fine, and the cattle were able to get accustomed to their new range and become hardened.

The boys at the sign camps took things easy. In each sign camp were two boys, one of whom rode days, and the other nights, when it was necessary in bad weather to hold the cattle from drifting.

In order to keep in touch with one another the riders started from their camps and met midway between, in order to exchange notes as to the condition of the cattle and other things necessary to the welfare of the whole herd.

There was another reason for this constant interchange of communication between the camps.

Ted had received a warning from the town of Bubbly Creek, a small cattle station, about twenty miles from the Long Tom Ranch, where there was a cattleman's hotel, a few saloons, and an outfitting store, to look out for the Whipple gang, which had its rendezvous in the Sweet Grass Mountains.

Edward C. Taylor

Fred Sturgis, in the last letter Ted had received from him, had also mentioned this gang of thieves and desperadoes, whose operations extended from Canada, into which they made extensive raids when the Canadian Mounted Police happened to be out of that part of the country, as far south as the central portion of Montana.

"I have had considerable trouble with the Whipple gang myself," Sturgis wrote, "but as yet I have never seen but one member of the gang to know it. I have had plenty of cattle stolen, and have always attributed the thefts to the Whipples. All I know about the gang is that it was founded by a fellow named Whipple, an outlaw on the scout, who attracted to himself a desperate gang of fugitives from justice who had taken refuge in the Sweet Grass Mountains.

"I have never seen Whipple himself, but from those who claim to know him he is described as an enormous man of prodigious strength, and a perfect brute, who has forced his men into absolute subjection by his acts of brutality toward them.

"With Whipple are a number of bad Indians, who have fled from the various reservations in Montana after having committed all sorts of crimes, from theft to murder. It is said that these are more to be feared than the white men, for they are terribly cruel, and when they get a victim he is tortured with all the horrible rites of the true savage. They know that the moment they are caught that is the end for them, so that they are reckless to the verge of insanity.

"I tell you these things, believing that you already know what ranching in northern Montana means, and with every confidence in Ted Strong's ability to take care of himself, and meet conditions when they appear. All I can say is, go after them if they molest you. I and my boys fought them so successfully that they gave us a wide berth toward the end. But when they learn that new hands have taken hold of the Long Tom they may think that they can start their funny business again.

"Knowing your reputation, and the ability you have shown in the past in wiping out, or at least breaking up and scattering, bands of bad men, I leave the Long Tom in your hands with the hope that when I take it over again in the spring there will be no more Whipple gang, and that the Sweet Grass Mountains will be as safe as one's own dooryard."

"A word in your ear about the Sweet Grass Mountains: It is known to a few men in Montana, and a few others in various parts of the country that somewhere in those mountains are rich mines of gold and copper, and at various times men have brought out beautiful and valuable specimens of sapphires and rubies in the rough, not knowing what they were, having picked them up solely because they were beautiful and unusual.

"If it were not for the Whipple gang the mountains would have been opened up to the prospectors long ago. Several prospectors, unheedful of the warnings, have gone in, but none have ever come out of the Sweet Grass Mountains."

"Whoever is at the head of the Whipple gang possesses more than the usual share of brains, courage, and luck. Keep your eye peeled, and good fortune to you."

This letter had been read to the boys one night in camp, and all were instructed to look out for strangers on the ranch and to inform themselves of the business of such.

One night Carl started from the sign camp to ride north to meet the rider from sign camp No. 2, which lay nearer the mountains.

The camp in which Bud and Carl were stationed was camp No. 1.

The distance between the camps was about six miles, so that each rider had to go about three miles to meet.

The night was clear and cold, and the air fairly sparkled with the frost in the brilliant white moonlight. It was a glorious night, and Carl, in a leather coat lined with fleece, and with a fur cap upon his head, and his feet in thick felts, started away from the camp on his ride.

There was no wind, but the temperature was very low.

To the north the Sweet Grass Mountains loomed, a black mass against the sky, while all about the world was carpeted with snow.

Carl had not progressed more than a mile from his camp when he saw a dark object against the snow some distance in front of him.

At first he thought it might be a bush or a rock, so still it was in the moonlight.

But he could not remember of ever having seen either a rock or a bush in that part of the range.

Then he wondered if he was late at the meeting place, and that the other line rider had got tired of waiting for him, and had ridden forward upon his line to meet him.

This stimulated him to greater speed, and he pricked up his pony.

But as he got nearer the black blot on the snow there seemed to be something unusual about it, and he unconsciously slowed his animal down to a walk.

At last he got within hailing distance, and saw that it was a man on horseback that he had been approaching.

The man on night duty at the second sign camp was a cowpuncher named Follansbee, a short, reckless, yet amiable fellow, whom Carl knew well.

The rider who was awaiting him was an unusually large man, and bestrode an enormous horse. The two were as if they had been carved from ebony, as they stood silent and absolutely still, outlined sharply against the dazzlingly white background.

Something inside of Carl began to sink as he went on, slower and slower, his hand gripping the reins tightly, and holding back on them.

"Vot it is?" he was saying over and over to himself. "Vot it is? Dot is not Billy Follansbee. Dot man vould make dree times of Follansbee, nit?"

Cold fear was slowly stealing over Carl, and he wanted in his heart to turn and ride the other way.

But something seemed to draw him forward, and, try as he would, he could not bring himself to turn back.

The man on the black horse could not be a member of the Long Tom force, for Carl knew every one of them well, as a fellow will who has camped with them for months on a cattle drive.

Now Carl was near enough to see the man's face, and he peered eagerly forward to get a glimpse of it.

Then his heart sank lower yet, for the man's face was as white as the snow beyond. There were no features; neither nose, nor mouth, nor eyebrows, only a pair of black eyes gleamed out of that dead-white face.

Carl clutched at the horn of his saddle to keep from falling, he was so frightened.

"Vot it is?" he kept repeating to himself.

His pony stopped of its own volition directly in front of this black apparition, and Carl swayed in his saddle and would have fallen out of it had he not clung to it with the unconscious strength of despair.

"Iss dot you, Follansbee?" asked Carl, in a weak, thin voice, well knowing that it was not his line partner, but trying to break the spell of fear that held him.

There was no reply, but the gleaming black eyes never left his own, nor did the figure on the horse move a hair's breadth.

"Vy don't you say someding?" said Carl, his voice sounding like the piping noise of the wind through a keyhole. "Speak someding."

Then it suddenly struck Carl that the man could not speak, because in that white, immovable face there was no mouth to speak with, only those black, blazing eyes.

"If you can't speak, make motionings," said Carl, in an imploring voice.

The sinister figure on the black horse slowly raised his arm, and motioned Carl toward him, at the same time swinging his black horse around and riding toward the mountains.

Chilled to the heart, Carl obeyed the signal, and sent his pony forward.

The man, apparition, demon, or whatever it was, sent his horse into a gallop, and Carl, with no volition on his own part, followed at the same speed.

But with the black and menacing eyes of the man with the dead face away from his own, some small part of courage oozed back into Carl again, and he remembered Ted's injunction to question every stranger met on the range, and if he did not give a satisfactory answer to drive him off.

But Carl had not got over the fright the sight of that face and eyes had thrown him into.

Suddenly his hand came into contact with the handle of his six-shooter, and a thrill of daring ran through him.

He looked ahead at the back of the man riding only a few feet in advance of him.

Should he take the chance? He knew that Ted or Bud or any of the boys would do so. Why not he?

If the man was only human a bullet would soon settle the matter. But if he should be a ghost or an emissary of the devil, as Carl strongly suspected, nothing like a ball from a forty-five would do him harm.

This had the effect of staying his hand, and the revolver stopped halfway out of its holster.

Then Carl thought of the boys, and what they would say if they knew that he had not nerve enough to pot the enemy when he met him.

Carl was not the bravest fellow in the world, and he was intensely superstitious.

Again the thoughts of the taunts of the other boys, should they ever know that he lacked the nerve to take advantage of the moment, came to him, and he gulped something hard that rose in his throat, and drew out his revolver.

At that moment the man in black turned and looked over his shoulder, his dead face gleaming white, out of which shone those terrible black eyes.

The revolver stopped suddenly in its upward course, and Carl's jaw dropped as he stared in abject fear at that white and expressionless face.

Then the man in black turned his horrible face once more to the fore, and rode on.

Something inside of Carl seemed to snap, and a great glow of courage swept over him. He fairly hated the sight of the grim rider in front of him, who was taking him he knew not where, and whom he yet dreaded with all his heart.

Up came the revolver again, and, almost before he realized what he was doing, Carl was firing, straight at the back in front of him.

The target could not be fairer, that black mark against the snow.

The first ball struck, for Carl heard the thud of it, as if it had struck and sunk into something soft.

The report of the weapon crashed through the still night, and was carried far on the frosty air, reverberating and echoing back from the distant mountains.

But the creature in whose body the ball had lodged did not seem to know it. The head was not turned, the body did not lurch or sway.

Carl, now blind to everything but the terror that had taken possession of him, fired again and again until every chamber in his revolver was empty, pausing after every shot to note the effect.

That every shot was fair he was sure, for he could hear the sound of the impact of the bullet.

The recipient of the bullets seemed not to know that they had been fired, for he did not hasten or retard the progress of the horse, nor did he take any personal notice that they gave him any discomfort.

But when Carl ceased firing he threw his head backward, looking over his shoulder again, and from that hideous face without nose or mouth came a gurgling noise that was like, and yet not like, laughter.

The laughter was worse on Carl's nerves than the silence, and he felt himself grow sick at heart.

How could he expect to fight or escape from a devil impervious to the balls from a Colt forty-five?

Then, to Carl's amazement and relief, the black horse sprang forward over the snow so swiftly that it seemed as if it was

Edward C. Taylor

flying rather than running, but this probably was due to the uncertainty and the illusion of the moonlight, and vanished into thin air, leaving Carl staring open-mouthed.

It was several minutes before Carl regained his senses and knew that he was sitting with his revolver in his hand, staring into space and seeing nothing.

Then he rode slowly forward to the brink of a deep coulee.

Here was where he had last seen the phantom rider, for such Carl had at last come to regard him.

Looking to the bottom of the coulee, Carl saw nothing but snow, where he had expected to find a dead horse and rider.

"Ach, vot a country," he wailed. "Vy did I effer come to it? Mutter, I vish you vas here to hellup your Carlos."

Then he heard a groan close at hand and looked about, expecting to see the phantom rider by his side.

A short distance off lay a black splotch on the snow.

It resembled the prostrate form of a man. Had he, after all, killed his horrible enemy? Cautiously he rode toward it. It was a man, and not the phantom, and it looked very much like a cow-puncher, for it was clad in leather coat and chaps, and there was a belt filled with cartridges, and in the snow beside it lay a Colt forty-five.

This at least was human, and Carl climbed stiffly from his saddle and bent over it.

He started back with a cry of surprise.

The man in the snow was his line partner, Follansbee.

That he was not dead was evident, for he groaned occasionally.

It was up to Carl to get him to camp as soon as he could, and when he tried to raise the insensible form he was stopped by a gush of blood from a wound in the breast.

But he heard a shot in the distance, then another, and another.

The boys had heard his shots, and were riding toward him with all speed.

Presently he heard the long yell, and in a few minutes Bud Morgan came dashing toward him at top speed, and soon they were joined by Kit Summers from sign camp No. 2, and the horror of the night was over for Carl.

CHAPTER VI

CAUGHT IN THE ACT

Follansbee was carried to camp No. 2, where Bud, who was a pretty good cow-camp surgeon, examined his wound. A ball from an automatic revolver had struck him in the breast, but on account of the thickness of the clothing he wore, and the fact that he had on a heavy vest of caribou hide, in the pocket of which he carried a small memorandum book, the ball had penetrated only a short distance.

While he had lost a lot of blood, and the shock of the ball striking had caused him to lose consciousness, he was not seriously hurt.

It did not take Bud long to extract the bullet and stanch the flow of blood, and Follansbee opened his eyes and looked about wildly.

"Where is he?" he cried in terror.

"Whar's who?" asked Bud.

"The man what didn't have no face," cried the cow-puncher.

"Carl chased him avay alretty," said Carl, bending over

his partner.

"All right, Carl. You saw him, too, did ye?"

"Sheur I sawed him, mit mine own eyes."

"Then it's all right," murmured Follansbee, sinking back on his bunk. "I wuz afeared the boys wouldn't believe me if I told them what I saw."

When Follansbee sank into a deep sleep, due to his weakness from loss of blood, the three boys sat before the fire while Carl told of his encounter with the faceless man, and of the six shots which he had fired at him and the ineffective bullets which had struck his body.

As the story was told a hush fell upon Bud and Kit. They were deeply affected by the fact that this unknown and terrible menace was upon the range which they were compelled to patrol, and which not even the balls from a heavy weapon could kill.

"I would hardly have believed it if both of you hadn't seen the creature," said Kit. "It sounds too much like a pipe dream."

It was morning before Bud and Carl left Kit's camp and rode to their own. Follansbee was apparently all right, and exhibited no symptoms of fever, for he had the iron constitution of a seasoned cow-puncher, who almost invariably recovers as if by magic from a gunshot wound if the missile does not penetrate a vital spot or splinter a bone.

Follansbee, when he awoke from his sleep, told Kit of his meeting with the "man without a face," as he called the man who had given him his wound.

"I wuz ridin' at a pretty good clip along the line to meet Carl," he began, "when I see a feller standin' waitin' for me by the deep coulee, about three miles south.

"At first I thought it wuz Carl, but soon I see that it wuz too big fer the Dutchman."

"I slowed down a bit, fer I saw it wasn't any o' our outfit. Ye see I had in mind what Ted said about that Sweet Grass Mountain gang, an' I wuz some skittish."

"As I rode along slowly the feller on the black hoss made a sign as if he wanted me to foller him. But I didn't like the stunt, so I stops still an' rubbers at him."

"Two or three times he makes his motions, an' I don't do nothin' but shake my head."

"Kit, that wasn't no human bein'. It wuz ther devil as sure as shootin'. I started to draw my gun, but shucks, I ain't got no chanct ter make a move before thar was a crash, an' a blaze o' flame come from his chest, right about the middle, an' I felt the ball strike me, I heard a queer sorter laugh, like a man bubblin' with his mouth in a basin o' water, an' then I went out, an' all I remember wuz fallin' out o' the saddle."

About noon of that day, Ted and Stella rode over from the ranch house on a tour of inspection, and stopped at Bud's camp, where they were told the story of Carl's strange encounter with the man without a face, to which he listened in troubled silence.

When Carl was through with his story, Ted looked for a long time into the fire without saying anything.

"Well, what do you think?" asked Stella, at last.

"I think it is the work of the Whipple gang," answered Ted.

"But why should they shoot Follansbee?"

"It is a piece of intimidation. Of course, they do not know us. Under ordinary circumstances an apparition like that, followed by the shooting of a man, would cause a panic among ignorant men on a ranch. It is a cinch that the Whipple gang has got it in for us, and this is just the beginning of it. You will soon see other evidences of their work."

"But why should they hev it in fer us?" asked Bud. "We ain't never done nothin' ter them."

"I don't know, but I have several ideas."

"What are they?"

"There are two or three things to be considered. In the first place they have it in for the ranch on general principles. You know Fred Sturgis said in his letter that he and his boys had driven the gang away from the ranch. That is reason number one. Then we are strangers in this part of the country, and they have seen us and have us sized up for a lot of boys, and, therefore, easy marks for them. Again, we have a big bunch of cattle, which Whipple and his bunch think we will not be able to protect against them.

"They may have learned that we are deputy United States marshals. That is enough to condemn us in their eyes. They are all old and fugitive criminals, and if we knew them I think that we would find that they are all wanted in one or more of the States and Territories, and that the aggregate amount of rewards which have been offered for them, dead or alive, would amount to a neat sum. They do not need marshals in this part of the country. There may be other reasons why they will make war on us, which we will learn later, but the ones I have mentioned are sufficient for them to make themselves very troublesome."

"So you think it is war, eh?" said Stella.

"I do, and I think that you will be a shining mark for them when they learn that you are here. For that reason I would warn you to be very careful where you go about the ranch, and especially ask you not to ride about alone, and to keep away from the mountains."

"Oh, dear, and just when I had planned to explore those mountains from one end to the other," said Stella, with a pout.

"Can't help it. You know what would happen if they should catch you and spirit you off as Shan Rhue did in the Wichita Mountains."

"Yes, I know, I'm a lot of trouble to you, Ted, but you know I don't mean to be."

"Of course I know it, but if you run into danger, and expose yourself to the attack of those who are avowedly our enemies, you run the chance of being caught, and then, of course, it is our duty to get you out of trouble."

"Well, I'll be good."

"The attempted killing of Follansbee was no accident," continued Ted. "It was the work of an exceedingly shrewd man, who knows the moral effect of his strange and mysterious appearance."

"Ain't it a ghost?" asked Carl, who had become all swelled

up at the thought that he had made a ghost run away from him.

"I should say not."

"Den vy shouldn't mine bullets haf killed him?"

"I'm sure I don't know. That is why I say that he is a remarkably clever man, and it is probably the cause of the power he wields that he is able to do such things. It wouldn't surprise me any if some day we learned that your visitor was none other than the renowned Whipple himself."

"What are you going to do about it?" asked Stella.

"What can we do? We wouldn't know a single member of the gang if we were to meet him. We don't know where they hang out, and if we did we know nothing about the Sweet Grass Mountains, and could not go to where they are. All we can do is to watch the ranch house and the cattle as a cat watches a mouse, and if anything more, such as the shooting of Follansbee, occurs, we will have to go on the warpath ourselves. But I don't want to do that. We are out here to winter feed our cattle, and not to fight."

"Shore enuff, but yer kin bet yer breeches I'm not goin' ter let no cave dweller or brush hider tromp onto my moccasins, an' turn ther other cheek ter be tromped on. Ther first feller o' that outfit I cotch sashay in' around me I'm goin' ter take a crack at him."

"Go as far as you like when it comes to an act of aggression on the part of one of them, but don't start anything, Bud, unless you can positively bring it to a successful end."

"I reckon I'm some of a fox myself. They ain't set no trap

what I've put my paw inter yet."

Ted and Stella rode on to Kit's camp to see how Follansbee was getting on, and found him doing nicely, but Stella laughed at the bandages Bud had put on the wounded cow-puncher, and insisted on redressing the wound.

Stella was a master hand at bandaging, because she was deft of hand and was naturally sympathetic.

When she had finished with Follansbee, and had sewed his bandages so that he could not rub or drag them off, he said he felt a hundred per cent better already.

Then they proceeded toward the mountains, where the third camp, under the direction of Ben Tremont, was situated.

It was almost the dying of the day when they left Ben's camp. He had not heard of the attack on Follansbee, and Ted made it an occasion to warn Ben against the attacks of the Whipple gang, as he was in the most exposed place, being so near the mountains.

When they turned their ponies' noses toward the south again it was to ride through a part of the herd.

Ted noticed that the cattle were feeding well and that there was plenty of good, rich, well-cured grass, and that it was free of snow in big enough patches to give the cattle ample room to graze.

As they were riding along Stella drew rein.

"What's the matter with that steer over there, Ted?" she asked, pointing to a steer that was dragging one of its hind legs.

Ted looked at the steer in question, which was moving slowly forward.

"See, there's another," cried Stella. "Why, I can see a dozen of them all limping in the same manner."

"That's strange," said Ted. "I wouldn't think anything of it if only one steer had gone lame, but I can't understand a dozen."

They rode slowly toward the lame steers.

"Great guns," exclaimed Ted, bending low in his saddle to examine the steers closely.

"What is it?" asked Stella excitedly.

"This is terrible," said Ted. "If this keeps up we might as well shoot all the cattle and let them lie out here on the prairie the prey to the wolves. We will never get them back to Moon Valley."

Stella looked at him with an expression of consternation on her face.

"These cows and steers have been hamstrung," said Ted, with a tone of suppressed rage in his voice. "Any man who would do a trick like that ought to be shot down in his tracks like a mad dog."

"Hamstrung! I don't understand."

"Some inhuman brute has ridden up behind these crippled animals, and with a sharp knife has cut the tendons or leaders behind the hoofs, or, rather, in the ankles, laming them and preventing them from being able to follow a drive. Where would we be in the spring if any large portion of our beasts were so maimed?"

"What a brutal thing to do!" exclaimed Stella, in indignation.

"Hello, what's that?"

Ted rose in his stirrups, standing and shading his eyes with his hand against the glare of the setting sun on the snow. With the other hand he was pointing off toward the east, where the cattle were milling uneasily.

"Something wrong over there," said Stella.

They rode slowly in that direction to see what was disturbing the cattle.

As they went, Ted was looking for other hamstrung beasts.

"By Jove! this is getting worse and more of it," he exclaimed. "See there! That steer has had the tendons of his leg cut to-day. The wound is fresh. It has hardly stopped bleeding. I wonder—"

But before he had finished the sentence he applied the quirt to his pony and was dashing through the herd, with Stella close behind.

He had seen something strange and out of the way in the milling herd, and while he thought he knew what it was he could hardly believe that it could be true.

As he rode he drew his revolver, and broke it to see that its chambers were filled.

Ted's face was pale and stern, and Stella saw at a glance that he was terribly angry, and had the look in it that she had observed there several times when he had seen animals being used with cruelty.

As he dashed into the milling herd he gave a cry of rage.

At the same moment a man sprang to an upright position in the midst of the cattle, and gave a cry of surprise.

Over his shoulders hung the fresh hide of a cow, with the skin of the head and the horns protruding above his head.

He gave one swift glance at Ted, then threw the hide to the ground and set out at a run through the plunging beasts.

Ted was hampered by the cattle getting in his way, and was not making much progress, but he was beating the horned beasts aside with his quirt.

It was possible even yet that the man who was running from him would escape, and this was what Ted was trying with all his might to prevent.

Ted knew why the man was among the cattle protected from them by his disguise of the cow's hide.

He had been hamstringing them by the wholesale.

In one day the inhuman brute could destroy for range use a whole herd.

In the meantime, the cattle were growing wilder and wilder from the pain caused by the hamstringer's knife, the wild career of the unmounted man among them, and Ted and Stella pressing through them from the rear with shouts and cracking quirts.

Edward C. Taylor

"Great Scott! They'll get him!" shouted Ted, reining in his pony.

The furious steers had turned their attention to the man on foot, and were surging about him with angry bellowings, charging upon him, and crowding him.

He was in a very perilous position, and it was only that the cattle were herded so close together that he had not gone down sooner.

But once the cattle got him down he would be gored and trampled to death. Nothing could save him.

Ted and Stella were trying to force their way to his side, but were unable to do so.

Notwithstanding the fact the fellow had been caught in the act of mutilating his cattle, Ted could not see him die without trying to save him.

Now they heard a cry of fear, and saw the man throw his arms up in the air.

The cattle were surging about him with wild and angry bovine cries, and with a great tossing of horns, and leaps into the air.

There were muffled yells of agony from beneath the tossing mass of horns.

"They've got him," muttered Ted. "They are wreaking their own revenge."

"Are they killing him, Ted?" asked Stella.

"They have got him down. The fool he was to go among them on foot. He should have known better."

Ted made another effort to get through the cattle, and at last succeeded in making a lane for himself.

"Stella," he shouted over his shoulder, "you stay where you are! This is nothing for you to see. Better let me attend to this."

Stella was aware that Ted always knew what he was talking about when he warned her away from anything, and she made her way out of the herd.

When Ted got to the spot where he had last seen the man, the cattle were still milling, but were getting calmer, and had no hesitancy in scattering when he rode among them slashing right and left with his quirt and firing his revolver over their heads.

When he had cleared an open space he rode back into it, and instantly recoiled from the sight presented to him.

On the ground lay the hamstringer, a mass of bloody clothes in which were torn flesh and broken bones. He was quite dead, and had been not only gored but had been trampled hundreds of times.

The vengeance of the maimed animals was complete.

CHAPTER VII

A NIGHT RAID

Ted bent over the mangled body of the hamstringer and turned him over. Then he leaped back with an exclamation of horror.

He had recognized the miscreant.

It was Sol Flatbush, the traitorous cow-puncher, member of the gang of cattle rustlers and gamblers headed by Shan Rhue, who had run off about five hundred head of cattle of the Circle S brand into the Wichita Mountains in Indian Territory.

But how had Sol Flatbush got into this part of the country? And where was he stopping? It was evident that the cow-puncher and desperado had hamstrung the cattle out of revenge for having been discovered and driven out of the broncho boys' camp.

Now that he was dead, however, Ted lost all his resentment, and was genuinely sorry for the poor chap because of the horrible means of his death.

Ted hardly knew what to do with him. It were better if his

friends could take charge of his body and bury it, but where were his friends?

Suddenly a thought occurred to Ted. Perhaps Sol Flatbush, following his instincts and habits, had come north after he and Shan Rhue had been outwitted by the boys at the Hole in the Wall in the Wichita Mountains, and allied himself with the Whipple gang in the Sweet Grass Mountains.

If this were true, the simplest thing to do was to send the body of Flatbush to the gang. It would serve, Ted hoped, as a terrible warning to the other members of the gang not to meddle with the affairs of the broncho boys.

Not far away Ted saw a pony, saddled and grazing quietly.

Mounting his pony, he rode up to it. Tied to the cantle of the saddle was a pair of blankets.

This was the very thing! Ted carried the blankets to where the body of Flatbush lay. Spreading them out, he rolled the remains of Flatbush into them, and bound them securely with a rope.

With some difficulty he lifted the bundle to the back of the outlaw's pony, and bound it securely with a lariat.

Then he tied the pony's reins to the horn of the saddle, gave the beast a slash with his quirt, and it started, snorting and jumping, toward the distant mountains.

Thus was the body of Sol Flatbush sent to his friends.

"What was it?" asked Stella, when Ted, having finished his gruesome task, returned to her side.

Edward C. Taylor

"The chap who was mutilating the cattle is dead," he replied. "The bulls turned upon him and gored and trampled him to death."

"Horrible! Do you know who he was?"

"Yes, I recognized him."

"Is that a fact! Who was he?"

"An old enemy of yours."

"An enemy of mine! I didn't know I had one."

"Not really of your own, for no one who knows you could feel any animosity toward you, Stella. But you have enemies through me. Those who would seek to hurt me do so by making trouble for you, knowing that they can hurt me worse by injuring you than they could by torturing me personally."

"That's why you have so often warned me to be careful where I go alone."

"That is why. It is not fair that you should be put to discomfort or in danger of death merely because I make enemies by trying to force men to obey the laws."

"I understand. But who was the man who was killed?"

"Sol Flatbush."

"Sol Flatbush! How does it happen that he is in this country?"

"I'm sure I don't know, unless he and Shan Rhue, after escaping from the Wichita Mountains, came directly here, having previously been members of the notorious Whipple gang."

"Then I suppose we shall see Shan Rhue one of these days. Ted, I'm afraid of that fellow. When they had me in the Hole in the Wall I heard him make the most horrible threats against you."

"Threats don't hurt, Stella. The threatened man lives long. You know the old proverb: 'The man I most fear is he who says nothing, but smiles in your face while he is planning to stab you in the back.'"

They were turned toward the ranch house, and as darkness was falling swiftly, conversation was suspended as they put their ponies to their highest speed, galloping across the snow-covered range toward where they could see the lantern of the house shining like a beacon through the gloom.

For the safety of the boys and the cow-punchers traveling toward the ranch house in the dark, Ted had placed a large lantern on the top of the flagstaff which stood in the front yard, so that it could be seen for miles at night to guide wanderers.

This had been suggested by his experience the first night they had spent at the house.

Those of the boys who were not riding line were stopping at the house, and they were all in the big living room awaiting the coming of Ted and Stella.

When Stella was late in arriving at the house, Mrs. Graham began to grow anxious and worried, and this was communicated to the others.

Edward C. Taylor

But when they heard Ted's ringing yell outside, as he and Stella galloped up, there were shouts of gladness inside, and the big door was thrown open, allowing a broad path of light to fall across the prairie, as two cow-punchers came bounding down the steps to take the ponies to the corral.

After supper Ted told of the maiming of the cattle and the death of Sol Flatbush.

It was part of the life at the ranch that bad news of any sort was never told at the table during meals, and if any of the fellows had a grievance or was in trouble he tried to keep that fact out of his face and look as merry as he could while the others were eating. If he wanted to tell his troubles later, and any one was willing to listen, all right and good, but mealtime was glad time where the broncho boys and their friends sat down together.

While they were sitting before the great fireplace after supper, Clay Whipple was looking into the flames with a preoccupied air.

He had been silent all evening, an unusual thing for him, for usually he injected humorously dry comments into general conversations.

"What's the trouble, Clay?" asked Stella, who was always the first to notice when one of the boys was not his usual self.

"Oh, I don't know," said Clay uneasily.

"Reckon he's worryin' some on account o' this yere mountain bandit bein' ther same name as him," laughed a cow-puncher named "Pike" Bander.

"I reckon you're only joshin', Pike," said Clay quietly, but growing a shade paler.

"Why, shore, Clay. Yer didn't think I wuz in earnest?" Pike hastened to say.

Clay's Kentucky blood would not permit him to receive without resentment any reflections against the South or the people of his family, while he could stand any amount of personal joshing without growing in the least touchy or angry.

"Then what's the matter?" asked Ted, as Clay returned to his gloomy contemplation of the fire.

"I'm worried some, that's all," was the reply.

"Tell your troubles to the policeman, that's us."

"Well, I might as well out with it. Only I don't want to appear as if I was gettin' panicky over nothing."

"What is it, Clay? You are so provoking when I am just dying to hear about it," cried Stella with a laugh. "Out with it."

"Injuns!" said Clay explosively.

"Indians!"

Every one around the fire sat up with a jump.

Clay nodded his head slowly without taking his eyes from the fire.

There was silence for a few minutes, for every one was turning this new menace over in their minds.

The danger from Indians in this far-away Northern country was very real. It was not that the Indians would make any open or daring attacks, but that they were lawless and fearless of the authority of the United States, and despised the "buffalo soldiers" at the near-by army posts.

"Buffalo soldiers" is a name of contempt given by the Indians to the negro troops who had been stationed near the Blackfeet and Crow Indian agencies, on account of their curly, woolly hair, which, in the fantastic minds of the Indians, resembled the short, curly hair on the shoulders of the buffalo.

The negro troops were too near their own color to demand much respect from the Indians.

But the danger did not come so much from the reservation Indians, as from the fugitive Indians who had left the reservations and had become outlaws, allying themselves with the white bandits in the mountains, and living by thievery from the ranchmen and sheep-herders.

Some of these Indians had rallied around Running Bear, a young Blackfeet, son of a chief, a graduate of the Indian School at Carlisle, in Pennsylvania.

Running Bear was a young fellow of magnificent physique, for he had been a member of the famous Indian football team of Carlisle that had a year or two previously cleared all white teams from the gridiron.

Running Bear was well educated also, and a man of fine address and manners, when he wished to be so. But he was unprincipled, and when he returned to the tribe lost no time in breaking all the laws imposed by the United States for the government and welfare of the Indians.

This brought him into conflict with the Indian agent, and certain penalties were imposed on him. This he would not stand, and soon persuaded other of the young men of the tribe to mutiny against the agent.

This led to further trouble, and after committing some unforgivable offense against the United States, Running Bear rallied his young men, and they fled the reservation and the ways and protection of the white men, and took to the mountains, where they lived by raiding the ranches in the neighborhood, and maintaining a sort of defensive partnership with Whipple's band of white outlaws.

After a silence, during which every one was turning these facts over in his mind, Ted turned to Clay, and said:

"What about the Indians, Clay?"

"I saw their tracks."

"Where?"

"In the coulee back of the house."

"Near the house!" exclaimed Ted. "That's getting pretty close to home. Did they see you?"

"I reckon they did. I took a shot at one of them, an' he left a red trail in the snow."

"That's bad, Clay. You shouldn't have shot at him."

"Shouldn't, eh? Well, you never saw a fellow from ole Kaintuck that would stand up an' let a man shoot at him without sending his compliments back—if he happened to be packin' his gun at the time."

"Did they shoot at you, then?"

"One of them did. It was like this: I was ridin' in from the west, where I had seen a small bunch of strays which I turned back to the main herd. As I was comin' up to the big coulee I saw something move against the snow. At first I thought it was a grouse, and was just going to take a shot at it when I looked again. Then, by jinks, I saw that it was the head of an Indian shoved up over the edge of the coulee.

"His back was turned to me, and he was watching the house. I pulled in my pony and kept my eye on him for several minutes."

"Then I saw Mrs. Graham come out of the house and stand for a moment on the back porch."

"The Indian rose up and brought a rifle to his shoulder. At that I let out a yell, and he turned to me like a flash, and pulled his trigger. But he was in too much of a hurry, an' the ball whistled over my head."

"I had my gun out, an' blazed away. The Indian yawped as if he had been hit, and disappeared. I got to the coulee as fast as I could, but he had disappeared."

"Was he the only one?" asked Ted.

"I reckon not, for there were any number of moccasin tracks in the coulee, and the footprints of white men or Indians who wore boots. There was a splotch of blood where the Indian had been, and a red trail leading to where there had been ponies. Then I came on to the house."

Ted was thinking deeply. At last he raised his head.

"This has been a day full of things that may mean a great deal to us," he said. "Follansbee has been shot by a member of the Whipple gang, Sol Flatbush was killed after mutilating our cattle, more Whipple gang; and an Indian prowler has been shot, some more of the Whipple gang. Boys, the war is on, and it depends on us whether it is going to last all winter and cause us to lose all our cattle, or whether we are going to be able to stamp it out right now. Which shall it be?"

"I reckon we'd better get busy. It'll be easier ter do the job now than fuss along with it all winter," said Pike Bander, who was an old Northern cow-puncher, and had had lots of experience with the Indians in Montana, the Dakotas, and Wyoming.

"I think you're right, Pike," said Ted. "And now off to bed with you. There'll be something doing to-morrow."

In half an hour the house was dark, and every one was asleep.

The moon which had been shining brightly during the early part of the night had become obscured by a heavy bank of snow clouds, which had been driven over the mountains by a north wind, and it had grown much darker outside.

In his sleep Ted seemed to hear the well-known voice of Sultan, whinnying shrilly. It was a dream, and Ted tossed uneasily. But again and again he heard Sultan's voice. It had a note of alarm in it, and Ted knew that Sultan seldom gave an alarm of this sort unless something serious was the matter. Ted's dream was of Indians, and the call of Sultan was very natural, for the little black stallion hated Indians, and whenever one came within smelling distance of him he grew uneasy and fretful, and always gave voice to his fear.

The dream had such a disquieting influence on Ted that it woke him, and he sat up in bed grinning to himself in the dark to find that, after all, it was only a dream, and that he was safe in bed.

But what was that?

He was awake now, and he distinctly heard Sultan. Then he had heard his pet give a warning, even in his dream.

Leaping from bed, Ted groped around the room, getting into his clothes, without lighting the lamp.

Grasping his rifle from the corner, and buckling on his belt and holster, he left the room.

As he passed Clay's room he entered and shook the sleeping Kentuckian, who was on the floor with a bound. Ted told him of the continued voicing of an alarm by Sultan, and Clay hurriedly dressed.

They passed into the living room, and Ted went to the windows on one side, while Clay went to the other side.

Hidden by the curtains, they stood looking out on the snow-covered plain.

"Hist!" It was Clay trying to attract Ted's attention.

Ted went swiftly to his side.

"What's that down by the corral?" whispered Clay.

Ted looked sharply.

"It's the Indians," said Ted. "They're trying to steal our

horses. Sultan knows what he's about. Come on, we'll have to rush them."

Ted heard a rustling noise behind him and turned.

It was Stella, fully dressed, and with her rifle resting in the hollow of her arm.

"I heard Sultan, too," she said. "We'll have to hurry if we're going to save the horses."

"You go back to bed," said Ted. "Yi-yi-yipee!"

His voice rang out in the old Moon Valley yell.

It was like a fire bell to a fireman, and brought the boys out of their beds like a shot, and they scrambled into their clothes and were in the living room with their arms in a jiffy.

In the corral a great commotion was taking place, to judge from the noise that came to them.

At the word of command they rushed through the door, and raced for the corral, turning loose the long yell.

They heard guttural shouts in the distance, and a band of ponies came through the gateway of the corral, scattering over the prairie.

Behind them rushed a band of Indians, who, seeing that there was no further occasion for silence, gave forth whoops of defiance.

Then Ted saw Sultan gallop out, and on his back was an Indian.

This was more than Ted could stand, and his rifle flew to his shoulder. There was a flash and a crash, and the Indian fell to the ground, over which he writhed in agony.

Ted whistled, and Sultan trotted to his side.

The ponies had scattered, and the corral was empty.

CHAPTER VIII

THE WAR PARTY

The Indians had fled in every direction.

They had been foiled in their purpose of running the ponies off in a band, as they had intended, by Ted's fortunate discovery of the raid.

How to gather the ponies together again was the question that puzzled Ted, for the broncho boys had no mounts with which to pursue the would-be thieves.

It was not long before the light appeared in the east, and by that time Ted had ridden to Bud's sign camp, and thence to camp No. 2, and had four more horsemen to assist him in the pony round-up.

These worked unceasingly, riding the snowy prairie, picking up the ponies which the Indians had not been able to round into a bunch to drive to their rendezvous in the mountains.

The attack upon them had been so sudden that they had taken no heed of where they were going. It was every man for himself, with the broncho boys' bullets for the hindmost.

Edward C. Taylor

About noon Ted and the boys from the sign camps rode up to the ranch house, driving before them a band of about twenty ponies which they had found grazing on the prairie or seeking the shelter of the coulees.

Not a sign of the marauding Indians had they seen.

"Boys, as soon as we can get something to eat we're going after those Indians," said Ted, dismounting and going into the house. "We've got mounts for nearly all of us, now. A guard will be left at the house, then we'll get on their trail. We can't afford to let this thing go. Those Indians must be taught a lesson, so that they will get over the idea that they can run in on us and take what they want just because we are boys."

"That's ther way ter talk," exclaimed Bud Morgan heartily. "Give 'em what's comin' to 'em, an' give it to 'em good an' plenty."

"I guess it won't be any snap to find them now," said Ben.

"They've scattered. But we can trail them. They'll leave a track like that of a moose, it will be so wide. They're in the hills somewhere, laying for another opportunity to raid the corral. They need ponies to ride, and beef to eat, and they have got the idea into their heads that we were sent out here to cater to their wants. It's our business to fool them."

"Oh, hurry up," cried Stella. "I'm so anxious to get started I'm all in a flutter."

"Who said you were going?" asked Ted, with a smile. "This is no pleasure trip. Trailing and fighting Indian outlaws is no matinee."

"I should say not," said Stella coolly. "But it's work for the broncho boys, and I'm one of them. Bud has promised to teach me the art of following an Indian trail, and there never will be a better time than this."

Ted could only shrug his shoulders, as he turned away to see if McCall was hurrying dinner. He knew that he would waste time arguing with the spirited young woman, who was as good a cowgirl as he was a cowboy, and for one of her sex quite as courageous.

So eager were the boys to be off that they fairly bolted their food, and rushed to the corral to saddle their cayuses.

Then they saw to their arms, and each took his rifle in the boot of his saddle.

Sultan had had such a hard day's work since daylight, rounding up the scattered ponies, that Ted left him in the corral, and decided to ride a fresh horse. The only serviceable animal he could find was the worst riding beast on the place, a vicious, half-broken Texas pony, which had to be roped and held before the rider could mount.

This, however, made little difference to Ted, who could ride anything that would fit a saddle.

While he held the saddle ready to throw it on Bingo's back Bud roped and held the rearing, raging, bucking beast, who was busy kicking holes in the air with his wicked heels.

After maneuvering around the corral several times, Ted managed to dodge the flying hoofs long enough to slip the saddle and tie the latigo.

Then it was up to him to mount.

Edward C. Taylor

Whenever he approached Bingo from the rear, dancing around to escape the pony's battery, and got to the side where he could grasp the horn of his saddle, Bingo would wheel in a circle away from him as if he was fastened to a pivot.

The performance was getting monotonous, for the boys were standing around in a ring waiting to start.

Ted was getting impatient also at the fool antics of the pony.

"Stop your fooling," he said to Bingo. "When I do land on your back I'll make you sorry you didn't stand still, my bucko."

He stepped back several feet and stood looking at the pony, who, with ears flattened and the whites of his eyes showing, stood still also, waiting for further developments.

He didn't know exactly what was coming, but wanted to be ready for it, whatever it was to be.

Suddenly Ted gave a short, swift run, leaped in the air, and before Bingo could gather himself for a plunge, Ted was astraddle of the saddle.

Bingo remembered his part then, but he was too late, for simultaneously he felt the sting of the quirt across his shoulder, and the prick of the spur in his flank.

A horse can think of only one thing at a time, while a mule can pay attention to the mule-skinner's lash and think of forty-seven varieties of devilment at the same time.

In trying to keep his mind on the sting of the quirt and the prick of the rowels at the same time, Bingo got rattled.

He leaped high into the air, intending to fall backward, and crush his rider. But Ted had been there before many times, and as he went up a stinging blow across Bingo's withers brought him down in a hurry.

Then he did some more plunging, but the spur in his side, and Ted's firm seat, soon convinced him that it was wasting time to fool with Ted, and he set off at a gallop across the prairie.

With a ringing cheer the boys followed, and soon caught up with him.

When they were together again, Ted paired the boys off to scout.

"I'll tell you how you will probably find it, fellows," said Ted. "The Indians ride in different directions. Whenever you hit a trail follow it, but go slow and keep your eyes peeled for an ambuscade. You will find that eventually all the trails will lead to the same place. If we are in luck, we will find them before they go on into the mountains, and we may have a skirmish. I hope, however, that we will be able to settle the matter without resorting to any shooting. Uncle Sam is mighty touchy about any one killing his Indians except his soldiers, no matter what an Indian does. We'll probably all come together where the Indians are. Kit, you ride with me. You other fellows choose your partners. Bud, take good care of Stella."

"You kin bet yer active an' useful life I will," said Bud, as he and Stella galloped off together.

Bud and Kit rode away to the north, while the other broncho boys spread out in pairs over the prairie.

Ted had been riding an hour without crossing a track.

"There's no use going in this direction any longer, Kit," he said. "They've probably gone farther to the west. I guess we'd better strike off that way, and take a chance of cutting them somewhere over there."

They had paused on the bank of a small frozen stream lined with willows, and Ted had dismounted to walk up and down the bank to find a place where he could break a hole in the ice to water the ponies.

"You'll have to rope Bingo and hold him when I go to get on," he said to Kit before he got down.

"All right," said Kit. "I'd get down and cut that hole in the ice myself, only my arm might give me trouble again. I've got to be mighty careful of it yet."

As Ted was looking for a safe place to lead the ponies down to the stream, with Bingo's bridle reins hanging over his arm, he was startled by a snort from the brute, and a sudden back pull.

He looked over his shoulder at the pony to see what was the matter with it.

Bingo was standing with his head high, his ears pointed forward, his nostrils as red as if they were lined with red silk, and the whites of his eyes like pieces of chalk, snorting as if in terror.

Ted read the symptoms instantly.

"He smells Indians," he muttered to himself.

He looked around for Kit, and saw him far down the stream, struggling vainly with the pony he was riding, which was running away in a panic of fear.

Kit was an expert and dauntless horseman, and not one of the broncho boys except Ted could excel him in horsemanship, but with his wounded arm he could not bring the brute under control.

"That settles it with me," muttered Ted. "I'm going to have a time getting on the back of this beast, for he will be worse than ever now that he has scented Indians."

He heard a noise behind him, and wheeled.

Coming out of the willows a few hundred yards away were a score of Indians, painted for war and all armed with rifles.

With a hasty movement the leader of the broncho boys loosened his revolvers and glanced to see if his rifle was ready for instant use.

The Indians had stopped, as much surprised as Ted, and stood staring at him in a stupid sort of way.

Ted saw that if he was to escape being murdered now was his chance, and turned to his pony.

As he did so the Indians let out a whoop that frightened Bingo almost into a fit, and, wheeling suddenly, he dashed away, almost dragging the reins from Ted's grasp.

But as he did so Ted was by his side, running with one hand clutching the long mane.

It was rough running over the rocks and hummocks with

Edward C. Taylor

which the bank of the stream was strewn, but Ted seemed to fly through space, so lightly did his feet touch the ground.

Rifle balls were now singing through the air above Ted, and on every side, which only served to increase the speed with which Bingo was running away from his enemies, the Indians.

Bingo had been trained in New Mexico, Arizona, and Texas to regard the Indian as his natural enemy, and whenever he smelled one it was his most earnest desire to get as far away as possible in the shortest space of time.

This was fortunate for Ted also.

While it was not an easy matter for Ted to mount while the pony was wheeling away from him, Ted was well educated in the cavalry drill as used at West Point, and mounting a running horse was one of the easiest of the many equestrian tricks with which he was familiar.

When he thought he was far enough away from the Indians not to afford them too good an aim for his body, he placed his hand on the cantle of the saddle, gave a smart upward spring, and the impetus of his running and the pony's speed took him through the air like a bird, and he settled in the saddle as easily, almost, as if he would have sat down in a chair.

As he reached the saddle he, for the first time, threw a glance over his shoulder.

The Indians were in full pursuit, yelling like madmen.

They were led by a young fellow dressed in a yellow buckskin shirt elaborately beaded, and trimmed with fringe, while on his head was a bonnet of eagle feathers, which trailed far behind him as he dashed on far in advance of his followers.

"Here's a chance to stop that chap," said Ted, swinging around in his saddle and throwing his forty-five over his shoulder.

The six-shooter cracked, and as the smoke floated away Ted saw that his bullet had gone where he intended it to go.

The pony on which the young Indian was riding stumbled and staggered forward a few feet, then dropped.

That brought the party to a halt, and Ted, turning his face forward, galloped on.

Kit had succeeded in mastering his pony and had brought it to a halt, and, as the report of Ted's revolver reached his ears, he turned and rode rapidly in that direction.

As the two boys came together and found that they were unharmed and that the war party of Indians had been halted, they dove into a coulee, followed it a short distance, and climbed again to higher ground.

The Indians were no longer in sight, and they set off at a gallop toward the west.

For half an hour they rode, when Ted suddenly pulled his pony to a stop.

On a rise far away he saw a black, slowly moving mass, which, at first, he had taken to be a band of buffalo, but when it strung out he discovered that it was a party of men on horseback.

Edward C. Taylor

As the sun was behind the riders, Ted could not distinguish whether or not they were Indians or whites, as he could have done if the sun had been shining upon them.

"If it's Indians I don't want any more of it," he said.

"I don't think they are Indians," said Kit. "Those fellows sit straighter than Indians. I believe they are either our own boys, or cavalry from the post."

"I believe you are right," said Ted. "Let's fire a few shots to attract their attention, and then ride to them."

The shots were fired, and presently they heard several faint reports, and knew that they had been heard and answered.

In a few minutes they had ridden to where the party was standing on the ridge of a rolling hill.

They were the broncho boys under the leadership of Ben Tremont. They had all come together on a broad trail that pointed toward the foothills in the north, and, as they rode, had picked up one pair of scouts after another.

"Where are Bud and Stella?" asked Ted, running his eye over the party.

"Haven't seen anything of them," said Ben, "although we have been keeping a lookout for them. They rode farther to the west, and probably will pick us up later. I think this trail leads into the hills, and that we will find the Indians in camp not far away."

This was Ted's belief also, and, taking the leadership, he ordered an advance.

"Halt!" Ted Strong had stopped his pony, and with his hand shading his eyes, was looking steadily to the front.

"What is it?" asked Ben, riding to his side.

"Smoke over the top of that hill right in front of us."

Ted did not take his eyes from the spot.

"By Jove!" he exclaimed. "The bunch of Indians who chased me have taken a short cut and beaten us in. I saw a band of Indians cross in front of us, and one pony carried double."

"Then we have caught up with them."

"I think so. Hold the boys here, I'm going forward to scout. When I signal, come forward as fast as you can ride."

CHAPTER IX

A BATTLE OF QUIRTS

Ted turned Bingo over to one of the boys to care for, and crept forward stealthily toward the hill behind which he had seen a thin thread of blue smoke rising in the still air.

No one but an Indian or a trained scout would build so small a fire. A tenderfoot would have made one that roared and sent a vast cloud of smoke toward the sky to attract any enemy that might be in the vicinity.

But an Indian builds his fire in a space not much larger than the hollow of his two hands, and manages to send up smoke that only a trained eye could detect, and at the same time have heat enough with which to warm himself and cook his food, with as little fuel as possible.

As he went forward, Ted was surprised that he came upon no sign of a camp guard.

The Indians evidently thought that the boys would not have the courage to follow them into their own country, and had grown careless.

So much the better. It would give him a chance to learn how

they were situated before making an attack.

He crept on his hands and knees to the ridge of the hill, and, removing his hat, peered over the edge.

Below in a small valley he saw about fifty Indians, who, from their dress and their manner of painting their faces, he knew to be of various tribes.

He easily recognized in the band several Blackfeet, six or seven Crows, some Sioux, who had come far north, and to his astonishment a few Southern Indians, such as Caddos, Cheyennes, and Comanches.

This alone was enough to convince him that the Indians were outlaws and renegades, and that they were plunderers and thieves, as well; probably murderers hiding out from the United States troops.

In the circle about the fire he soon discovered the young fellow whose pony he had shot beside the frozen stream.

The young Indian, for he did not appear much older than Ted himself, was holding forth to a number of other Indians.

Probably he was boasting of his pursuit of the white boy, and the unfortunate mishap that brought down his pony and prevented him from bringing a white captive into camp.

Not far away from this group Ted observed a man dressed in Indian garb, who yet did not act like the other Indians. An Indian has a peculiar, slouching walk, while this man strode about with the smarter, quicker, springier tread of a white man.

Presently the supposed Indian drew from his belt a pouch of

Edward C. Taylor

tobacco and some cigarette papers, and proceeded to roll a cigarette.

Northern Indians do not roll cigarettes; they smoke pipes. It is only the Indians of the Southwest who take their solace from tobacco through the little homemade paper tubes.

"That's a fellow who has been a cow-puncher," said Ted. "He's a white man disguised as an Indian. Probably one of the Whipple gang. I've got my opinion of a white man who will play Indian, and live with the dirty scoundrels," said Ted to himself, with disgust.

He had seen all that was necessary, and had laid his plan of attack in his mind.

Creeping down the hill, he threw his hand in the air as a signal for the boys to come to him, also signaling for silence.

In a few minutes they were by his side, and, while one of the fellows held Bingo safely, Ted sprang into the saddle.

"Now, fellows, we're going to ride around the end of this hill and plump into the Indian camp. The snow will deaden the hoofbeats of the ponies, but keep as still as possible. We'll surprise them, and probably be able to settle the whole thing without firing a shot. But don't bet on it, and keep your hands on your guns, but don't fire until they make the first crack, then rush them and drive them into the hills, and bring down all you can."

With this advice they rode forward by twos, Ted and Ben in the lead.

It did not take long to round the hill, and then, as suddenly as if they had opened a door and stepped into a room, they were in the midst of the Indians.

No such surprising and sudden attack was ever made. The Indians stood as if they were carved of wood as the boys rode up to them, staring open-mouthed.

Only one of them made a break—the young Indian whom Ted had dismounted.

For several moments not a word was said.

Ted saw instantly that the broncho boys had all the best of it, and that the Indians had been taken completely by surprise, for not one of them was armed. Their rifles and guns were either still on their saddles, and the ponies were standing some distance away, or they were stacked beside a ledge of rock twenty or more feet from the fire, where most of them were congregated.

The young fellow whom Ted had foiled stared for a moment with a look of contempt and dislike.

Suddenly he made a rush to where the guns were standing.

"Stop!" Ted's voice rang out sharply. But the youth continued to run.

"Stop, or I'll kill you!" shouted Ted again.

Then an old Indian cried out something, in the tongue of the Blackfeet, and the young fellow halted suddenly and came walking back with a sickly look on his face.

The old Indian who had stopped the youth now stepped a little ways forward, and, holding up his hands in a peace sign, began to talk.

"You are my brothers," he said, "and Flying Sun, the medicine man, welcomes you to our camp."

Ted held up his hands in a sign of peace also, but said nothing.

"He's a darned old hypocrite," said Ben, in an aside to Ted. "He has murder in those little red eyes of his, if ever a man had."

"I'm on to him," said Ted. "Keep your eyes on that bunch, and give it to them if they start anything treacherous."

"My white brothers come with peace for their red brothers. Join us at the fire. Warm yourselves; eat of our meat."

"We are willing to be brothers," said Ted. "But one brother does not steal the ponies from the corral of the other."

"That was the work of the young men, and they are now sorry for it," said the medicine man.

Ted looked at the young fellow whom he had unhorsed, and saw that his face was distended in a sarcastic smile.

"The young brave yonder is the one who led the raid on my corral. He does not look sorry," said Ted, pointing to the offender.

Flying Sun threw a glance in the direction of the young man, and said a few words sharply in the Blackfeet tongue.

"Crazy Cow is young and the son of a chief. His blood is hot within him, and he does not know what he does," said Flying Sun.

Crazy Cow's face at once assumed a look of sadness.

"I have not come for war," said Ted gravely, "but I want to warn you and your tribe that I will not stand for any raids on our ranch. You will find that we are good fighters, and that we can kill just as well as the soldiers. The ranch is ours, and the cattle and horses are ours, and do not belong to the young men of your tribe. They must leave us alone, or we will be compelled to deal out justice to them in our own way, which is a hard one."

"Very well, my brother," said the wily old chief. "We desire to live in peace with our white brothers. Your cattle and horses shall be sacred to our young men."

"I mean this," said Ted, looking at the old man severely. "Keep your young men away from our ranch, or they will be killed."

At this Crazy Cow drew himself up to his full height, and looked at Ted with scorn.

"Two can make killing," he said, in perfectly plain English.

"Perhaps they can," said Ted quickly. "But I want to say to you particularly, that if you are ever seen within the lines of the Long Tom Ranch again you will be sorry that you ever were born. I have said enough. Get on your horses and go. You are now on the ranch. Get beyond it."

The young Indian gave a short, harsh laugh, and strode toward a pony, decorated after the fashion of war ponies with feathers and bits of red flannel woven into his mane and tail.

The other Indians were not slow to follow his example, and soon they were all mounted.

"Now look out for treachery," said Ted in an aside to the boys.

"Keep your eyes peeled, fellows," said Ben, passing the word along back.

"Ride up in open order so that we can surround that bunch if they get gay," said Ted, in a low voice, and the boys rode out and scattered themselves in a long line.

The Indians were bunched pretty well together.

It was a critical moment.

The slightest suspicious move on the part of the boys might have alarmed the Indians and started a fight.

While the boys kept their hands on their weapons not one was drawn.

The Indians rode off to a distance of a few hundred feet, then halted. All had their rifles or guns in their hands, but not in a hostile way.

They were well aware that the white boys were much better armed than they, and were not in a temper to stand any foolishness.

It seemed as if the Indians had stopped to say good-by before riding away into the mountains.

But when they stopped, Crazy Cow rode out from them a short distance and stopped.

"I am Crazy Cow," he said in a boastful way.

This was in the manner of a personal challenge, as if he had said: "Who the deuce are you? Knock the chip off my shoulder if you dare."

Ted looked at him for a moment, for Crazy Cow was staring at him with an impertinent look in his face.

"I don't care who you are," said Ted, who was disgusted with the fellow's airs. "If you were the chief himself, I would tell you to keep away from my cows and ponies. What is the son of a chief? Nothing!"

The tone in which Ted said this was such that the young Indian flushed a deeper red, and grasped his rifle harder.

"I am an educated Indian," said Crazy Cow, "and as good as any white man. This is my country, and I shall go wherever I please."

"Go where you will, except on my ranch. Keep off that."

The Indian shrugged his shoulders.

"I go where I please. You, whoever you are, have no right to prevent me from going anywhere. Who are you to talk to me like that?"

"My name is Ted Strong. I am a deputy United States marshal. Do you know what that is?"

"Yes. I spit on them."

"Well, here's one you won't spit on. That's a cinch. You ought to be ashamed of yourself, a man who got his education free from the United States, to talk that way."

"Bah! I hate the United States which robbed my people of their lands, and then made treaties only to break them. Since they have driven me into the mountains they owe me a living, and I'm going to collect it."

"Very well, only be careful how you do it. I have said enough."

"Ted Strong talks big and much, but does nothing. He is a coward who is afraid of the Indian."

"I am not afraid of you. I think I have shown it."

"Yes, but you ran when I surprised you by the stream."

"My pony ran, and to keep from losing him I clung to him."

"It was a good thing for you that he did run. If he hadn't, you would never have gone home again, and the buzzards and vultures, assisted by the prairie wolves, would have you by now."

"Big talk means nothing. You are not a fighter, you are a squaw. You are a fool and a boaster."

"No, I am a chief, and a warrior. I have seen the blood of the white man flow, and I drank it. I am brave."

"You're full of hot air. Run along now; I'm disgusted with you."

"Hah! White squaw afraid to fight. Go back to your camp, and cook the meals and wash the clothes in the tub."

Crazy Cow made motions, of scrubbing at a tub.

At this the other Indians burst into laughter.

"You are but an idle boaster, Crazy Cow. You make much noise like the wind in the trees. That is all it amounts to. You do not make me feel bad by what you say."

Crazy Cow, seeing that he could not get Ted angry with his banter, tried a new tack.

"Hah, little bay pony," he cried, addressing Bingo. "Are you a squaw pony?"

He paused in a listening attitude as if he was paying close attention to what the pony was saying.

"Yes, you are ashamed to be ridden by a squaw who does not fight, but only talks. Come over here, squaw pony, and be ridden by a man."

Again his speech was greeted by the laughter of the Indians, to whom it was interpreted by the disguised white man.

"So you think I will not fight, eh? You think I am a squaw, do you?" said Ted quietly.

The Indian only laughed.

"I will show you who is the squaw. I will thrash you with my quirt until you cry out with pain. You may keep your gun. I am not afraid of it."

"Now you begin to talk a little like a man. But you won't fight. Little pony, you are ridden by a squaw. Why don't you throw him off and come to me, who is a fighter?"

"Fellows, stand fast," said Ted to the boys. "I'm going to give that young buck such a licking as he never thought possible. If they don't play fair, shoot."

Ted threw his rifle to Ben, so that he would not be burdened by it, and rode toward the Indian, who also threw his weapon to one of his followers. In his right hand he carried a long, braided Indian whip of thongs. It was a cruel weapon, for the Indian is cruel to everything in his power, from his squaw to his dog.

This he grasped firmly in his right hand, and awaited Ted's coming with a satirical smile on his face.

Ted had been coming on quietly, but when he was a few feet from Crazy Cow he suddenly gave Bingo the spur, and the astonished horse reached the Indian's side in two jumps.

Without a moment's hesitation Ted reached forward and grasped the Indian by a collar of leather which he wore laced around his throat, somewhat after the fashion of the white linen chokers worn by young white men.

Furiously the young Indian lashed out with his quirt, which struck Ted across the shoulders, and made him wince with the burning sharpness of it.

But Ted was back at him like a flash, and his quirt sang through the air and slapped upon the buckskin shirt worn by the Indian.

Crazy Cow, whom the lash had not hurt in the least, only laughed.

Ted saw that he might go on thrashing the Indian all day upon his shirt, and that it would have no more effect than if he whipped a covering of iron.

The other Indians also saw the humor of the situation, and joined in the laughter.

Meantime, the Indian was plying his quirt with all his force, and every time the lash struck Ted across the shoulders or neck it left a blue welt.

Whipping fights are common among the Indian lads, and are merely tests of courage, and the power to endure pain without crying out. The Indian boy who cries out unexpectedly at some particularly stinging blow is called a squaw, and sent into Coventry by the others for varying lengths of time, during which none of them will speak to him.

Crazy Cow had often indulged in the whipping sport, and knew how to wield the quirt most effectively.

So the battle of the quirts went on, the blows falling as fast as their arms could fly, but Ted plainly was getting the worst of it on account of the protection which the buckskin shirt gave the Indian.

Ted saw that this soon must change or he would be ignominiously beaten. He had not shown that he suffered any pain from the blows he received, although the Indians watched his face closely for any sign that he was weakening.

At last Ted thought that he had discovered a vulnerable spot.

With a sudden wrench of his strong wrist upon the leather collar which he grasped, he whipped Crazy Cow flat across his saddle and held him there.

Then with all his strength he brought his quirt across the seat of Crazy Cow's blue flannel trousers, which were drawn tight, and upon the tender part of the back of his legs.

The Indian struggled furiously, but could not release himself, and all the while the cruel blows were raining upon him.

A huge burst of laughter rose from the broncho boys, but the Indians could not see the joke, and with angry exclamations started forward to rescue their young chief.

But at this sign of hostility Ben Tremont let out a roar, and every broncho boy threw his rifle to his shoulder, and the Indians shrank back in silence.

Ted thrashed the Indian until his yells of agony and his struggles ceased, then threw him aside.

"Go back to your people and tell them that you are no longer fit to be chief. That you have been whipped with a quirt by a white boy until you cried. It is you who are the squaw," said Ted, riding back to his party.

CHAPTER X

SILVER FACE

As Ted released the badly punished young Indian and rode back to where the boys were waiting for him, Crazy Cow painfully raised himself to a sitting position in his saddle. But the pain was too great, and he slowly and painfully slid to the ground. But the backs of his legs were so seamed with welts that he could not walk.

He was, indeed, an object for pity, but he had been defeated, and not only that, but had been whipped on the most shameful spot, in Indian fighting, and his friends would have none of him.

When he looked toward them for sympathy they only pointed the finger of scorn at him, and laughed.

Now Ted rode out in front of the boys, and, raising his voice, said to the Indians:

"Go back to your village. Do not come to my ranch again. Next time it will be something worse than quirts with which we fight, and dead men, instead of squaws with sore legs, will be the result. Go!"

Edward C. Taylor

The old medicine man turned his pony toward the mountains, and in a guttural voice gave the command.

Without a word, and without looking back, the Indians started on their way, Crazy Cow following dejectedly on foot, leading his pony.

He had been conquered and humiliated, but his heart burned with hatred for the young white chief who had been the cause of it.

When the Indians were out of sight, Ted returned to the boys.

"Well, that's over for the present," he said.

"Yes, but we'll have trouble with those fellows later, you may be sure," said Ben. "Look out for a ball or a knife in the back from Crazy Cow."

"I don't fear him as much as I do the cunning and treachery of that old villain, Flying Sun, who plans these raids and lets the young men execute them while he stays back in a safe place."

"What interests me more than anything else just now is Stella and Bud. I propose that we drop everything else and hunt for them. You know that since the appearance of the man without a face, and now this encounter with the Indians, to say nothing of sending Sol Flatbush's body home on his horse, the members of the Whipple gang will be pretty keen after every member of our party."

"True, Ben. We must be very careful of Stella from now on. I would not have taken this ranch had I known that it was menaced by such a gang of thieves as seems to be in the mountains."

"Where had we better scout?" asked Ben.

"Do you think Bud and Stella went farther west?"

"Yes. As we started away from the ranch house I heard Bud say to Stella, 'When the gang came out of the corral just before daylight I saw that most of them headed into the west. If we go that way we're sure to beat the others to the trail.' Then I saw them slip away quietly back of the house, and later they disappeared over a rise due west."

"Then that's where we must look for them. Forward, fellows. We're going to find Bud and Stella."

"Do you think it is necessary for all of us to go?" asked Kit.

"No, I don't. The ranch must have a guard of some sort. About half of you turn back to the lines, and two of you ride to the ranch house to see that all is well, and guard it."

Ben sorted out the fellows who were to go back to the ranch, keeping all the broncho boys to start on the hunt for the missing ones.

No one felt exactly uneasy for the safety of Stella and Bud, but it was proper, under the circumstances, to see that they were safe.

"As before, we will split up into couples to search for Bud and Stella," said Ted. "You better come with me this time, Ben."

To the west of the line of the Long Tom Ranch the land became more broken. At first the hills ceased to be rolling and broke off into canons, more or less deep, with sometimes sides that assumed the dignity of precipices.

The sides of the foothills were clothed in small tracts of scrubby pine timber, and altogether it was not a pleasant country to travel over in winter.

*   *   *   *   *

When Bud and Stella left the ranch house, Stella was bubbling over with joy at the prospect of being in the hunt for the Indians, and the prospect of Bud teaching her the mysteries of the trail, particularly the war trail.

"Don't say a word," said Bud, with a wink, "an' we'll fool 'em all. Them Injuns never went nowhere except inter ther east. I threwed out a blast o' hot atmosphere erbout them goin' west. That wuz ter fool ole nosey Ben, who had his neck stretched out like a spring chicken's ter hear what was bein' said, an' git ther advantage o' my sooperior knowledge.

"Well, when I see that I thort I'd give him somethin' ter chase, so I hands out the west p'int, when I mean ter go ter ther east. When we start out we'll ride ter ther west until we come ter ther first draw, then foller it ter ther south until we come ter a break leadin' east, then foller that, an' we'll be fust onter ther red man's tracks."

"All right," laughed Stella. "That will be a good joke on Ben. He didn't like it because he couldn't go with us."

Now it will be seen that Bud's little fiction in the hearing of Ben was not the proper thing, and, as it turned out, Bud was mighty sorry for his apparently innocent fib before the end of the day, or the dawning of the next.

They did as Bud planned, and when they were well out of sight and hearing of the other boys they turned to the east, and, when well out on the prairie, turned their ponies' heads to the north.

As they cantered across the prairie, on which the snow was like dry sand and only about an inch deep, they could see bands of their cattle here and there pawing the snow off the grass, or "rustling" for their fodder, as the cowmen call it.

"I shore believe thar's somethin' wrong on this yere range," Bud remarked, after they had gone a few miles.

"Why?" asked Stella.

"Somethin' wrong with ther cattle."

"In what way?"

"Thar ain't half enough o' them here."

"Do you mean that some of them are gone?"

"Yep. Thet's jest what I mean."

"Strayed, probably?"

"No. Stole."

"Nonsense. Who could have stolen them? The Indians?"

"No. I reckon not. The Injuns is keen after ponies. In the fust place thar ain't nobody what kin wear out a pony as fast as an Injun. They work their ponies ter death, starve 'em, beat ther hides off'n 'em, neglect 'em, and when they're wore out turn 'em loose fer ther wolves. Second, they kin run off a bunch o' ponies in a hurry, but they balk some at rustlin' cattle because they move so slow. If we aire shy on beeves ther white men has got 'em."

"When we get back we ought to round the cattle up and count."

"That's ther only way ter do it. I've got a pretty good eye fer a herd, an' it's my idee thet we're losers here, an' that ther rustlers is gittin' rich off'n us."

About noon Bud pulled in his horse, and examined the snowy ground carefully.

He had struck a trail.

Winding across the prairie in a northeasterly direction was a broad trail, the tracks of many cattle and horses.

"Here we are," said Bud. "Thar's whar some o' our cattle and several ponies have passed."

He got down to the ground, and, stooping over the trail, regarded it carefully.

Suddenly he straightened up.

"This is not an Injun trail," he said.

"It isn't?" asked Stella.

"No. Here are the tracks of cattle, an' on top of them those of horses ridden by white men."

"How do you know they were not Indians?"

"Here's an impression o' a horseshoe, an' here's another o' a different size. These were made by animiles ridden by white men."

"I can understand why you should know that they were white men's horses because Indians do not shoe their ponies, but I'm blessed if I can see how you know that white men were riding them."

"Easy enough. These horses were ridden straight. An Indian, in spite of stories to the contrary, is not a good horseman. He rides all over the ground instead of straight ahead when he is going anywhere, seemin' as if he wanted to get his money's worth of the ride. If it had been Indians who were driving off these cattle, you would see pony tracks all over the prairie about here."

"Then we've struck the wrong trail."

"Well, we've missed the Indians, but we've struck another and a better lead. Ther boys under Ted will most likely git in ther trail o' ther pony snatchers, but we're on another lay—cattle thieves."

"This is something of a surprise, isn't it?"

"You bet. If we hadn't run ercross this yere trail we mightn't have got on ter ther fact thet our steers wuz bein' lifted ontil so many o' them wuz gone thet it would make a big hole in our herd."

"Have they much the start of us?"

"I reckon they have." Bud was down on his knees, looking closely at the tracks.

"Yes," he continued, "they went by here shortly after midnight."

"How do you know?"

"Against ther east side o' each o' these leetle depressions made by a hoof is some fresh snow."

"I don't see how that tells the time."

"I do. Along about midnight last night a wind come up an' blew from ther west fer half an hour. It drifted a little snow before it, which settled inter these depressions an' banked up against ther east side o' these tracks."

"That seems reasonable. Bud, where did you learn all these things about trailing?"

"Never learned them nowhar. It's jest thinkin' about what yer see what makes a scout an' trailer. These cattle is somewhar up in them hills yon. They probably drove until sunup, an' then stopped ter give ther critters a rest before shovin' them inter ther mountings."

"Then I suppose we better hurry. We may be able to find out where they are."

"Righto, we'll mosey. I reckon we've struck a good thing."

"How many beeves do you suppose there were in that steal?"

"Oh, I reckon fifty er sixty."

"Whew! That's worth going after."

Bud had mounted, and they galloped along the trail, which was broad and deep. It led them through coulees and over hills and down into valleys, and the sun was high and the trail apparently endless.

"Bud, let us stop and eat our lunch. I'm hungry," said Stella.

"All right. I'm a bit peckish myself," was the reply.

They were in a narrow valley which was strewn with great bowlders, and on the sides of the hills grew a great many scrub pines. Through the center of it ran the broad trail.

The lunch was tied to the cantle of Bud's saddle, while Stella carried a canteen of coffee, for she was a great favorite of McCall, the cook, and when she started out for the day he invariably put up the best lunch a cow camp could afford.

Bud, in the meantime, had found a spring on the hillside and had watered the horses, then made a fire of pine boughs over which they heated the coffee and warmed themselves. Then they began their luncheon.

Bud was so busily appeasing his hunger that he did not say much, and did not think it strange that Stella said nothing. They were seated on opposite sides of the fire, and Bud, thinking that perhaps Stella might need something, looked across at her.

What he saw caused him to stare.

Stella was looking over his head with an expression of horror on her face. Her wide, staring eyes were filled with an unspeakable horror.

Her hand was poised in mid-air, just as if she had been going to put something into her mouth, when the action was arrested by the sight of something that froze her with terror.

"Stella, what's ther matter?" Bud managed to blurt out.

Stella's lips moved, but no sound came from them. She was too frightened to speak.

Then Bud, observing the direction in which she was looking, turned his head.

In an instant he was on his feet. He had become very pale, and his hand shook as he reached slowly toward his holster.

Standing behind him was a creature such as he never had seen before.

It was a man of great stature, clad entirely in black, over which was thrown a long, black cloak.

But the horror of the creature was the face. Out of an expressionless mask of silver, without nose or mouth, gleamed a pair of fierce, black eyes, that twinkled maliciously. Midway of the face were two holes, nostrils through which he breathed.

It was the man at whom Carl had fired his six harmless bullets—the man with the silver face.

Bud stood staring at him like one frozen, but Stella, when she saw that Bud was as frightened as herself, was able to take her eyes away from those terrible orbs that shone through the silver face, and regained her composure, and now was able to look at him without terror and with curiosity.

There was something fascinating in that blank, rounded, shining, white face, lighted only by those remarkable eyes.

What was behind that mask? A face, or only a blank?

Bud had somewhat recovered from the ague of terror into which the sudden appearance of the man with the silver face had thrown him, for he was a brave fellow, and not easily shaken from his courage.

"What do you want?" he asked at last, but yet with a little tremor in his voice.

There was no answer, but the eyes continued to burn in a very suggestive way. It seemed as if the man behind the mask was trying to speak, but could not.

Presently, however, he made a motion with his hand that told them to follow him.

"I'll be derned if we do," said Bud stubbornly. "Who aire yer, anyway, an' what business hey yer buttin' in on us this away?"

A strange, inarticulate, bubbling sound came from behind the silver face, but Bud could not understand it.

Again came the signal to follow.

"Not on yer life," said Bud firmly. He drew his revolver, and a look of decision came into his face. When Bud took on this look he meant business.

"Oh, Bud, don't oppose the terrible creature," whispered Stella, to whom fear had come again from looking on that blank but fascinating face.

"No, by jing, I ain't goin' erlong with thet freak. If I could see his face an' knowed who he wuz I might talk business."

As he said this the eyes behind the silver mask fairly shot forth sparks of anger, and again that horrible bubbling noise was heard.

The creature raised his arm. There was a sudden rush, and Bud felt his arms grasped from behind.

But as this happened he had presence of mind enough to point his revolver at the man in the silver mask and pull the trigger.

The weapon crashed, and, as the smoke cleared away, Bud saw the thing of horror still standing unharmed where he had been, although the revolver had been pointed directly at his heart, while from behind the mask came again that sickening, bubbling laugh.

At another signal from the figure Bud was dragged a little way up the hillside, and his wrists were securely tied, his arms embracing a tree.

While this was being done Stella, too frightened to make an outcry, was led away, and, looking over his shoulder, Bud saw her mount Magpie and ride away surrounded by four men, led by the man with the silver face, who bestrode a splendid black charger.

Bud was left alone to survive, if he could, the perils of frost and hungry wolves.

CHAPTER XI

LOST IN THE WILDERNESS

Stella could not keep her eyes from the silver mask of the man who rode by her side. She was wondering continually at the mystery of him.

For an hour or more they rode up one valley, then across a hill or stretch of prairie, and through valleys again, the black mountains coming nearer all the time, until at last they entered a forest of pines, which they traversed until night began to fall.

At a gesture from "Silver Face," as Stella had named the man who rode by her side, the party came to a halt.

Stella now saw that it was the intention to camp, for, while some of the men cared for the horses, others cut down several small pine trees and built a shelter of pine boughs, into which she was ushered, and before which a blazing fire had been lighted.

It had grown very cold, and Stella was grateful for the heat that filled her shelter.

One of the men had brought food, and a pan and coffeepot

from a pack on one of the horses, and now began to cook supper.

Stella fully realized the peril of her situation, but particularly that of Bud, who had been left alone, bound and helpless, in that wilderness.

If he had not given the impression to the boys that he was going west instead of east, things might have been easier for them, but now Bud might perish of cold or be the prey of wild animals before Ted could come to their rescue, which she was sure he would do soon.

After she had eaten the supper which the man with the silver face brought her with his own hands, she felt better and more cheered, and began to take a brighter view of the situation.

The floor of her lean-to shelter had been thickly strewn with pine boughs, which were soft and aromatic, and Stella reclined upon them, and gazed into the fire, listening to the strange sounds that filled the forest, for the camp was absolutely quiet.

After eating their supper the men had silently smoked their pipes and then curled up on their blankets, which had been spread on mattresses of pine boughs, and were asleep.

Only Silver Face was awake, and he sat wrapped in his cloak near the fire, his eyes taking on a fiercer gleam as the flickering lights struck them.

Stella wondered who he was. Evidently the mask concealed a horrible mystery. Could he talk, and would not? Was that eerie, bubbling laugh of his the only articulate sound he could make?

Stella wished she knew more about him, and that he would talk to her.

The night was growing on, but Stella did not feel like sleeping.

Occasionally Silver Face arose and replenished the fire with resinous pine logs, and for a while the flames leaped high, filling the woods with strange shadows and ghostly, wavering spots of light.

Then afar, it seemed, there sounded the night cries of wild animals, timber wolves, those dreaded monsters of the lupus tribe, and occasionally the scream of the cougar, like a woman in agony. Then, close behind her shelter, there sounded a horrible, snarling shriek. It was the night cry of a bobcat close at hand, attracted to the camp by the scent of the meat which had been cooked for supper.

It was so near and clear that for a moment Stella's heart seemed to stop beating altogether, and she felt as if she would suffocate, and buried her face in her hands, expecting every moment to feel the claws of the terrible animal sink into the flesh of her back.

But at the sound Silver Face leaped to his feet, and was coming swiftly around the fire.

Through the silver mask his eyes were gleaming wickedly.

Stella heard him, and looked up. He was standing before her at the corner of her shelter, his blank face turned toward the place from which the cat's cry had come.

Suddenly a strange thing happened. From the breast of the black garment worn by Silver Face leaped a flame, followed

Edward C. Taylor

by the crash of a revolver. This was succeeded by another, and a third.

The sleeping men had been aroused, and were sitting up in their blankets, blinking stupidly.

Behind her shelter Stella heard a thrashing among the frozen underbrush, while Silver Face stood immovable, the blazing eyes in the mask staring in that direction.

Meanwhile, Stella was marveling at those shots which had seemed to spring from his very body, and without the apparent use of his hands.

But soon the noise in the brush ceased, and Silver Face stepped out of sight.

In a moment he was back, and threw into the circle of light about the fire the body of an enormous mountain cat.

The men had fallen back into their blankets and were sleeping again, while Silver Face resumed his place before the fire.

Soon Stella, began to yawn, and her eyes grew heavy with sleep.

But she did not want to sleep. She had a foreboding that if she slept she would be in danger.

However, the dancing flames and the soft, comfortable heat which came from the fire were too much for her resolution, and her head began to droop, and presently her body sank gently down, and, as she pillowed her head on her arm, she fell into a deep sleep.

How long she slept she did not know, but when she awoke it was light.

The fire had burned low, and she felt cold and numb.

Staggering to her feet, she looked around. The camp was deserted.

The men were gone, and so were the horses. Beside the fire was a considerable pile of wood, and Stella hastily pulled the embers of the fire together and threw several sticks upon it. As the fire blazed up and she grew warmer, she tried to review the situation.

Why had the men who had captured and brought her thus far deserted her? Had they been frightened away by the proximity of the boys? No, it could not have been that, for the boys were far away.

Then a thought of horror flashed across her mind. She had been brought here to perish in the wilderness. Probably Silver Face and his men, desiring to wreak vengeance upon Ted, and feeling that keeping her a prisoner would be too much of a burden, had brought her into this dangerous place to leave her a prey to the wild animals that she knew infested the forests.

If they had only left her Magpie, she might have stood some chance of escaping.

But her fortitude soon returned to her. She was not dead yet, and, while she had a fighting chance, she would not despair.

Something of pity must have moved the men, for she found that they had left her revolver and her rifle beside her in the lean-to, and that in a pile not far from the fire was food enough to last her for several meals.

She set about cooking some breakfast, and caught herself singing as she did so.

After she had eaten she sat down in her shelter to think a way out of her predicament.

She was in the midst of a reverie when she was brought to her feet by that most dreaded of sounds—the howl of the timber wolf.

For a moment she stood trembling, trying to think what her best course would be.

The wolves had smelled the frying bacon from afar, and had been attracted to it, for the scent had carried far in the clear air.

From another direction came another wolf cry, and presently they seemed to come from every direction.

They were far away as yet, but the wolves were gathering.

Without trying to reason further, Stella gathered up what food she could carry, and, grasping her rifle, struck out into the forest in the direction away from that from which the howls of the wolves came to her.

Suddenly to one side appeared a slinking, gray form, which slunk along, apparently dodging behind the trees, but following her.

As it came from behind a tree in fair sight, she swung her rifle to her shoulder and fired.

It was a strike, for the wolf, with a howl of pain sprang in the air, then rolled over on the snow and lay still.

As the report of the shot reverberated back from the mountains, it was followed by a perfect crescendo of wolf howls.

They sounded louder and nearer now, and Stella's heart began to beat rapidly with fear.

Too well she knew what would happen if they caught her.

But suddenly a thought came to her, and she stopped.

Surely Ted and the boys would come to find her. They might even now be on the way, and who could say they were not far away?

If she could only send them a message to let them know that they were on the right trail!

Her face lighted up with an inspiration. She had the means.

Breaking a stick from a low-growing tree, she began to write in the snow:

"I am followed by a wolf pack. Hurry." "Stella"

These were the words she left behind her for Ted to read should he come that way.

Then she hurried on with all speed.

Every few minutes the howls of the wolves assailed her ears as she struggled on through the snow.

Edward C. Taylor

Her burden of food was becoming very heavy, and she cast away a part of it.

Perhaps, she thought, it would serve to stop the wolves for a while when they found it on her trail.

Every moment seemed to bring the cries of the wolves nearer.

They were following in her footsteps now, for the noise was all behind her, not scattered over the forest, as it had been at first.

The brutes had gathered into a pack, and Stella shuddered as she pictured in her mind the gray band coming upon her with long, loping, tireless strides; with red, long, lolling tongues and slavering, sharp-fanged jaws.

Presently she heard another noise behind her, and looked over her shoulder.

The sight that met her eyes caused her to almost faint.

Not twenty yards behind her was an enormous gray wolf, loping along easily but as swiftly as a horse.

His eyes were blazing like green lamps, and his great body was scarred and torn. Evidently he was the king of the pack.

Stopping suddenly, she drew her revolver and fired two shots at him.

He came to a halt with a snarl of rage and began biting at his shoulder.

Then Stella turned and ran again, with the clamor of the pack close behind her.

But she was failing, and her run had become a painful stagger, and her breath came in gasps.

She was near the end, and she realized it. She fancied herself falling into the midst of that ravenous crew and shuddered. What could she do to save herself?

Not far ahead was a tree with a forked branch growing low enough for her to reach it if she still had strength to get so far. With almost a superhuman effort she continued her flight toward it.

As she reached it the great, gray king of the pack was only a few feet behind her, so close that she could hear him pant from his long run.

She reached up to the branch and tried to pull herself up, but it was an impossible task burdened with food and rifle and her coat, which she had removed at a time when she had stopped long enough to write another message in the snow for Ted.

She threw the rifle in the snow and tried it again, but she could not, and then cast aside the food and the coat, and succeeded in clambering into the sheltering nook just as the great wolf, leaping into the air, swept past her, carrying in his teeth a shred of her skirt. She was safe, but by a very narrow margin.

She looked up into the tree, for the branch upon which she was perched was so near the ground that she was not safe from the leaps of the savage and famished brutes.

But the next higher branch was far beyond her reach or her

ability to climb to.

She must defend herself as best she could.

Fortunately she had retained her revolver and had a good supply of ammunition.

As the old wolf leaped again she fired, and knew that the ball had entered his neck. If she could shoot him often enough, she ought to kill him after a while.

But now the clamor was all about her. The pack had arrived, and was leaping about the foot of the tree like waves upon a storm-tossed shore.

Her red coat had been torn to shreds, and, in the fight over the food she had cast aside, more than one of the brutes had met his death by the razorlike teeth of his comrades.

Suddenly, through the din about her, Stella lifted her head and listened, while for a moment the wolves ceased leaping and howling and stood listening also.

From afar off, and very faintly, there came to her a subdued cheer. Her heart leaped with hope. Could it be the boys who were signaling to her?

But now the wolves, even more savage than before, were leaping at her, their saber teeth snapping within an inch of her, as she fired into their faces, and laughed as she saw them roll upon the snow in their death agony.

Again she heard a faint cry in the forest. Oh, if she should be wrong, and it was not the dear old Moon Valley yell, she would die.

Now the old king of the pack returned to the attack.

He was bigger and stronger than any of the others, and when he snapped at them with his terrible teeth they made way for him.

He began a succession of leaps at her, and every time she planted a bullet in his massive and seemingly invulnerable body.

But each leap brought him closer to her perch.

The next jump might be the one by which he would reach her, she thought, and that surely would be the end, for, if he ever succeeded in getting his hooked fangs fastened in her clothes, she would be pulled from the tree in an eye twinkling, and she shuddered as she thought of the sequel.

The end seemed very near, and she had about given up hope of holding out until the boys could reach her, when a well-known yell was wafted to her on the frozen air. The boys had come.

She felt the fangs of the king of the pack fasten in her skirt, and she knew that she was being pulled out of her perch when, through the woods came Ted and Bud and Ben, and the rest of her friends, yelling like mad and amid a perfect fusillade of rifle shots.

Then she began to slide out of the tree. But she did not reach the ground, for Ted was there, and she slipped naturally and without harm into his arms, as the last of the pack that remained alive escaped into the forest.

Edward C. Taylor

CHAPTER XII

WHO WHIPPLE WAS

There was great rejoicing when Stella so far recovered from the strain which she had been undergoing, to learn that Bud was safe, although he had passed a very uncomfortable as well as perilous night tied to a tree with the cold numbing him, and wolves sniffing and snarling at him.

These he had been able to keep off for several hours by kicking them whenever they got close enough.

But he was rapidly becoming exhausted when in the distance he heard shouts.

Ted and the boys had ridden to the west until they realized that it was useless to go any farther, for they had not come upon the trail of Bud and Stella, and Ted came to the conclusion that they had gone in the opposite direction.

But it was almost night when they turned their faces to the east, and day was dawning when they heard Bud's cry for help, and rescued him by driving the snarling pack from his heels.

When they had heard his story about the man with the silver

face and his crew, and the fact that they had taken Stella away with them, the boys waited only long enough to make a fire to thaw out Bud, and to make some coffee, and took up the broad trail.

When they came to the deserted camp they were almost sure that Stella had gone on with her captors, and were about to follow the trail.

Had they done so, Stella would have perished in the woods. But Ted had one of his "hunches" that Stella was not far away, and rode around the camp in a wide circle.

He was soon rewarded by finding the prints of Stella's shoes in the snow, and, concluding that she had in some manner escaped from her captors, he called the boys together and started on her trail.

They had not gone far when they, too, heard the howls of the wolf pack, and knew that Stella was in great danger.

Presently they came upon Stella's message in the snow and obeyed her injunction to hurry.

They had been compelled to leave their horses at the camp, for the forest was too dense to permit them to ride.

When Stella told them of her adventure and about Silver Face and the stolen cattle, they decided to push forward on the trail, and, if possible, regain their stolen property.

At the camp they remounted, and, having to ride double where Bud and Stella were concerned, made but slow progress.

But the trail was broad and good, and they made good time

as compared with a slow cattle drive.

Early in the afternoon Ted became conscious, in that remarkable way of his, that not far ahead some one was on the trail.

Stella was riding behind him, for the boys had taken turns in carrying her so as not to burden any one horse too much, and he transferred her to Kit's pony, and, telling the boys to move forward slowly, rode on ahead to scout.

Ted wanted to see for himself this wonderful Silver Face, who was impervious to bullets, and who could fire them from his chest with no apparent effort on his own part.

Ted was also affected as the others had been who had seen him; that is, by the mystery of the creature.

He had ridden quite a distance ahead of the party, and had just entered into the pass of a canon which seemed to broaden out into a respectable valley farther on, when he was brought to a halt by the scream of a rifle ball close to his head.

This was warning enough, and he scurried into the shelter of a huge rock that jutted from the canon wall.

In a few minutes he emerged from it and rode back over the trail.

When the party came up with him he told them of the shot.

"It's my opinion," he said, "that Silver Face and his men and our cattle are in that canon or valley, but how to reach them I don't know."

"S'pose we go scoutin' on ther hills above, an' take a look," said Bud. "Stella an' ther boys can cache ther hosses an' hide, er come erlong with us."

"Very well," said Ted. And so they did. Hiding their horses in a thick glade of cedar trees, they climbed in single file up the side of the mountain, and were soon in an advantageous position, from which they had a good view up and down the valley.

A curious sight met their sight.

In the center of the valley they saw their bunch of steers close herded by several cowboys, while not far away two men were butchering one of the steers.

"They're going to have beef for dinner," said Ted, with a grin.

"I hope it chokes 'em," growled Bud.

"Or that they never get a chance to eat it at all," said Stella.

Lounging around the fire were a party of Indians, but, though Ted could not see from that distance whether or not they were the followers of Crazy Cow, he thought most likely they were.

The great figure of Silver Face could easily be picked out from among his followers, even were it not from the reflected light from his silver mask whenever the rays of the sun smote it.

Close to the west wall of the valley, and huddled under its shelter, were a number of Indian tepees, while farther on were several white canvas tents.

"Boys, we've stumbled upon the permanent camp or rendezvous of the outlaw Indians, and the members of the Whipple gang," said Ted.

As they were looking they saw a young woman, dressed as cowgirl, and with long, blond hair hanging down her back, come out of one of the tents, and look over the scene.

Silver Face strode to her side, and then began a strange pantomime between the pair with her hands. This convinced Stella that the man with the silver mask was unable to talk.

"I don't see how we are going to get at those fellows," said Ted.

"They do seem to be pretty well fixed to defend themselves," said Ben, who was lying flat on the rocky edge of the canon wall, looking into the scene below.

"Oh, Ted," cried Stella, grasping the arm of the leader of the broncho boys. "Look there. It is Magpie, my pony. There isn't another like him in the world. We must get him back, Ted. Think of letting a dirty Indian outlaw ride and abuse the splendid fellow."

"All right, Stella," replied Ted. "Show us how to do it successfully, and we'll go down and tackle the whole mess."

"See, there's an Indian throwing his filthy blanket on Magpie's back. I can't stand that."

Stella put her rifle to her shoulder, and was about to pull the trigger when Ted's hand closed down over the lock of the weapon.

"Not on your life," he said. "This is not the time for anything like that. If we were to get them after us right now we'd last about as long as a snowball on a hot stove. Wait a while."

While Stella said nothing she was angry clear through. It hurt her like a blow to have her pony ridden by another.

The Indian, having fastened his blanket on the pony's back to his satisfaction, sprang upon his back, and began to lash him with a quirt.

"Oh, the brute!" exclaimed Stella. "I hope Magpie throws and kills him for his cruelty."

Magpie wheeled and bucked under the unusual punishment, and the Indian continued to beat him.

"I can't stand it any longer," cried Stella, gnashing her pretty, small, white teeth.

This time she got her rifle to her shoulder, and, before she could be restrained, had fired a shot. Perhaps Ted knew that the provocation was great, for he did not interfere this time.

At any rate, the ball flew close enough to knock the hat from the Indian's head, and cause him to dismount and scurry to the shelter of the rock wall.

But it caused the greatest excitement in the camp.

The man with the silver mask rushed forward, rapidly scanning the cliff for whoever had fired the shot.

He did not have long to search, for the smoke hovering over the spot where Stella was lying on the top of the cliff was advertisement enough.

A man by his side handed him a rifle, which he sighted, then took down as a puff of smoke rose above him.

Then there followed the smash of a bullet on the rock, a foot below where Stella was lying.

"Pretty close work," said Ted. "That fellow is a corking good shot. Look, he's coming to shoot again. Duck! I'll bet he gets the range this time."

Every head went out of sight. Then came the sharp report of the rifle, and the ball from it shattered the edge of the rock not far from Stella's head.

"That'll be about enough of that," said Ted, picking up his own Winchester. "We'll have to stop that fellow's fun, or he'll end by hurting some of us."

Ted poked the barrel of his Winchester over the edge of the rock, adjusted the sights, took a short aim, and fired.

Then he looked to see the result of it, and saw the man with the silver face drop his rifle, stagger to the side of the canon, and sink down.

"By jove! I got him," exclaimed Ted. "I believe that from here we can drive that whole bunch out of the valley and get back our cattle and horses, if we dodge back and shoot straight. We'll try it. Every fellow get ready to fire."

On seeing their leader fall, the men, both white and red, in the valley, ran hither and yon in a state of great excitement.

But when the boys began to fire systematically at them, kicking up the snow about them with every shot, it became a veritable panic.

Shouts of terror were heard, and, as the young woman raised the man with the silver mask to his feet and helped him walk to the tent, the others hastily saddled their ponies, and prepared to decamp.

All the while the boys were pumping Winchester balls into them, and occasionally a horse dropped, or with a yell a man would grasp a leg or an arm and fall to the ground.

"We've got them going," shouted Ted. "Keep it up until we get them on the run."

The boys fired their rifles until they got hot, then waited for them to cool, and resumed firing.

It was like bedlam in the valley, and not one of the men attempted to retaliate by firing back. They were in a panic of fear.

As soon as one got his horse saddled he dashed away toward the head of the valley out of the way of those spiteful bullets which sang about them like enraged hornets.

Not one of them stopped to burden himself with his baggage, nor did they pay any attention to the stolen cattle.

They were in too much of a hurry to get away safely themselves.

The Indians left their tepees standing, and ran for their lives.

Soon the valley was clear of men. All that remained in sight were the bunch of cattle, a small band of ponies in a rope corral, and the tepees and tents.

"I guess we're safe to go down now, and take possession of

our own," said Ted.

"Don't forget that Silver Face and the young woman are in that tent," said Stella warningly. "Look out for treachery."

Without further delay the boys and Stella climbed down the mountain to where their horses were, and, mounting, rode fearlessly into the valley.

As they approached the tents the flap of one of them was pushed back and the young woman came out.

Her hand was raised for silence, and the tears were coursing down her cheeks.

"Hush!" she said. "He is dead."

"Who is dead?" asked Ted, with the greatest respect.

"Silver Face," was the answer.

"Who was he?" asked Ted.

"I don't know. I found him lying in the mountains almost dead from an accident a few months ago, and nursed him back to life, but he never spoke again, and he has never been able to let me know who he was."

"Pardon me, but who are you?" asked Ted.

"I?" said the woman, drawing herself up proudly. "I am Whipple."

"What? Leader of the Whipple gang?" asked Ted, almost incredulously.

"The same," said she. "I have laughed many times at the fear I inspired among you ranchmen in the valley, and the officers of the law, to say nothing of the soldiers. But that was because they had never seen me, and believed me to be a man."

They all looked their astonishment, for she was an exceedingly pretty woman, and spoke in gentle tones.

"But it is all over now," she continued sadly. "If those steers and ponies are yours, take them. I am going to leave the mountains, and my men are scattered and will leave also. I told them to go. And now that Silver Face is no more, there is no reason why I should stay here."

"You loved him?" asked Ted, nodding toward the tent.

"Yes," she answered quietly. "He was my husband. When I had nursed him back to life I sent my boys out and kidnaped a preacher. I had him brought here blindfolded, and made him marry us, then sent him back, not knowing where he had been."

Ted and the boys looked their sympathy.

"Can I be of any assistance to you in caring for him?" asked Stella, very sweetly.

A look of terror crossed the woman's face.

"No, no," she cried. "Leave me with my dead. Take what belongs to you and go."

She retired into the tent, and they heard her weeping, and turned away.

The boys started immediately on the back trail to the ranch, where they arrived with their cattle and ponies.

That was the last of the Whipple gang, for the members of it left the country, and the outlaw Indians were gathered in by the troops and the Indian police, and imprisoned on the reservations.

But on winter evenings, as he sat before the big fire in the Long Tom ranch house, his big snow camp, Ted Strong often turned over in his mind the facts about the death of Silver Face, the man of mystery.

Somehow, away down in his heart, he did not believe that the man with the silver mask was dead, but that he would some day meet him again and solve the mystery that surrounded him.

In the early part of December, however, the members of the Moon Valley outfit left the Long Tom Ranch for Phoenix, Arizona.

CHAPTER XIII

AN UNEXPECTED GUEST

Although it was winter, the air was soft and pleasant, and at noon the sun shone with some fervor.

It was Arizona, and as Ted Strong sat on Sultan and gazed across the wide valley, over which the sun's warm rays shimmered above the sand and cactus, greasewood and sage toward a low-lying ranch house in the far distance, it did not seem at all like Christmas.

But it was Christmas Eve, in spite of the fact that there was no snow, no sleigh bells, no apparent use for Santa Claus, and that roses were blooming in yards where there was sufficient black earth for them to thrive.

Behind his saddle Ted had a great bundle wrapped in burlap and securely tied.

For many miles on the way Ted had cast anxious glances behind him, and occasionally reached back to assure himself that he had not lost his freight.

This argued that it was a very precious burden.

Edward C. Taylor

"I guess that must be the place," mused Ted, as he looked at the apparently deserted house.

Not a live creature was to be seen about the place, neither man, woman, nor beast.

"Cheerful-looking prospect for Christmas," Ted continued to soliloquize, as those who travel or ride on mountain or plain in solitude often get in the habit of doing.

"Wonder where the folks are?" he continued. "Hope they got here all right. But, of course, they did. Bud is too good a leader to let them get off the trail. Besides, they have been long enough on the way to have got here and back again." Again he paused, musing.

"Well, Sultan, old chap, it has been a long, dry drive, hasn't it?"

Sultan, on hearing his name, gave a toss of his head and a soft snicker, and Ted's hand passed gently over his beautiful, glossy mane with a caressing gesture.

"Hello, here comes some one. Wonder who it is. That's the only sign of life, except a few rattlesnakes and horned toads I've seen since I left the railroad at San Carlos."

Shading his eyes from the sun, Ted looked for several minutes at the dark speck bobbing along in the distance, a mere shadow against the yellow surface of the earth.

"He's taking his time," muttered Ted. "Reckon he's wondering who I am, and what I'm standing here for. It can't be one of our fellows. I guess I'll just wait for him to come up and say howdy."

There was a faint trail, or road, which skirted Sombrero Peak, the mass of multicolored rock at Ted's back, over which he had come on his way from San Carlos to the Bubbly Well ranch house, which he was now facing in the distance. But where he was now standing the road branched off to the west, while a fainter trail lay straight before him to the ranch house.

Bubbly Well was the ranch of Major Caruthers, an Englishman, and a retired officer of the British army, who had come to America to pass his remaining days in the open. He was a well-preserved man, tall, stalwart, with white hair and a red, fresh-looking face, who could ride well and was an excellent shot, but who knew nothing about the cattle business.

Ted had met him in Phoenix, at the hotel, and had dropped into "cow talk." When the English major learned that Ted knew so much about the cattle business, he told of his ranch at Bubbly Well, confessing that his own knowledge of steers, cows, round-ups, and the like was so limited that, instead of making the ranch pay, it had been steadily losing money for him.

It was then that the major had invited Ted to visit him at the ranch, look the situation over, and give expert advice how to better the condition of things.

"I'll tell you what we'll do," said the major; "let's make up a Christmas party for Bubbly Well. The holidays are so beastly lonely out here, don't you know, and Christmas knocks me all of a heap. Come out and help me make things cheerful."

"I'd like to," Ted had said, "but I'm not a free agent. I am with a party of friends, who are also my partners in the cattle business and other enterprises. You see, my first duty is to them. I don't know what their plans are."

At this the major looked considerably crestfallen. Then Ted, as briefly as he could, told the Englishman all about the broncho boys and their plans and principles.

As he talked, Major Caruthers occasionally interjected such exclamations as "Extraordinary!" "Very remarkable!" "Fawncy!"

He was intensely interested in Ted's accounts of some of the adventures which the members of the Moon Valley outfit had gone through, and when Ted stopped, with an apology for having consumed so much time in talking about himself and his friends, the major assured him that he could listen with pleasure and profit all night if Ted could only go on telling him such stories.

"My boy, I have the very thing," said the major, after a moment's thought.

Ted looked at the Englishman inquiringly.

"Do you think your friends, not knowing me, would accept an invitation to spend Christmas at Bubbly Well, and as long thereafter as they can and will?"

"That's a very kind thought," said Ted. "You see, we generally contrive to be at our Moon Valley Ranch at Christmas time, but this year we had business in this part of the country, and could not finish it in time to get back home, and were planning to get as much joy out of the day in the hotel here as we could."

"Christmas in a hotel!" exclaimed the major. "I can't think of anything more dismal. I'd spend Christmas in my own place even if there wasn't another live thing there, and nothing to eat but cheese and crackers."

"I feel very much that way myself," laughed Ted.

"Then you'll come?" asked the Englishman eagerly.

"I think my friends will be very glad to accept the invitation," answered Ted. "I am sure I should like to, personally, and I thank you for the privilege and the honor."

"Don't speak of it."

They talked of other things; about sport, and about the dangers of ranching in that country.

Before they parted it was decided that the broncho boys should visit Major Caruthers' ranch. They were to take their own mounts on the train to the nearest railroad station to Bubbly Well, where they would be met by one of the major's men as a guide.

It was three days before Christmas when all of them, except Ted, arrived at the ranch and were given a hearty welcome by the Englishman. That is, all arrived there except the leader of the broncho boys, who had remained in Phoenix to attend to some business details and do some shopping, agreeing to follow them later and arrive at the ranch Christmas Eve.

At the opening of this chapter we find him within sight of Bubbly Well, with a pack of Christmas presents for all hands on his back, waiting patiently for the approaching rider.

In the course of a few minutes, the stranger rode up, and, with a cold and quiet greeting, pulled in his mount, a beautiful chestnut mare, and looked Ted over from top to toe in a cool manner.

He was a handsome young chap, dressed in such a manner that Ted could not quite determine what he was. He had not the appearance of a cow-puncher, nor was he a town man, for he was bronzed by the sun, and he sat his mare like a born horseman.

His clothes were dark, save for a tan vest which buttoned close around his throat; his boots were of the very best quality, and fitted the calf of his leg snugly, and on his head was an expensive Stetson, with the skin of a rattlesnake for a band.

But it was his face that affected Ted with a sort of dislike that yet had something of fascination in it, while at the same time it puzzled him, it was such a strange mixture of good and bad.

"Can you tell me what ranch house that is over there, and who owns it?" said the stranger, in a well-bred manner that yet had the freedom of the West in it.

"Yes," answered Ted. "That is the Bubbly Well Ranch, and it is owned by Major Caruthers."

A strange expression passed over the young fellow's face.

"Jack Caruthers—do you happen to know?"

"I have never heard him called Jack," said Ted, smiling. "He signs himself 'John Stairs Caruthers.'"

"It must be the same," said the young fellow musingly.

"Do you know him?" asked Ted.

"Well, no. That is, not exactly." The stranger thought a moment. "I suppose I'll have to put up somewhere for the night; it's a dickens of a way to anywhere out here. I started from Rodeo, across the mountain, early this morning, thinking I could make it to San Carlos by night, but—"

"You couldn't get there before morning if you rode at top speed," said Ted, as the other hesitated.

"Are you going to the ranch house?" asked the stranger suddenly.

"Yes."

"Do you think your friend would put me up for the night?"

"I haven't a doubt of it. And to-morrow, too. You know this is Christmas Eve."

"So it is. I hadn't thought of it. My name is Farnsworth— Hilary Farnsworth."

The young fellow looked defiantly at Ted, who had started slightly at the name.

"Do you want to take me to the house now?" asked Farnsworth, with a slightly contemptuous smile.

So this was Farnsworth. "Fancy" Farnsworth, as he was called in the Southwest. Ted looked at him with new interest, and the other stared back with his gray eyes, which were as handsome as a woman's, and yet had in their depths a wicked, cruel gleam.

"I don't see why not," said Ted.

"You know me?" asked Farnsworth, with a smile.

"By reputation."

"May I ask your name?"

"Certainly. I beg your pardon. I am Ted Strong."

At this Farnsworth suddenly pulled his horse to its haunches, at the same time throwing his hand backward, and, with almost incredible rapidity, whipping out a revolver.

His face was white, and had as suddenly assumed an expression in which fear and determination were equally present.

"No, you don't!" he said slowly and coldly. "You don't get me that way. I'm not as easy as that."

Ted had made no move to draw his revolver, and was smiling in an amused sort of way.

"I'm sure I don't want you," he said.

"You're a deputy United States marshal, aren't you?"

"I am, but I'm not after you."

"Then you haven't heard?"

"Nothing about you recently. When I was in this part of the country before I heard—"

"Oh, you can always hear a lot about a fellow in this rotten part of the world—except the truth. Then you haven't heard the latest news from Rodeo?"

"Not a word."

"And you don't want to arrest me?"

"Not now. I wouldn't know what to arrest you for, and I haven't seen a United States warrant for months."

"I believe I can trust you. You seem to be a square chap, in spite of what I've heard of you. But I want to tell you one thing: I've got eyes in the back of my head, and there isn't a quicker man on the draw in Arizona, so no monkey business. This is not a boast, but a warning."

"I have nothing against you now," said Ted quietly; "but if I ever have, you'll know it, and have your chance. But I don't see any use in standing here in the sun palavering. Let's hike to the house yonder. I've been riding since daybreak without a drink, and I'd like to sample the major's famous Bubbly Well."

Farnsworth looked sharply at Ted for a moment, then replaced his revolver, and signaled to lead the way.

They rode in silence along the trail toward the ranch house for several minutes.

"How shall I introduce you to the major—as Farnsworth?" asked Ted, at last.

Farnsworth paused to think before replying.

"I think not," he said at last. "If I am to stay there for the night, there may as well be no unpleasant feeling. Call me anything you like but that, and I will fall in with it. They may know something about me, and, while I would be safe while Major Caruthers considered me a guest, still, it might cause some restraint."

"Probably you are right. How will Mr. Dickson do?"

"As good as any. Say, Strong, you're a brick! I won't forget this."

"This is a sort of truce. Anyway, it's Christmas, and a fellow should put away malice at such a time."

"Have you malice toward me?"

"No, I can't say that I have. But I have heard things about you that haven't prepossessed me in your favor."

"Have you ever thought that perhaps you have heard more than the truth?"

"Of course; I know that men are usually painted worse than they are."

"That's true. It's especially true with regard to myself."

For a moment Ted said nothing. He was running over in his mind several of the stories he had heard about this handsome and daring young fellow.

"Well, I'll take your word for it because it's Christmas," he said at last.

"I'll make you believe that I'm telling the truth before our acquaintance ends," said Farnsworth. As Ted looked into his eyes he saw that they had changed in expression. Now they were bold and brave and truthful, where before Ted had seen only a cold, cruel, relentless look.

Ted threw back his head, and the Moon Valley yell issued from his mouth.

It instantly transformed the slumbering ranch house. Out of doors, from around corners, and even as if they sprang out of the ground, appeared the broncho boys, and the air fairly rang with their shouts of welcome.

"That's the way I'd like to be greeted," said Farnsworth, a little bitterly.

"Then why don't you fix it so that you are?" asked Ted, smiling.

CHAPTER XIV

CHRISTMAS AT BUBBLY WELL

Ted introduced Farnsworth as Mr. Dickson, whom he had met on the road, and the boys made the newcomer welcome in their usual characteristic style.

In a few minutes Major Caruthers rode up to the house, and Ted brought Farnsworth forward. From the question Farnsworth had put to him when he had first mentioned the owner of the Bubbly Well Ranch, Ted was anxious to see the meeting between the two men.

Major Caruthers received the young fellow cordially, and told him, with true Western hospitality, that he was welcome to stay as long as he wished.

But Ted was watching Farnsworth.

As he put out his hand to grasp the major's, a peculiar look crossed his face. It was rather wistful, too, and it seemed as if he wanted to say much more than the few formal words of thanks which he returned in exchange for the major's greeting.

Ted looked curiously at the two men, and started with

surprise at a peculiar resemblance Farnsworth bore to the older man.

Ted had not particularly noticed the major's face and eyes before, but now he noticed that his eyes bore a remarkable resemblance to those of Farnsworth.

There was a resemblance, too, in the shape of the head and the turn of the jaw, but there it ended; and Ted surmised that the major must be at least fifteen or twenty years older than the stranger.

During the rest of the day there was much mystery about the house that always precedes Christmas.

Stella was particularly busy, and flew here and there, whispering with Bud, who seemed to be in some secret with her.

Behind the big ranch living room was a bedroom which had been used for casual guests.

Stella had possession of it, and had taken the bed down and banished it until after the holidays.

Within this room certain mysterious things were going on, and whenever Stella or Bud left it, the door was always locked behind them.

Not all the teasing of Ben and Kit, nor their efforts to get past the door, were successful in finding out what was going on.

Along toward evening, Bud, who had not met Farnsworth, or Dickson, as he was known to Bubbly Well, came across that young man pacing up and down the veranda alone.

Edward C. Taylor

When Bud saw him he stopped as if shot, took a long look, and then passed on.

But he set out to find Ted, which he did at last at the corral.

"See here, Ted," said the golden-haired cow-puncher, "whar did yer pick up ther maverick what's up at ther house? I hear he come with yer."

"I met him on the road, and he wanted to know if the major would put him up for the night, and I told him I thought he would be welcome," answered Ted.

"Of course he'd be welcome. Ther major would welcome a yaller dog with ther mange, out in this yere lonely place. But say, boy, does yer know what yer brought?"

"Why? I don't understand you exactly, I'm afraid."

"Yes, yer do. Who is that feller? He's not Dickson. Who is he?"

"Search me."

"That's what I'm tryin' ter do, an' if yer don't give up peaceful, I'm goin' through yer, minute."

"Do you know who he is?"

"I've got my suspicions. I see a feller up to Phoenix what's ther dead ringer fer him, an' his name wasn't Dickson then."

"What was it?"

"It was Fancy Farnsworth."

"I guess you're on, Bud. But Mr. Farnsworth asked me to keep it dark, and, as it is Christmas, I consented to do so. Remember, this is the time for brotherly love and peace toward all men. It wasn't much to do, and I invented the name of Dickson for him myself. What's the matter?"

"Oh, nothin', if yer like ter bring cattle like that ter our Chrismus festivities. Fer me, I wouldn't."

"I guess he's not as bad as that."

"He's worse."

"Explain."

"Well, if yer don't know, I will, an' let yer chew on it, an' see if yer want ter take any chances on him. Now, Farnsworth ain't his real name, neither. D'y'ever hear tell o' ther Somber Pass massacree, where a tenderfoot immigrant named Spooner an' his family was killed, an' their wagons an' horses, an' a pile o' money what Spooner had brought with him ter start a cattle ranch an' buy stock with, wuz taken? D'y'ever hear tell o' that?"

"Sure. It's part of the history of the Territory."

"D'y'ever hear any suspicions cast upon nobody?"

"I never did. That is, I never heard any one specifically charged with the crime. Did you?"

"I did, an' his other name was Farnsworth, only that wasn't ther name he went by at that time. He's ther feller who was p'inted out ter me as ther devil what led ther band o' cutthroats what killed ther Spooner family fer a measly few thousands o' dollars. That's what I meant if yer knew who yer was bringin' ter yer happy home."

"Why, that crime was committed five years ago, and Dickson or Farnsworth, as he calls himself, was too young then to be engaged in anything of that sort."

"He looks young, but he ain't. He's ther feller. Look out fer him, Ted."

"Don't you tip off who he is, Bud. I brought him here because it is Christmas, and he's going to stay. He's going to get a square deal here if I have to fight for him."

"Oh, I won't say nothin', but I'd like ter slip a pair o' handcuffs onto them smooth, white wrists o' hisn, jest ther same. But why is he here? What's he doin' in this part o' ther country?"

"I don't know, Bud. He asked me when he met me and knew who I was if I had heard the news about him. I hadn't, and told him so, but he did not volunteer any information on the subject."

"Whar did he come from? Did he tell you?"

"Yes, he said he had come from Rodeo; starting early this morning."

"Then look fer a big piece o' news from Rodeo right soon."

"How do you know?"

"I know this, if Farnsworth left Rodeo airly this mornin' thar was some good reason fer it. I reckon it's a killin'. But he's a chump ter stop off here. If anything has been pulled off at Rodeo, ther whole country will be out after him, fer Fancy, so called fer his passion fer good clothes an' high-colored poker chips, they don't like none too well, he's too almighty quick an' slick with his six-shooter, hez got a list o' killin's ter his credit as long as yer arm."

"Well, he's here; let's forget it until after breakfast. But as long as he's here as a guest, he gets all the protection I can give him."

Supper that night was a very merry function in the Bubbly Well ranch house, full of mysterious whisperings and jokes which were only understood by two or three at a time.

Mr. Dickson, as the latest guest, occupied a seat at the left hand of the host, and Ted again noticed the remarkable resemblance between the two, although it did not seem to be apparent to the others; at least, no one mentioned it.

After supper was over, and the Chinese cook and waiter had cleared the room, the major brought out a violin, and asked if any one could play it.

"Clay kin jest make a fiddle sing!" shouted Bud, dragging the modest Kentuckian forward.

There was a piano in the living room, and Stella and Clay went to it, and while Clay played the violin, Stella accompanied him.

Lively airs were demanded, and the ranch house fairly rang with the clapping of feet as Bud and Carl and Kit danced reels and jigs and cake walks, and the laughter of the boys at Bud's jokes and Carl's lingual mistakes.

But at last they became tired of music. It was ten o'clock, and the major disappeared for a few minutes, then entered, leading the way for the two Chinamen, who bore between them baskets of rosy apples, dishes of nuts and raisins and candies, and pitchers of cider.

Although the day had been warm enough in the sun, the night was cool, and the fire that leaped high in the fireplace made the room cozy and comfortable, and one could well imagine that outside was the snow glistening under the stars, and hear the far-away jingle of the sleigh bells.

They sat around the fireplace eating apples and cracking nuts, talking nonsense and laughing at Bud's comic antics, until even Farnsworth relaxed from the air of anxiety he had borne all evening, and once or twice laughed.

But Bud kept his eye on him, for he was distrustful of him, and believed that he was up to some trick.

At the end of the living room, between two massive deer heads, hung a big clock, and, while they were still cracking nuts and jokes it began to toll the hour of midnight.

Instantly every one was on his or her feet shouting "Merry Christmas!" and shaking hands all around. Farnsworth was not neglected because he was a stranger, and Stella was the very first to wish him happiness on this Christmas Day.

Ted was the last to press forward and with all sincerity wished him happiness, and, as he did so, he noticed that the young fellow was very pale, and that his eyes were filled with unshed tears as he looked from Ted to the major, who was fairly beaming with happiness and joy at the great success of his Christmas Eve party, which, he said, was the finest ever held in Arizona.

Then Clay sat down to the piano and began to play a march,

and Bud, with a great flourish, unlocked and threw open the door of the guest room.

Every one started back in surprise, while a shout went up that shook the roof; but the old major hadn't a word to say. He simply stared, growing pale and red by turns. He was deeply affected, and Farnsworth had retired to a far corner, with his face buried in his hands. What memories stirred him that this desperate young man should be so shaken?

Inside the room all was aglow with myriads of candles which sparkled from a small pine tree, which was hung with numerous packages and strings of popcorn. Now every one understood the mysterious movements of Bud and Stella.

But the most marvelous thing of all was the enormous figure of Santa Claus, dressed in a coat of red, liberally trimmed with fur, and a long beard sweeping his breast, sitting on the back of a splendid little bay pony that was none too quiet in the midst of the light and noise.

"Where did it all come from?" asked Ted of Stella, as they were standing together admiring the tree.

"Oh, Bud and I thought it out for a surprise for you and the boys before we left Phoenix, and one afternoon, when you were busy, we went shopping and brought all these things. If we hadn't come here, we were going to have the tree in the dining room of the hotel," she answered.

"It was a great idea, and just like you, Stella. It has made this like Christmas, indeed. We couldn't have had a better one at Moon Valley."

"But look at Major Caruthers," said Stella, pulling Ted by the sleeve.

The old major was actually on the verge of tears.

"I have never been so near the dear home of my boyhood as this evening, with all you happy, generous young people around me," he said.

"Who in the world is Santa Claus?" asked Ted.

"Why, just Santa Claus, you goose," said Stella, laughing.

But now Santa Claus got down from the pony's back and stepped to the front of the tree. Every one gathered around and kept silent.

"Good evening, children," he said, in a gruff and husky voice.

"Ach, it iss Kris Krinkle!" shouted Carl Schwartz, in glee. "Py Chiminy, ain't he noble? How you vas, Kris?"

"Children, I have a few seasonable gifts for you which I will give you before I hurry away, for I have many more young friends whom I must visit before the dawn. But first I will turn over to my young friend Ted Strong this beautiful pony, which has been intrusted to me by Major Caruthers." He led the pony forward and thrust the bridle into Ted's hand.

Ted was so astonished that he did not know what to say, but managed at last to mumble his thanks to his host.

For Stella there was a beautiful necklace of New Mexican turquoises from the major, who also had not forgotten one of the boys.

Then mysterious packages, well wrapped, were handed off the tree, and as they were opened, shouts of laughter greeted them, for nearly every one of them contained something meant as a joke on the recipient.

Carl got a noble-looking parcel, and when he opened it, found a nice red bologna sausage. Every one screamed with laughter, but Carl promptly turned the joke by taking out his knife and cutting up and devouring the sausage.

There was a lemon for Kit from Ben, and a Joe Miller joke book, full of antiquated chestnuts, for Bud, who proceeded to get square by reading all the most ancient ones, such as the chicken crossing the road, and similar gems.

While the laughter and fun were at their height there was a sound on the veranda, and they all stopped to listen.

Ted instinctively turned to where Farnsworth was sitting alone in the corner, for there had been no presents for him, and saw him sitting up, listening intently.

Being a guilty man, or, at least, aware that he was being pursued, he was alert.

"What's the row out there?" asked the major, who was loath to have the evening's fun disturbed by outsiders.

"Don't know," said Ted. "Sounded like some one walking on the veranda and trying the door."

He had no sooner spoken when the door was thrust open and four men sprang into the room and looked around.

At the same instant, Farnsworth leaped to his feet, drawing his revolver and backing into the center of the room.

Farnsworth was as pale as paper, but his eye flashed fire as he glanced swiftly around.

Apparently there was no way of escape, for the intruders barred the only outside door.

The sudden entrance into the brilliant light had temporarily blinded the men, so that they stood uncertainly for a few moments, looking from one to the other of the figures that almost filled the room.

Major Caruthers now stepped in front of them, his face red with anger.

"What do you mean by intruding on me like this?" he thundered.

For answer, one of the men threw back his coat and displayed the star of a deputy United States marshal.

"We're officers," he said gruffly, "an' we want Fancy Farnsworth."

"You've come to the wrong place," said the major.

"Oh, no, we haven't. We traced him right here, an' he's in this house."

"What crime has he committed?"

"He killed a woman over at Rodeo last night."

An exclamation of horror arose from all parts of the room.

"There he is! Get him!" almost screamed one of the men, pointing to the pale but resolute figure standing under the chandelier.

There was a rush, and confusion indescribable followed.

Crash went the chandelier, shattered into a thousand pieces by a dozen bullets.

Rushing, struggling forms turned the smoke-filled room into a perfect bedlam.

Two of the intruders went to the floor, sent there by swift and powerful right-handers from Ted.

But they were up and rushing through the room in the direction of the Christmas tree.

There Santa Claus met them, and again they were bowled over.

Ted saw the slender, black-clothed figure of Farnsworth slip past him in the smoke.

Then followed the sharp hoofbeats of a pony on the wooden floor, a crash of glass, and the swift patter on the earth outside, and all was still.

Farnsworth had leaped upon the back of Ted's Christmas-gift pony and escaped.

CHAPTER XV

THE THUGGEE CORD

Several moments following the dramatic and sensational escape of the Christmas guest passed in silence, to be broken at last by Kit.

"That was about the smoothest get-away I ever saw," he said, with a grin, for he had assisted in it by deftly tripping the chief deputy while he was on the way to intercept the pony.

"What in thunder did they want to stop my star performance for?" asked Santa Claus, pulling off his beard and revealing the rubicund face of Ben Tremont, who was slowly baking beneath the heavy robes and hairy disguise.

"Well, he's gone, and only taken a pony and a window with him," said the major, "and he's welcome to both. And now, you men, we'll try to dispense with your company. You see, this is a private party, and had I known that you were in this part of the country, I probably would have invited you to be present. But I regret to say that the guest list is full."

The leader of the posse of deputy marshals looked up with a scowl. Apparently, he was mad clear through at the sudden and unexpected loss of his prospective prisoner.

As he looked about his eye encountered that of Ted Strong, in which he saw laughter, which did not tend to lessen his anger.

"I've a good mind to arrest the whole bunch of you for conspiring at the escape of a United States prisoner," he growled.

"You'd stand a fine show to do that," said Ted quietly. "On the other hand, I've a mind to arrest you for the forcible entry of this house."

"You have, have you?" sneered the other. "You make me laugh, young feller. You couldn't arrest a fly!"

Ted threw open his coat and showed that he, too, wore a star.

The leader of the posse leaned forward to read the authority on it.

"Who are you?" he asked huskily.

"I am Ted Strong."

"Then why didn't you stop Fancy Farnsworth?"

"What for? I have no knowledge of his having committed a crime, and, besides, I have no warrant for him. Have you?"

"No. Didn't have time to get one. But that makes no difference. He killed a woman, and as soon as I heard of it I got my posse together an' hit his trail. If it hadn't been for you fellows I'd have got him."

"I don't think you would."

"Why wouldn't I?"

"Because he'd have killed two or three of you first."

"What about this crime, and why are you so sure he committed it?" asked Major Caruthers. "I thought him a fine, gentlemanly, quiet young fellow, and I'm somewhat of a judge of men myself. I can hardly believe that a man of that stamp could commit so terrible a crime as woman murder. That is the lowest degree of killing."

"He done it, just the same," said the deputy marshal positively.

"Why are you so sure?" asked Ted, taking up the interrogation.

"Well, in the first place, he skipped the town just before the body of the woman was found. He was seen to ride out of town along the road on which her house stood."

"Is that all the evidence you have against him?"

"No; he was seen coming out of the house about three hours before he was seen leaving town."

"H'm! Is that all?"

"It comes pretty near enough. But, besides that, it was known that the woman, who was young and beautiful, had recently received a lot of money as her share in a mine, and that the money had been taken to her that morning by one of her partners."

"And it is believed that the young fellow you call Fancy Farnsworth killed the woman for her money?"

"Sure."

"In what shape was the money? Currency, gold dust, ingots, or gold coins?"

"It was in ingots."

"Anybody know how much of it there was?"

"Yes; her partner, Billy Slocum, was at the hotel, intendin' to go back to the mine to-day, and I went to see him."

"And did he give you any idea of how much the gold weighed?"

"Yes, it weighed about thirty pounds. Billy brought it in on his saddle, and he said it weighed quite considerable."

"But Farnsworth, as you call him, had nothing of the sort when he arrived here."

"That may be. He'd be too foxy to do that. He's cached it somewhere in the mountains, most likely."

"How was the woman killed?"

"She was strangled by a cord."

"What was her name?"

"Helen Mowbray."

"What sort of a woman was she?"

"She was a mystery to most the folks at Rodeo, an' all over the mountains, for that matter. Nobody knew where she came from. She didn't mix much with the folks, but lived in a swell house, what she had built for herself, with only two servants, a Japanese man and woman."

"Was she rich?"

"Said to be. Had interests in a good many mines, an' owned the Cristobal Turquoise Mine."

"Anybody ever learn where her mail came from?"

"Yes, she frequently got letters from England, and occasionally sent large drafts to a bank in London to her credit."

"How do you know this?"

"Early this morning, when the crime was discovered, and every one was talking about it, Mr. Rossington, the banker, told that much to a crowd at the hotel."

"Had she any particular friend in Rodeo?"

"Only Farnsworth, who came to the town at intervals and put up at the hotel. When he was in town he generally spent an hour or two at her house in the afternoon or evening, and then faded away as mysteriously as he came."

"Did he appear to be in love with her?"

"All I know about that is what I have heard since Miss Mowbray's death."

"There has been gossip, then?"

"Not what you would call gossip, exactly. Only folks who had seen them riding and driving together a few times seemed to think that, while she was very much in love with him, he never made any fuss over her."

"How long have you known Farnsworth?"

"About three years. Ever since he has been traveling through this part of Arizona."

"Don't you know that he is a very undemonstrative man, and that if he really cared for any one he is not the sort to exhibit it?"

"Yes, I reckon Fancy is a cold sort of a proposition."

"How have you got him sized up?"

"I'd hardly know how to tell it. He's some of a mystery to me, and he ain't never let no one as I know of snuggle beneath his jacket."

"But, as an officer, you must have kept some sort of tab on him."

"Sure. I know Fancy as well as most. I always looked upon him as a crook, and a very dangerous man with a gun."

"Has he ever been convicted of a crime?"

"Ain't never been able to land him. Generally he gets away by some slick trick, just as he did to-night, or he bluffs off the fellows who go after him with his guns."

"Has any crime ever been fastened on him so positively that there was no doubt that he committed it?"

"Can't say there was; but that don't cut no ice, for he's been in several killings where no gun got busy but his, an' we've been able to track him right up to crimes, but there we lose him. He's too slick to get caught."

"Something like the murder of Miss Mowbray? He is seen leaving the vicinity of the murder, and is immediately suspected of the crime, although probably fifty other men in the town were near the house or on the road before the murder was discovered, eh?"

"That's true enough. I passed the house myself on my way home, just before midnight."

"Why don't you arrest yourself as a suspect? But how was the murder discovered?"

"Some one passing saw a flame at the corner of the house, and, looking through a window, saw that the house was afire. He gave the alarm, and the blaze, which was in a corner of the library, was put out before much damage was done."

"Then the body was discovered, I suppose?"

"Yes; a fireman found it in the bedroom on the floor."

"In what condition?"

"She was dressed for bed, and around her neck a cord was tied so tightly, in a peculiar slipknot, that she could not breathe, and her face was black and her tongue protruding."

"Simply strangled to death, eh?"

"That's about it, I reckon."

"What became of the two Japanese?"

"Disappeared."

"Where are the ingots of gold?"

"Gone."

"What became of the cord by which she was strangled?"

"I have it."

"How does it happen that you have it?"

"At the alarm of fire I left my home and ran to the scene. As I entered the house by the front door, one of the firemen came running out of the bedroom, crying that he had found a dead woman. I ran into the room, and saw Miss Mowbray lying on her face on the floor, at the foot of the bed."

"She was dead then, I suppose?"

"I thought so. I placed my hand on her bare shoulder, and it was cold."

"She had been dead several hours, then?"

"Two or three hours, perhaps, but maybe less, for the room in which she lay was cold, there being no fire in it or in the adjoining rooms."

"What did you do when you found that she was dead?"

"I turned the body over, and saw by the discoloration of her face and the protruding tongue that she had been strangled. Then I discovered the cord, which was sunken deeply into the flesh of her throat, and so hidden that I would not have discovered it had I not seen the end of it."

"What did you do with it?"

"In the hope that she might not be dead, and that something might be done to revive her, I managed, with great difficulty, to get the cord untied and off her neck."

"What authority did you have for that? I suppose you know that it is the coroner's duty to do things of that sort?"

"Yes; but, besides being a deputy marshal, I am also deputy coroner."

"I see. What did you do with the cord?"

"I don't remember. Oh, yes. I think I put it in my pocket. Yes, here it is."

"Let me see it. Why, this is very peculiar. Do you know what sort of a cord this is?"

"I don't. I never saw one like it before."

"I have. Notice its thickness, and how closely it is woven, and that it is strong as a piece of wire."

"Yes, I noticed that when I found it. What sort of cord is it?"

"Japanese."

"Japanese, eh?"

"Yes, and a very rare sort of Japanese cord, too, fortunately."

"Why fortunately?"

"This is the cord that is used by the Japanese and East Indian secret societies known as the Thugs or Thuggees."

"How do you know?"

"I have seen cords like this before in the Orient, where they were used by Japanese murderers."

The cord passed from hand to hand as the major and the boys examined it with curiosity and some degree of horror, while Stella positively refused to handle it, or even look at it.

"Tell me more about Miss Mowbray's servants," said Ted, again taking up his line of interrogation. "What were the names of the two Japanese?"

"The man was called Ban Joy, but generally was known as Joy."

"Was he pretty well known in the town?"

"No, he was uncommunicative, and spoke very little English. The only persons who had much to do with him were the storekeepers of whom he bought supplies for the house."

"And the woman?"

"Her name was Itsu San, I believe. I only saw her once, and that was in the yard back of the house. She appeared young, and was very pretty for a Jap, I guess. She is the first Jap woman I ever saw."

"What were her duties?"

"She was Miss Mowbray's maid, while Joy was the cook."

"And you say they are gone?"

"Yes. I saw Joy about eight o'clock, but when I searched the house after the discovery of the body they were not there, and I could find nothing that belonged to them."

"What are you going to do now?"

"I'm going to hit Farnsworth's trail, and I won't leave it till I run him down and send him to the gallows."

"I don't think you will."

"I won't, eh? Why shouldn't I?"

"Because Farnsworth did not murder Miss Mowbray."

"Then who did?"

"I don't know; probably the Japanese, but I'm not too sure of that. I believe you will pick up a surprise at the end of the string you are following. At any rate, me for Farnsworth, and I give you fair warning that I'm going to help him all I can until I am persuaded of his guilt."

"That's a fine way for a deputy United States marshal to talk."

"A better way than you are talking, for it is as much our duty to protect men from injustice as it is to bring them to justice."

"That's enough of you for me then. I'll say good night. Come on, boys."

The four deputy United States marshals marched in single file from the house, mounted their horses, and rode away into the west just as the sun poked its head above the eastern horizon.

CHAPTER XVI

A LETTER FROM THE DEAD

Ted was brooding over the appearance of Farnsworth, and the startling events which followed, and particularly the crime at Rodeo, of which the young fellow had fallen under suspicion.

Ted believed that Farnsworth was innocent of the crime.

But his flight from the town, and the question he had put to Ted when they met in the road, as to whether Ted had heard the news from Rodeo, were enough to convict him in the mind of any person prone to suspicion.

But Ted looked at matters of this sort differently than most people. In the first place, his experience had taught him that actions which seemed most suspicious often proved most innocent.

That Farnsworth knew of the murder of Helen Mowbray before he quitted Rodeo his question to Ted left no doubt, and the shadow of suspicion under which he had lived was reason enough for him to leave the town before its discovery. He knew the dangerous temper of the people, and that it would take very little to arouse them against him, and

Edward C. Taylor

precipitate them into a lynching, with himself as the central figure.

Ted had heard that Fancy Farnsworth was the worst man in Arizona, and that he had the most ungovernable temper, the quickest eye, and swiftest "draw" of a gun in the Territory.

He was a gambler against whom nobody seemed to be able to cope, for he invariably won. It had been said that he was not a straight gambler, but those who said it did so only once, as they were incapable of saying it twice, for by that time they had been shot full of holes by the card sharper.

Why it was that Farnsworth always escaped punishment at the hands of the authorities no one knew, except that they lacked the nerve to force prosecution against him, and that he invariably had a good excuse for killing a man; at least, one that made good in that rough country, where every man was of a size because all carried revolvers.

But even while Ted believed that Farnsworth was innocent of the murder of Miss Mowbray, he felt that some day he and the dashing young fellow would meet on the battlefield as enemies.

But it was the strange resemblance between him and Major Caruthers that affected Ted more than anything else, and he often wondered that the major had not noticed it himself.

Major Caruthers found Ted on the veranda turning these things over in his mind after breakfast. Coming to his side, the old gentleman threw his arm around Ted's shoulder and said:

"Ted, I'm rather worried about that young chap Dickson, or Farnsworth, whichever he is. I was greatly attracted to him, and intended to invite him to stay with us several days, when those deputy marshals entered and accused him of a crime that horrifies me. Somehow, I feel that he is guilty, although I want to believe in his innocence, as you so bravely advocated when we all were too cowardly to do so. But if he was innocent, why did he not stay and face his accusers, and go back to Rodeo with the marshals and prove himself innocent?"

"He never would have got as far as Rodeo," said Ted quietly.

"Why not? He was under arrest and in the guard and custody of four deputy marshals, officers of the United States."

"They would have prevailed no more than if they had been dummies, which I strongly suspect they were."

"Um, how is that?"

"They were sent out from Rodeo as marshals, but the mob that would have met Farnsworth at the outskirts of the town, to hang him, was the real boss. Those marshals would no more dare defy that mob than they would fly. In the first place, they were not of the real stuff, as was proved by their conduct when they entered your house and saw Farnsworth in the middle of the floor and dared not go to him."

"Well, I'm glad he got away, but I am sorry he had to steal your pony to do it."

"That's all right about the pony. I'm betting I'll get it back one of these days. And, besides, there was nothing else for him to do."

"Ha, ha, ha!" laughed the major. "That was the neatest thing I ever saw, the way he got into that saddle and deliberately put that pony at the window."

"It sure was nervy," said Ted, with a reminiscent smile.

"Wasn't it the most dramatic thing you ever saw? I can see it yet. Farnsworth dodging those deputies and their bullets, and before any one knew what his plan was, leaping upon the pony and jumping through the glass. By Jove, it was fine. I never was so excited in my life."

"It certainly was very dramatic. Almost like a thing one would see in the theater."

"Yes, but a lot more exciting, because it was the real thing. By the way, Ted, there was something about that young fellow that I cannot explain to myself. I was quite strangely affected when he took me by the hand. And every time I looked at him it gave me a feeling as if he was somehow mixed up in my life, or would be in the future."

"That is strange. I wonder who he is. His name is not Dickson, nor is it Farnsworth. Of course, there is a mystery behind him somewhere, and he has a name which he is concealing. Suppose we take a look through his effects. He had a saddlebag in which there may be something by which we can identify him."

"Very well. I don't believe it would be unfair to him to do so. You know, we might be able to help him if we know his real name and address."

They went into the room which had been assigned to Farnsworth, but which he had had no opportunity to occupy.

In one corner they found his saddle, a very ornamental and expensive piece of horse furniture, trimmed with silver and made of the most expensive leather.

Beside it lay a bag which could be fastened to the cantle of the saddle.

It fastened with a snap lock, which was easily opened, and then Ted, at a nod from the major, began to turn out its contents.

First came a pair of silver-mounted hairbrushes and several toilet articles, showing that even in the desert young Farnsworth did not neglect his personal appearance. There were some clean shirts and handkerchiefs, and in the bottom of the bag another leather case.

"If he has anything by which he may be identified, it is in here," said Ted. "But this is locked. Shall I force it?"

"I believe you'd better," answered the major.

"I don't care much about doing it," said Ted, "but as it is to help him I suppose I might as well."

The major nodded, and with the blade of his knife Ted soon had the bag open.

The first thing he came to was a photograph of a beautiful woman, at which he looked intently for a few moments.

It seemed to him that he had seen her, or some one very like her, somewhere before.

Then he passed it over to the major, and reached his hand into the bag once more.

Suddenly he was interrupted by a startled cry, in which there was a tone of pain and surprise, from the major.

Looking up, he saw that the major was as white as a sheet, and that his hand trembled violently.

"What is it?" Ted asked, striding to the major's side.

But Major Caruthers was too shaken by emotion to reply at once.

He continued to stare at the picture with devouring eyes, his face alternately flushing and paling. He was gasping as if he would speak, but the words would not come.

"Do you know her?" asked Ted gently.

The major nodded his head for reply.

"What else do you find?" he managed to ask finally.

Ted emptied the contents of the bag upon the bed.

Among them was a package of old letters carefully tied.

"Look at those letters," commanded the major hoarsely.

Ted untied the string, and took one letter from the pack and opened it. It had been opened and folded so many times that it was with difficulty that Ted could open it now without having it fall to pieces.

"You read it before I do," said the major, who was suffering from a great, nervous strain, and showed it in his face and trembling hand.

Ted spread it on the bed and bent over it.

In the upper left-hand corner was a faded crest of a tower, over which was a coronet.

"My dear, wandering boy," the letter began, "I do not know where you are, or if you are well and alive, or are in trouble, for I have not heard from you for many months. I am sending this at random into that great America in the hope that it may reach you some day to tell you that your mother is constantly thinking of you. Your brother Jack is still in India with his regiment, but will soon retire and come home. Your sister Helen and her husband are I know not where. Mowbray turned out very badly, as your father believed he would, and he had to run from his creditors, and the enemies he had made through his dishonest practices. I don't know where they are, but it is my belief that they have gone to America. I wonder if you will ever run across them? If you do, tell Helen to leave the beast and come home, and both her father and I will forgive, and she can take her place here as if she had never met him. And this leads me to tell you that your father has greatly changed since you left us, and has even said that he was sorry for his harshness, and wished you had stayed with us. We are very lonely with all of our children away from us. Come back to your mother, and all will be different."

There were many expressions of mother love in the letter, which was signed and dated from The Towers, Huntingdon, several years before.

After reading the letter Ted passed it to the major without comment, and walked to the window, that he might not be a witness to his emotion.

He was now very sure that by the strangest of circumstances Major Caruthers had come across a bit of personal history, and that it was giving him a heart-tearing experience.

In a moment he heard the sound of a sob behind him, followed by others, which, however, subsided gradually, and he heard his name called.

Ted came to where the major sat on the side of the bed, holding the photograph in his hand.

"It is the picture of my sister," he said quietly, for he was now the master of his emotions.

"Then Farnsworth is your brother," said Ted.

"Yes, my brother, poor chap," answered the major, gulping down a sob.

"It is strange, very strange," muttered Ted, almost to himself. "I felt sure you were related, there was such a strong resemblance between you."

"I didn't notice it. Why didn't you speak of it?"

"Farnsworth knew that you were his brother, and I have no doubt he would have made himself known to you had he not been compelled to flee before the deputy marshals. I know that he was deeply affected at meeting you, and saw that he hesitated to make himself known."

"I didn't know him. I had not seen Fred since he was a little boy, when I went into the service. Then he went away to school, and I to India. I am much older than he, so we did not meet. When I returned to England from India he had disappeared on account of a foolish row with our father. Our only sister, Helen, had married a scamp against the wishes of the family, and had left England also. Shortly after that both our parents died, and I came to America with the intention of finding both my sister and brother, and this is how it has turned out."

Tears were coursing down the major's pale cheeks.

"Don't you see how it is?" he asked, holding out the photograph to Ted.

Suddenly it dawned upon Ted, and he took the photograph and gazed at it eagerly.

It was Helen Mowbray, the sister of the major and of Farnsworth, or Fred Caruthers, to give him his real name— the woman who had been strangled to death in her house at Rodeo.

This was a shock indeed.

The complications which had arisen in these few hours were sufficient to shatter the strongest nerves, and Ted himself trembled a little at the possibilities unfolded by this unforeseen and unexpected knowledge, while it entirely unnerved the major, and left him as weak as a child.

What was to be done? It was not likely that Fred Caruthers could be found at once. That he knew that it was his sister who had been murdered, and that he was charged with the crime, would be sufficient to spur him on and on, his brain and heart filled with horror. And that he had just found his brother, who might have given him all the moral support he needed at such a time, only to be driven from him by the fear of mob law, which he knew would give him no chance whatever for his life, was an additional sting.

The major sat on the edge of the bed with drooping head, holding in one hand the letter from his dead mother, and in the other the photograph of his murdered sister.

He was too dazed with the suddenness of the shock with which the revelation had come to him to stir.

Ted saw that he must be roused from this immediately.

"Come," he said, placing his hand gently, on the major's shoulder, "we must do something at once."

"What can we do?" asked the major, in a stifled voice.

"In the first place, we must ride to Rodeo with all speed. Do not forget that your sister lies there dead, and that it is your duty to care for her."

"Of course. I had forgotten. All the ghosts of the past crowded in upon me until I forgot my duty to the dead. We will go at once. Will you take charge of things? I am not able yet to do so."

"Certainly. Leave it all to me."

Ted left the major with his relics of the dead and the revelations of the present to compose himself, while he went out to make arrangements for the ride to Rodeo.

Ted knew the difficulties and prejudices they would meet when they got to Rodeo, and feared that before the unpleasant details attending the burial of the dead woman were finished they might clash with the authorities or the townspeople.

Therefore, he decided that they should go well able to defend their rights, and, calling the boys together, he told them as briefly as possible the story of the major and his newly found brother and sister, as the reader knows it.

"Now, fellows, we must help the major straighten out this tangle, bury the dead, defend the innocent, and punish the guilty," he said gravely. "Arm yourselves and saddle, ready to take the road to Rodeo as quickly as you can."

CHAPTER XVII

BESIEGED

The broncho boys galloped into the town of Rodeo early in the afternoon, having put their horses to full speed, only stopping now and then to give them a blow.

Ted had done his best to restore the major to whatever cheerfulness was possible under the circumstances, and the sturdy Englishman had regained his courage and forcefulness.

As they were riding up the main street, Ted in the lead, flanked by Stella and Major Caruthers, they saw one of the deputy marshals who had so unceremoniously entered the ranch house at Bubbly Well to arrest Farnsworth look hard at them, then set off on a run down a side street.

"That fellow has gone to give warning of our approach," said Ted.

"Well, let him. What difference does it make to us?" asked the major.

"It may mean something to us before we get through here," said Ted.

"I imagine they will be suspicious of us," said Stella. "At least, they know that we are not their friends, since we went to such trouble to defend their favorite victim."

"True," said the major. "But we are strong enough to meet them, and we feel that we have the right on our side."

"What shall we do first?" said Ted, deferring to the major's wishes in the matter.

"Who has charge of the body of my sister, do you suppose?" he asked.

"Probably the coroner."

"Very well, let's look him up at once. That, of course, will be my first care."

It did not take them long to find the coroner, who told them that the deputy marshals had taken possession of the house, the property, and the remains of the dead woman, to be held for the appearance of some friend of hers, who had notified them to do so.

"Who is this friend?" asked the major stiffly.

"I'm sure I don't know. You'll have to see the deputy marshals. The inquest has been held, and I have nothing more to do with the affair."

"Now for the deputy marshals," said the major, who had recovered possession of himself, and was now all decision.

They went immediately to the chief deputy, who was also deputy coroner, and whose name, they learned, was Jack Burk.

But they could not find him, neither were any of his men to be found, although Ted was convinced that he was in town.

"There is only one thing to do," said Ted.

"What is that?" asked the major.

"Go to the house, and take possession of it yourself."

"But suppose we find it in the hands of the authorities?"

"That makes no difference to me. The remains of your sister belong to you, and you have the first right to her and her possessions."

"But her husband? I do not know where he is, or whether he is dead or alive."

"As long as he is not here, it is up to you, major, to assume whatever authority is necessary."

"Perhaps you are right. But we cannot gain our point without some show of force."

"I know it, and have come prepared for it. The broncho boys will back you to the limit. Do whatever you think best, major, and you will find the boys and myself right behind you."

"Then we will go to the house," said the major firmly.

In a few minutes Ted and the major dismounted before a handsome house on the outskirts of the town. It was surrounded by a high stone wall, and the gate, which was of iron, was locked.

Ted shook the gate vigorously, and called out for admittance.

Presently the door of the house was opened a crack, and a voice demanded to know what was wanted.

"Come and unlock the gate," demanded Ted.

After a moment's hesitation the door slammed, and there was silence.

"Evidently whoever is in charge of the house does not intend to open to us," said Ted, "and I suppose this will have to be the first act of aggression on our part. Shall I smash our way in?"

"By all means," responded the major. "I don't propose to stay out here and cool my heels in front of my sister's house at the behest of a stranger."

"That's enough for me."

Ted picked up a big stone from the road, and with a vigorous blow or two shattered the massive iron lock, and the gate swung open.

Ted and the major entered the garden in front of the house and walked up the path.

As they were about to ascend the steps to the veranda they were stopped by a voice.

"Halt! What do you want?"

"We want entrance to the house," said the major.

"You can't get in without an order from Deputy Marshal

Burk," said the voice behind the door.

"The deuce I can't!" growled the major, whose fighting blood was coming up at this opposition. "Do you know who I am?"

"No, and it don't make no difference who you are. Them's my orders from the chief."

"I am the brother of Miss Mowbray."

A silence followed this.

"Can't help it," said the voice again. "I can't let you in."

"Open that door instantly, or we'll break it in."

"If you try that you'll be sorry. I warn you, I am armed, and have orders to shoot."

"Shoot, and be jiggered!" shouted the major, who was thoroughly angry by this time, for he was not used to having his orders disobeyed.

"I will if you attempt to break into this house. If you get an order I'll let you in. Without an order you get in only after I am down and out."

"Stay here, major. I'll be back in a few minutes."

Ted Strong was angry also at the delay, and at once suspected that Burk, the deputy marshal, had some sinister reason for putting the house in charge of one of his men, but he could not imagine what it was unless his purpose was not honest.

Ted's experience had taught him that all men in authority as deputy United States marshals were not honest, and that they often used their office to graft.

He had no faith in Burk, whose looks and actions he had distrusted at their first meeting. If Burk knew that the broncho boys were in town it would be sufficient excuse for him to annoy and impede their movements all he could.

No doubt Burk knew that they would come to Rodeo in the interests of Farnsworth, but he did not believe that the deputy marshal knew anything of the newly discovered relationship between Major Caruthers, the dead woman, and the so-called Farnsworth.

What, then, was his reason for holding the house and the remains of the murdered woman against all comers?

There were two inferences: Loot of the woman's house, unprotected by friends and relatives, and the awaiting of the woman's husband.

Ted had thought out these two possibilities thoroughly. He had no doubt that there were many valuables in the house, for the woman was reputed rich, secretive, and probably kept her personal property about her. From what the major had said the husband, Mowbray, evidently had been cast off by Helen Mowbray on account of his rascalities, and, being a bird of prey, would swoop down upon her property as soon as he learned of her death.

Could it be that Burk was holding the house awaiting Mowbray's arrival?

With these thoughts running through his mind Ted had gone around to the back of the house to find, if possible, something with which to smash in the door.

In a shed he found a sledge, and returned to where the major was still arguing with the guard inside.

"Open or we'll break in the door," called Ted, in a stern voice.

"Take the advice of a fool, and leave the door alone," answered the guard.

"Then, for the last time, will you open?"

"No."

Ted swung the sledge and brought it down with all his strength on the lock of the door.

There followed a crash, and the door flew open suddenly.

Then came another crash; this time from a revolver, and a ball whistled past Ted, penetrating the brim of his hat and burying itself in the door casing.

But it was not repeated, for before the guard could wink twice a tan-colored figure shot through the opening, and he fell to the floor with a smash that shook the house, and looked up to find a stalwart youth astride of him, slowly shutting off his wind with strong and inexorable fingers.

Then he was relieved of his revolver, and before he could indicate that he was willing to surrender he found himself trussed like a fowl, with his arms behind his back, and the hall full of young fellows.

"Why didn't you let me know that you had brought a regiment with you?" he said sullenly. "Maybe I'd have let you in."

"You had your chance to open, and was a fool not to take it," said Ted.

"I believe you."

The major had left the party and walked into a room on the left, and in a moment they heard sobs issuing from it. He had found the remains of his sister, and, at a signal from Ted, the boys hustled the deputy marshal into the back part of the house and retired, leaving the major alone with his dead sister.

In a few minutes Ted heard his name called, and went into the room where the major was standing beside a bed, on which was a form covered with a sheet.

"We must get ready to remove her to my house," said the major, in a hushed voice.

"Leave it to me," said Ted. "I will take charge of everything."

"And I want you to help me search the house, for I intend to remove all the valuables she left to Bubbly Well until such time as the courts can handle her property. I don't propose that it shall fall into alien hands."

In the room at the foot of the bed was a small steel safe, which Ted found was fastened with a combination lock. He knelt before it with his ear to the lock, turning the handle of the combination, listening to the click of the tumblers, while the major searched the drawers of the handsome dressing case and other articles of furniture in the room.

Everywhere were evidences that Helen Mowbray had been very wealthy.

Edward C. Taylor

On top of the dressing case were sets of gold and silver toilet articles, and ornaments, boxes, and bottles handsomely chased in silver and gold, and set with jewels.

In one of the drawers the major found a bunch of keys, probably to open other drawers in the console and other articles of furniture.

"I have it, major," said Ted quietly, as he flung open the door of the safe.

"See what is in it, Ted," said the major.

In the bottom of the safe lay a pile of gold ingots representing a value of many thousands of dollars. A drawer was filled with bank notes of large denomination. Other drawers were crowded full of the stocks of mines and other enterprises.

"Whew!" said Ted, as he revealed the dead woman's possessions. "Did you know she was so rich?"

"I had no idea of it," answered the major. "Helen was always a capable woman, and when she left England my father gave her her patrimony outright, that he might never be compelled to see or communicate with her husband again, and this looks as if she had increased it many times."

"This would have made fine plunder for the thieving fellows who had taken possession of the place if fate, in the hands of your younger brother, had not turned up to put you in command."

"What else do you find?"

"Here is a package addressed 'To be sent to The Towers,

Huntingdon, England, to Robert Caruthers, Esquire, or Major John Stairs Caruthers, upon my death, unopened.'"

"Give it to me," said the major huskily, thrusting the package into his pocket.

"And here's a bank book," said Ted. "It bears the name of the Bank of London."

He handed it to the major, who put it also into his pocket.

"Anything else?" he asked.

"That is all."

"Then take this bunch of keys and examine the contents of the drawers."

The first drawer of the console which Ted unlocked and opened was full of jewels, rich and beautiful, a fortune in themselves.

"Poor girl," said the major, in a low voice. "Why did she risk murder by keeping such a fortune about her?"

"Probably she didn't want some particular person to know that she was so rich," suggested Ted.

Drawer after drawer revealed other valuables, such as priceless laces and articles of gold and silver.

"We must get all this away as soon as possible, and guard it carefully," said the major.

"Yes, it is a great temptation, I sup—"

As Ted was speaking he chanced to look up.

Framed in the window was a face.

But as Ted met the blazing eyes in the face it vanished, and he ran into the hall and out onto the veranda, but could see no one in the garden.

At that moment, however, he was brought back into the house with a jump by the sudden slamming of the back door of the house and a cry of warning from Bud, followed by shouts from the other boys. Then a shot outside, and a crash of glass.

The house was being besieged.

He heard a rush in the garden, and turned to see several men race around the corner of the house toward the front door.

They had almost reached it when he slammed it in their faces, putting his shoulder to it, and calling for help.

In the lead of the besiegers he recognized the face he had seen at the window.

As he was still holding the door against those who were striving to push it in from without there was a shot through one of the panels, and Strong sank to the floor insensible.

CHAPTER XVIII

TED SAVES THE HOUSE

But as Ted Strong fell to the floor there was a rush through the hall, and in a moment he was surrounded by the broncho boys, who held the door while Bud and Ben picked Ted up and laid him on a sofa.

As he was laid down Ted opened his eyes.

"Barricade that door with the furniture," he commanded. "Never mind me. I'm all right. Defend the house first. We must not let the thieves get Helen Mowbray's property."

While several of the fellows held their shoulders to the door, which was bulging with the power without to force it in, Bud and Ben carried a heavy sideboard across the room and placed it against the door.

This held it for a while until other heavy articles made it secure.

They had no more than finished their work when a shot crashed through a pane of glass in the dining room in which Ted lay, attended by Stella, who was trying to stanch the blood from a wound in his side.

Edward C. Taylor

Kit gave a muffled groan, and put his hand to his arm. The blood was trickling through his fingers.

"Keep out of range of the windows everybody," shouted Ted, from the lounge.

"Them fellers is quick an' peevish!" shouted Bud. "I'm goin' ter git one er two, shore's my name ain't John Henry Thomas Quackenbush."

There was a stairway in the hall, and Bud went up the steps three at a time.

They heard his step overhead, then his voice in a roar of angry surprise.

"Jumpin' sand-hill fleas!" he yelled. "So that's yer game, is it?"

Outside there was a crash, and through the window they saw a falling ladder; then two men hurtling through the air.

In a moment there was a thud on the earth, and yells of agony.

"They were trying to surprise us from above, but good old Bud got there in time to fool them," said Ted. "Bully for him. Ben, go up and help him. He may need it."

Several shots outside broke the silence that followed the fall of the ladder, and the breaking of glass in the upper windows.

Then came a fusillade in the upper rooms.

"Bud and Ben are giving them as good as they send," muttered Ted.

From the yells that came from the garden the shots from above had evidently done some execution, for they were followed by a rush of feet, then silence.

"Look out, Kit," said Ted, "and see what's doing. But be careful; do not expose yourself."

"No one in sight," said Kit, peering around the corner of the window casing, having first put his hat in an exposed position to draw fire if there were any sharpshooters on guard outside.

"Wait! Great Scott, they're going to set fire to the house!" yelled Kit, running from the room.

In spite of the protestations of Stella, Ted staggered to his feet and followed Kit.

He swayed from weakness as he ran, but appeared to grow stronger with the excitement.

Two men had rushed to the shelter of the side of the house, and were now safe from shots from the windows.

One of them had trundled before him a tar barrel, while the other had his arms full of shavings.

This was the sight that had caused Kit's exclamation.

"Gee whiz, this is bad," said Kit. "In a minute they'll have the stuff blazing, and the house will go in this wind as if it was made of oiled paper. What are we to do?"

Ted, who was holding himself up against a table to keep from falling, thought a moment.

"They're watching for us to stick our heads out of a window to take a shot at those fire bugs, and, if we do, that's the end," said Ted to himself. "But we must get them before the house catches."

Suddenly he straightened up. A spasm of pain crossed his face, and he clutched his side.

"Ted, you must not exert yourself," said Stella, springing toward him. "Ted, remember you are wounded; you do not know how badly."

"I'm all right," answered Ted, with a grim smile. "Let me alone for a while, Stella. Then you can fuss over me all you like. I've got to think of some way to circumvent those devils."

Suddenly he drew his revolver from its holster.

"I have it," he said briskly. "It's taking a risk, but it must be done. If they set the house afire it's all off with us. Kit, stand ready to throw open the door when I give the word. Then shield me from shots from the shrubbery on the opposite side of the garden. The gang is hiding behind those bushes."

"What are you going to do?" asked Stella breathlessly.

"I'm going out to stop those fellows with the tar barrel."

"You are not. I will not let you," cried Stella.

Ted gave Stella a peculiar look that she had never seen in his face before, and she rather quailed from it, it was so full of authority and force.

"Sorry, Stella, to do anything against your wishes," he said quietly. "But some one must do it, and Kit is wounded in his pistol arm, and the other boys are busy."

"Oh, fiddle!" cried Stella. "You are wounded yourself."

"But I'm going, just the same. Stand ready, Kit."

Kit sprang to the door.

Already they could smell the burning tar.

"Hi, deir der puilding firing up alretty," shouted Carl, bursting into the room, pale with apprehension.

"All right, Carl. Stand back from the door, and do as Kit tells you," said Ted. Then, with a look at Stella, which seemed to ask her forgiveness for acting against her wishes, he got ready for a rush.

"Open!" he yelled.

Kit threw the door wide, and Ted Strong sprang out into the garden, and ran swiftly along toward the rear, keeping close to the wall.

He was firing toward the shrubbery as he ran, and those on guard inside heard yells of agony.

Evidently Ted was making good with his bullets.

There came a return fire from the shrubbery, directed not at the open door, but at the flying figure of Ted.

Stella, Kit, and Carl poured a hot fusillade into the bushes, but did not seem able to silence the fire from them.

Then Stella did a foolhardy thing. Without a word of warning she leaped through the doorway, and stood on the step outside, looking after Ted.

She saw him running weakly toward the corner of the house, where two men were bending over the tar barrel, into which they had put the shavings.

They had set fire to the shavings, and were lifting the barrel to place it against the side of the house.

And now the barrel was blazing like a gasoline torch, and the flame was licking the side of the house.

But Ted was upon them. They did not see him, as their backs were toward him, and in a minute both had gone sprawling over the barrel, falling in a heap on the ground.

In a flash Ted had sent the barrel rolling down the yard, and with a piece of canvas, which he had picked up from the ground, was beating out the flames which were creeping up the side of the house.

But the men were on their feet now, and, seeing the cause of their discomfiture, they ran toward Ted with howls of rage, and reached his side as Stella, who had started toward Ted when she saw that the men were about to attack him, was still some distance off.

Ted was not aware of the presence of the men until they were directly behind him. Then he turned, only to be met with a blow on the head with the butt of a pistol, and he sank to the ground with a groan.

Meanwhile, Kit, whose duty it was to cover Ted's attack on the house burners from the doorway, was not able to get a shot because Stella's body was between him and the corner of the house.

As Ted went down with a groan Stella drew her revolver and blazed away.

At her first shot one of the men ran off, limping and yelping like a kicked cur.

The other, conscious that the bullets from her revolver were singing unpleasantly near to his head, made a dash for the shrubbery.

Bending over Ted, Stella tried to see how badly he was hurt.

"You reckless boy," she was saying. "See how you run into danger. Now you have two wounds for me to nurse, if you are not killed."

She was trying to lift him to a sitting posture when she felt herself grasped around the waist, and before she could make a motion in her own defense, was borne swiftly across the yard, and into the shrubbery.

Her scream rang out piercingly, and the boys ran in a body into the garden.

But by the time they got there Stella was out of sight, and they were met with a fusillade of bullets from the shrubbery, causing them to retreat into the house again and close the door.

None of them had noticed Ted lying unconscious at the corner of the house.

They were no sooner out of sight than three men sped from

Edward C. Taylor

the shrubbery across the yard, and, seizing Ted by the heels and shoulders, ran back with him into the place of concealment.

As they threw Ted down on the grass none too gently, the pain brought him back to life and wrung a groan from him.

When he opened his eyes he saw Stella sitting beside him trying to hold his head from the ground.

Several men were there, too, lying flat, peering underneath the shrubbery toward the house.

Every man was armed either with a rifle or a revolver, and occasionally one or the other of them would fire a shot at the house, which would be answered by the boys.

"They fire too high," muttered Ted to himself, "because they do not know that these rascals are lying flat. Every ball goes a foot too high. Wish I could let them know, but then they would probably hit Stella or me."

Lying beside him was Burk, the deputy marshal, his greenish-gray eyes looking coldly at the house, and whenever he saw a chance for a shot his rifle flew to his shoulder.

He became conscious that Ted was looking at him, and turned with a grin on his face.

"So we got you at last, eh?" he said to Ted, with a sneer. "You thought you could put this thing through because you are a deputy United States marshal, did you? Well, you won't be a marshal much longer."

"I think I'll be longer at the job than you will," Ted replied slowly.

"Not after your attempt to loot a dead woman's house while her body still lies there under guard of a United States officer."

This caused Ted to think of the situation in a different light. True, he believed that Burk was a crook, and that it was he who was conspiring to rob the house, but he had authority on his side, while Ted's belief, after all, was based on surmise, and he would have difficulty in proving anything criminal against the marshal. At the same time, he did not fear for his own part in the affair, because behind him was the brother of the dead woman.

"I say, Burk, I'm tired of this nonsense, lying here and potting away at the house," said a drawling voice, the owner of which could not be seen, being hidden behind the shrubbery.

"Can't help it," answered Burk. "We've got to take our time. The house is full of them, and they can shoot some."

"Rot! So can we. I propose that we rush them. But first I want the pleasure of putting my revolver against the head of that young bully there and the girl, and getting rid of them. Think what's at stake. We must get away from here soon."

"Don't talk nonsense," growled Burk, in reply.

"I'm getting tired of it, I tell you. Three of our men are wounded now, and that red-headed beggar is going to die, and he was such a good cook."

The speaker laughed unpleasantly at his gruesome joke.

"Well, we can't do it now, because we don't know how they're situated. We'd have had them when they all rushed out a few minutes ago if you hadn't shot at them so soon, and driven them indoors again. Why didn't you let them get into the open, where we could have shot them down?"

Stella shuddered at the cold-blooded tone in which these men discussed the killing of the boys, but Ted only smiled, for he knew that Burk was at heart a coward, and that he did not care to rush, nor would he stand a rush should one come.

He wished he was back in the house and knew the enemy's situation as well as he did now. He would not give them time to run very far.

If he could communicate to the boys in some manner the exact situation, he felt confident that the thing would be over in a very short time.

"I say, Strong, I've a proposition to make to you," said Burk, after a silence.

"Well, out with it," said Ted coldly.

"There's no use of any more of us being hurt or killed," said Burk, looking at Ted out of the corner of his eye.

"Then why don't you quit shooting and vamose?"

"That's not for me to do," said Burk hotly.

"Oh, I see. You want us to quit, eh?"

"Sure. You're the fellows who broke in there over our guard. But if you'll call your fellows off and get out of the house, I'll agree to turn you and the young lady loose. But nothing must be taken from the house."

"That seems right generous of you," said Ted, with a sarcastic smile, which Burk didn't see because his head was turned the other way.

"It's a darned more than you deserve, but I don't want any more of my fellows shot up."

"What do you want me to do?"

"Just step out there and holler to your boys to quit firing, and tell them that you're going to quit, and then—"

Ted just laughed, and Burk turned upon him with a scowl.

At that moment there was a cheer from the direction of the house; then a few scattering shots from the men in the shrubbery.

Ted heard the doors of the house open, and the swift patter of running feet. The old Moon Valley yell was in his ears. All the men in the shrubbery had sprung to their feet, and were running wildly about. A man crawled through the bushes— the man with the face he had seen at the window.

As he crawled close to Ted the expression of his face was awful to contemplate.

Such fiendish, murderous hatred he had never seen in a human countenance before.

When he was so close to Ted that he could hear his feverish breathing, the man suddenly thrust forward a pistol until the muzzle was within an inch of Ted's head.

Ted struggled to grapple with him, but he had grown so stiff from his wound that he could hardly stir. He was looking death close in the face.

The man was just about to pull the trigger when close at hand the major's voice rang out in an exclamation of amazement:

"Mowbray! You here?"

The man with the pistol sprang to his feet and faced Major Caruthers for a second. Then, with a wild cry of fear, he sprang away through the shrubbery and escaped.

CHAPTER XIX

HELEN MOWBRAY'S WILL

By the time one could have counted ten there was not a man of Burk's force in sight, but, on looking down the road where it led to the plain that lay before the mountains, the dust of their retreat hung in the air.

"We've got 'em on ther run," said Bud, throwing his hat into the air with a joyous yawp. "Sufferin' tomcats, but them fellers has their nerve, aber nit."

Ben and the major had carried Ted into the house, and the major, who was a good surgeon, had Ted's coat off and was examining his wound.

When the shot had been fired through the door at him the ball had been deflected by a piece of iron, and, instead of penetrating his heart, as it surely would have done otherwise, it struck a rib and ran around toward the back, coming out near the spine, and, although an extremely painful wound, it was not at all serious.

A ball had passed through the fleshy part of Kit's forearm, but when the major had washed it in warm water and dressed it, it ceased to pain, and he could use it handily. But Ted's wound was different, and the impact of the ball on the rib had made him so sore that he could not breathe without suffering agony.

Stella had one of the boys make a fire for her, and, having found the house well stored with provisions, she began to cook supper for them, for they were all tired and hungry.

It was evening before they knew it, and it was decided to stay at the house all night, keeping a careful guard against the return of Burk and Mowbray.

"I never was so surprised in my life as when I saw Mowbray in the bushes out there just in the act of murdering you," said the major after supper, as he sat on the sofa beside Ted.

"It was a surprising meeting," said Ted. "I had no idea he was in this part of the country. His was the face I saw at the window when we had all that money and gold and jewels out."

"Then he knows we have found it?"

"Sure. He knows we have it, and if he is the chap I think he is, he'll not rest until he gets it, or—something else."

"Meaning?"

"Death or imprisonment."

"He richly deserves either, or both. He made the life of my sister most unpleasant."

"By the way, major, what do you know about him? It might be handy to know something in the future if he tries to make trouble."

"Precious little."

"Oh, by the way, have you looked into that packet I took from the safe and handed you? The one addressed to your father, I take it, or to yourself."

"Haven't thought of it until now. Must take a look at it, by Jove. It may tell us a lot we want to know."

The major pulled the envelope from his pocket, and after examining the writing on it closely for a moment tore off the end of it and drew out several business-like documents.

"You'll excuse me, Strong, while I look these over, won't you?" he said.

"Certainly. Don't mind me," replied Ted, sinking back comfortably among the cushions.

As the major's eyes traveled over the documents they began to light up with a new intelligence. Then a look of pain followed, and the tears ran slowly down his cheeks.

Finally he turned to Ted:

"It is her will, and some history of her adventures in this country since she left home, and an account of the abuse and indignities heaped upon her by her husband, Mowbray, from whom she was divorced some months ago."

"Then Mowbray has no right to her property?"

"Not a penny's worth. I shall not bore you by reading all she says on the subject. She tells how he beat her after stealing from her all he could. Then she goes on to tell of his crimes."

"He is a bad egg, then," said Ted, as the major paused.

"You would scarcely believe how bad he was if I were to read the story of his career."

"I suppose he had been bothering her since in order to get more money from her."

"Yes, she says that he made her life miserable, and that he often threatened to kill her if she didn't give him all she had."

"Hearing of her death, he came here to steal everything he could lay his hands on; is that it? But I don't quite see why the authorities here, knowing of her divorce from him, would permit him to take possession of her effects, from any ownership in which the courts had barred him."

"I don't suppose the people here knew anything about it, for she says in this paper that she got her divorce secretly, and that there was no publicity about it. She simply had her lawyers notify Mowbray to that effect, at which time she sent him ten thousand dollars in settlement of all claims against her, which he agreed to accept with that understanding. But later he wrote her a letter in which he said that the agreement meant nothing to him, and that he would expect more."

"But why didn't she make the fact that he was no longer her husband public? It would have saved this trouble."

"She didn't want the news of it to travel to our parents in England. That was her pride."

"I see. Does she leave him anything in her will?"

"Yes. Her will is a curious document. It was evidently made immediately after her divorce from Mowbray, and leaves all her property to our mother, and, after her death, to my brother and myself, with a small bequest to silence Mowbray. But there is a codicil which leads me to believe that she had heard of mother's death, in which event she leaves almost everything to her brother, Frederic Caruthers. He is the one known as Fancy Farnsworth."

"Nothing to you?"

"Oh, yes, but not so much as to Fred, whom she puts in my care, asking me to see that he is properly treated and that he gets the justice which is his due."

"Evidently she knew, then, that he has many enemies who were trying to put him within the clutches of the law."

"Evidently. But there is a section which I do not understand."

"Read it. Perhaps we can figure it out between us."

"All right, I will. The paragraph is as follows: 'I desire that my elder brother, John Stairs Caruthers, shall take charge of my property in the event that the said Frederic Caruthers shall not be present when my will is opened, and that he shall be found as speedily as possible. For several years Frederic Caruthers has been my only protector, defending me from the abuse and greed of my former husband, and, further, sustaining my credit and honor by assuming the misdeeds of Mowbray, to his own discredit and danger. Had it not been for his watchful care, I would long ago have been stripped of all I have been able to accumulate, and have been in my grave at the hands of Mowbray. But of this latter I am in constant dread, and I feel such will yet be my fate. If my dead body is found with marks of violence on it, and my house robbed, it will have been the work of said Mowbray. Therefore, in the way of a tardy reward for the loyalty, care,

Edward C. Taylor

protection, and love given me by my brother, Frederic Caruthers, I leave to him the bulk of my property, personal and real, in mining stocks, jewels, money, and the turquoise beds in New Mexico, as well as the San Fernando Ranch. I especially charge my brother John Stairs Caruthers to find his brother, and to defend him and clear his name, should it be necessary, and to put him in full possession of his property.'"

As the major finished reading he looked at Ted inquiringly.

"Well, what do you make of it?" he asked. "I confess it puzzles me."

"I can see through it. But you have your work cut out for you, major."

"In what way?"

"You will find this fellow Mowbray a hard customer."

"Pshaw! I am not afraid of him."

"Neither am I, for that matter; but it is not he alone that is to be feared in this matter."

"What do you mean?"

"Just this: Mowbray evidently is an archvillain, but he could not do all his dirty work alone."

"You think he has accomplices, then?"

"Exactly. And of the most dangerous sort."

"For instance?"

"I have been thinking the matter over, and I am convinced that Mowbray has got about him the most dangerous sort of a gang to carry on his work for him. Do you know if he is a man of any particular force and cleverness?"

"When I knew him, which was before I went to India, he was already beginning to practice his shady transactions in England, but he had never been directly caught at it. This led to the greatest opposition on the part of my family to his marriage to my sister."

"But, in spite of it, she married him?"

"Yes; she had an idea that he was abused and misrepresented, and flew to his defense by secretly marrying him. After that he got worse and bolder until he was caught not only cheating at cards, but actually stealing by means of forgery and in other ways, and they had to flee from England."

"Then, of course, he is a master in crime by this time."

"It would not surprise me to learn it. But you spoke of his being especially dangerous because of the men he had gathered about him?"

"Yes, and I mean it. I am sure now that in his gang are several men who are especially dangerous, because they can defy the law without much risk of running counter to it."

"I don't see how one man can break the law with less danger of punishment than another."

"It is this way: Mowbray has in his gang several deputy United States marshals. These men have advance information of any action to be taken by the law against the suspected perpetrators of crime. This information is at once at the disposal of Mowbray, and he can escape the consequences of his crimes without difficulty. He is protected, also, by his partners rigging up accusations against innocent persons, and convicting them by manufacturing evidence against them."

"What a villainous system!"

"It is. And it is just this thing that has enabled Mowbray to prey on his wife for so long a time."

The major uttered an exclamation of anger.

"Another thing," continued Ted: "I am sure now that it was these very pals of Mowbray that made the accusations against your brother, known as Farnsworth, at the instance of Mowbray. They nursed public resentment against the young fellow until every hand was against him, and he was forced to become an outlaw, or fall into the hands of the authorities and be forced into prison, or to the gallows, through the perjury of these same deputy marshals. It is an infamous thing, and I am going to try to sift it to the bottom and clear your brother, and see that Mowbray gets what's coming to him."

"You are very good, and I shall never forget what you have done for me already."

"That's all right. It's my duty as an officer of the United States in this Territory of Arizona to do it. Never fear; there will be more to this than the beginning, and a race is not won until it is ended."

All night one or the other of the boys patrolled the grounds, hiding in the shrubbery, ready to give the alarm should any of Mowbray's party return to attack the house and capture the treasure.

But dawn broke without an alarm, and the boys were astir, making ready for the abandonment of the house and the return to the Bubbly Well Ranch.

Ted was feeling so much better after a good night's rest that he was able to climb into his saddle and go into the town.

His object was to get a wagon and a span of mules in which to transport the remains of Helen Mowbray and the valuables she had left behind to her brother's house.

At a livery stable he met the proprietor, a garrulous old man, whom, when he had explained his mission, looked at him strangely before speaking.

"What's doin' at the Mowbray house?" he asked. "We all uptown was some curious last evenin' when we heard so much shootin'."

"Nothing much," said Ted. "Just a little pistol practice."

The old man grinned.

"Yuh musta kep' ther targets warm some from ther way ther poppin' sounded up yere," he said dryly.

"Yes, it was rather warm for a while. Well, can I have the wagon, and a driver to bring it back?"

"I don't know whether I can spare one or not. Yuh see, it's some dangerous ter take sides in this town."

"I don't want you to take my side. All I want is to complete a business transaction with you. I want you to hire me a wagon and team for a day. You understand what I want?"

"Yes, but, yuh see, that would be considered as givin' succor ter ther enemy."

"I don't understand why."

"It's this way: Judge Harris owns this stable an' rents it to me by ther month. He could kick me out to-morrow if he wanted to. He's a queer dick, an' him an' Burk, what, I understand, was at ther Mowbray house yesterday, and what had ter run away, is as close as two sheets o' sticky fly paper."

"He is, eh?"

"Yes; an' the coroner, the jailer, the mayor, the sheriff, an' everybody else what has any power er authority, is in the same boat. They all hang together, an' they're all friends o' Mr. Mowbray. Lord Mowbray they calls him."

"Ah, ha!" thought Ted. "If that is the case, it behooves us to get out of town and to Bubbly Well with our property as soon as we can."

After some further talk Ted was still unable to get the old man to rent him a wagon. Then he changed his tactics.

"Well," he said, in a firm voice, "if you won't rent me the wagon and team I'll be obliged to confiscate it for the United States."

"Eh, how is that?"

"I said I would take it for the uses of the United States. Come, roll it out and hitch up before I have to resort to violence."

"I don't know you, bub. I'm from Missouri. You'll have to show me."

Ted exposed his star of authority.

"Does that go?" he asked. "Because if it don't, this will."

His revolver was out of its holster like a flash, much to the surprise of the liveryman, who had been somewhat of a bad man himself in his day, and gun plays were not uncommon at Rodeo.

He gazed mildly into the bore of the big, silver-mounted forty-five, and then murmured:

"It goes, pal."

CHAPTER XX

KNIFE AND FANG

Several days had passed since the fight at Helen Mowbray's house, and Ted Strong and the broncho boys were again at the Bubbly Well Ranch.

The remains of Helen Mowbray had been laid to rest near the major's ranch house in a little lot surrounded by a low fence, and her treasure was safely stored away in the safe in the major's bedroom.

The period of their visit to the ranch house was past, but still they stayed to help the major to get word of his brother Frederic Caruthers, alias Fancy Farnsworth, alleged to be the worst man in Arizona.

Where he might be none knew, of course, but Ted was of the opinion that he was still somewhere in Arizona, and not far away, either.

He could not have told why he believed so, but he had one of his "hunches" to that effect, and believed it as surely as if he knew it for a fact.

Ted had seen his hunches turn out true so often that he did

not attempt now to distrust them.

Somehow, he felt that everything was to come out all right some day, and that he would find Farnsworth, or Frederic Caruthers, to be more exact, and Ted always reproached himself when he thought of the young fellow by his false name.

One morning Ted awoke before the dawn, sitting upright in bed, listening for a sound, but heard nothing unusual.

This was one of Ted's habits—to be aroused by some unknown sense in the night when danger threatened.

Hearing nothing, he got out of bed, and sat on its edge and listened again.

"Wonder what waked me?" he muttered to himself. He was not in the least sleepy, as he would have been if he had wakened naturally.

"I don't think I was dreaming," he continued to mumble to himself. "And it wasn't a noise. Must have been a hunch. Guess I'll get up and see if there's anything wrong about here."

He slipped swiftly into his clothes, and sauntered through the living room.

It was just beginning to get light outside, and the windows were gray, while all else in the room was still dark.

He opened the door and stepped out into the chill morning.

Then he heard a noise, but so faint that it couldn't have been that which had disturbed him from his sound sleep, he thought.

But as the sound came nearer on the clear, thin morning air, and he recognized it and realized its significance, he knew that it was this fine, almost indistinguishable sound that had penetrated in some mysterious manner to his inner ear and called him from his sleep.

It was the cry of a hungry and angry wolf.

At last he located the sound off to the east, but as yet he could see nothing, for it was not yet light enough, and a thin mist, like a mirage, hung over the surface of the sandy prairie and obscured the view.

For a long time he stood listening to the long-drawn and savage howl, thinned out by the distance and mist, but he knew that it was coming nearer, and that the animal that was making it was not only hungry, but that it was a master wolf. It was none of the gaunt, half-starved, cowardly brutes that follow in the pack and take what the master wolf leaves of the scraps of the murdered calf or sick cow or sheep which the leaders of the pack have pulled down.

He had heard before the yells of these kings of the packs of savage prairie wolves, and they were masterful indeed, and could easily be distinguished above the feebler pipings of the wolf rabble.

Suddenly the sun came up and the mists disappeared as by magic, and it was light.

Ted looked steadily toward the place from which the howls had come when it was dark, and saw a spot against the earth.

It was either a pony or a cow, and it was in trouble, for it came on very uncertainly, running sideways, stopping for a moment to kick, then running on again.

Ted immediately saw what was the matter. It was being pursued by the wolves he had heard.

The wolves were running with it, perhaps had been chasing it all night, and were snapping it its heels, trying to hamstring it.

He thought it was a small, lean cow from this distance, and wondered at its courage, and if it would last until it got close enough to where there were human beings to be safe from further pursuit.

At first he thought of going inside and putting on his coat and boots and getting his arms and starting out toward it on his pony. But this was too much trouble, and he stood watching the tragedy of the plain, hoping for the plucky animal that was doing its best to outrun and outwit the wolves, for they were close enough now for him to see that there were four of the gray devils of the prairie.

But only one of them was worthy of a second look—a great, gray brute much larger than his mates and twice as courageous.

Ted thought it strange that the wolf king was not doing as the others did; that is, running up behind their victim and making a slash at his legs with their razorlike fangs, then retreating with a whining howl when they felt the heels of the poor brute they were tormenting.

No, the big wolf was leaping high into the air from the side, evidently trying to reach something that was fastened to the pony's back—for now Ted was able to distinguish what it was.

It was a bay pony, rather small, and almost all in with fatigue.

Something baggy was tied to its back, which resembled a bundle of old clothes.

Once, as he watched, Ted saw the pony go to its knees, actually tired out and weak.

But it was up again, and struggling bravely on again.

"Plucky little beggar," muttered Ted, in admiration. "Wish I had taken my first hunch and ridden out to help it. By Jove, it's not too late yet!"

Without going into the house Ted jumped to the ground and ran out to meet the pony and its enemies.

It did not occur to him that he was not armed until he was halfway to them. Then he felt in his pocket and found his big-bladed knife.

Taking this out, he sprang open the big blade and carried it loosely.

He had stooped and picked up a large stone, which he carried in his hand.

When he came close enough he hurled the stone at the wolves, and a dull thud, followed by a shrill, dog-like howl of pain, told him that he had countered on the rib plate of one of the nasty brutes. Then he let out a wild yell, and three of the wolves turned and fled.

Not so the king of the pack.

He stopped for a moment and stared at Ted with his pale-green eyes. Then, with a long howl of defiance, he sprang again at the pony, which had picked up courage at hearing a human voice and was coming on more briskly.

Suddenly Ted recognized the pony.

It was the major's Christmas gift, and Ted once more gave voice to an exultant yell, which only served to increase the fury of the wolf's attack at whatever was fastened to the pony's back.

Ted knew that Fred Caruthers, as he tried always to call the young brother of the major, would send the pony back some day, and now his faith had been rewarded.

When he became aware of the identity of the pony he ran faster, and was soon within a few feet of it.

He naturally expected that the wolf would now beat a retreat, as wolves met singly and in this fashion generally turn tail and split the wind for home when attacked by man.

But the big wolf simply turned his attention from the pony to the boy, and stood as if carved out of gray granite, his head held high in the air, and his eyes blazing like two pale-green lights.

"By Jove, I think the brute is going to stand and fight!" said Ted to himself.

Taking advantage of the situation, the pony trotted past Ted, who scarcely gave it a look, and went on to the corral back of the house.

"So it's going to be a fight," said Ted, advancing cautiously toward the wolf. "All right, old chap; I'll give you something to think about, if I do not leave you on the ground entirely incapable of thinking. I wish I'd gone after my Winchester now. That would have made it too short, though. Come on, now. All I have is a short knife blade against four sharp fangs, and you are as brave as the devil himself."

The wolf had not stirred except that his nose was constantly working as he sniffed the air for Ted.

Ted knew that a wolf that will stand and fight a man by himself is possessed of more than ordinary courage and brains, and, therefore, he was on the lookout for the tricks of the fight.

It was well that he was so versed, for before he was quite ready for it the wolf, without a sound, leaped straight through the air at his throat. He had just time to dodge aside, and make a vicious swipe with his knife.

But his blade did not touch the wolf, whose leap carried him several feet past Ted. Had the wolf succeeded in striking Ted, they would inevitably have gone down together, and Ted would have had none the best of it.

But the battle between Ted, the skilled huntsman and wolf exterminator, and the wily wolf, whose scarred hide told of many battles with bull and dog, wild cat and man, serpent of the desert, and the eagles of the mountains, when, in his dire hunger, he had raided their families.

The wolf slid a few feet, then swung himself around like a top and came at Ted again.

Ted was wiser this time, and dodged just out of the way. At the same time he gave a vicious side lunge with the knife, and he felt it enter the wolf's hide. There was a ripping sound, and he knew he had added a scar to the brute's large collection.

The wolf was now thoroughly angry, and snarled its fury as it wheeled once more to the attack.

Ted turned to meet it as it rushed toward him, but as he did so he heard a shout from the ranch house and turned his head in that direction for an instant.

But that instant was the critical one, and before he could get around again to face the wolf it was upon him.

Ted felt it strike his chest a mighty blow with its head, and staggered backward.

It suddenly came to him that if he got under the wolf its teeth surely would get to his throat, and that one snap of those saber-sharp teeth would settle the business for him.

He tried to protect his throat with his left arm as he felt himself toppling, but could not get it up far enough because the wolf's body and head interposed.

But he was slashing away with his knife in a frenzy of despair, and, apparently, was doing some execution, for every time he struck the wolf let out a little whine of angry pain.

But the wolf had all the best of it now, and as Ted's foot slipped on some pieces of dry grass he went down with the heavy brute on top of him.

He could feel it nuzzling at his neck for a toothhold on his throat, but he kept his chin pressed close to his neck, and, although the wolf chewed his shirt to pieces, it had found no room to get its teeth into the boy's flesh.

Ted had no time now to play with the knife. It was not up to him to conquer the wolf now, but to keep it from taking his life.

Had his revolver been with him he could have ended the fight with a couple of shots, even if the brute seemed to have a dozen lives, for he knew that had any one of the knife thrusts which he had planted in the wolf's body been given to an ordinary specimen of the species the fight would have been over long since.

The wolf was standing on him, and its weight crushed him.

All he could do in self-defense was to try to get the wolf by the throat with his bare hands and to choke it.

But the hair about its throat was a thick, almost impenetrable mass of heavy, thick-growing bristles, on which Ted's hands had apparently no effect at all.

Ted was in a pretty tight place, and he fully realized it.

The wolf was working hard to get at his windpipe, and the teeth were getting closer and closer to the vital spot.

Ted's arm, where he tried in vain to get it between himself and the wolf, was gashed in a dozen places, and the blood was all over him. His clothes had long since been torn into shreds.

The wolf was getting tired also, as well it might, for, probably it had been running all night, and had been long without food, so that it was no discredit to its enormous strength that it was weak and weary.

But neither was Ted as strong as usual, for the ball which had creased his rib had cost him lots of blood.

In the hearts of both of them, however, there was strength enough, and it was that which kept them fighting long after both of them were tired and winded.

The wolf knew, as well as did Ted, that if it ever got to his throat there would be strength enough for it; the strength that comes from blood.

Ted was wishing that some one would come.

He had heard a cry. Why didn't whoever had called out come at once?

He couldn't last more than a minute longer, and the strong, murky smell of the beast was turning him faint, as the wolf seemed to be gaining in strength and savagery.

Presently he knew the reason. He felt that his side was wet.

His wound had opened again, and he was bleeding.

The wolf had smelled his blood, and it had renewed its strength and courage, while it weakened and took the life out of Ted.

Suddenly there was a crash of hoofs on the sod. Stella's clear voice rang out, and the swish of a quirt came through the air.

That was all Ted remembered, except that he felt relieved of the weight of the wolf, which was running like a streak of gray lightning toward the hills.

His eyes opened, and he saw Stella bending over him, and managed to stagger to his feet, congratulating himself as his hand went to his throat that he had at least saved it from the white fangs of his enemy.

CHAPTER XXI

'WARE THE GRAY WOLVES

As Ted and Stella were walking slowly back toward the house they heard a series of shouts from the direction of the corral.

They then saw Kit at the corral gate waving frantically to them.

"Something wrong there," said Ted. "I'll get up behind you, and we'll hurry to the corral."

He jumped upon the pony's back, and Stella rode as fast as possible to where Kit stood holding the gate of the corral.

Inside the corral was a scene of confusion.

The ponies were running around and leaping in the air, snorting and edging away from the little bay pony which had come across the plain chased by the wolves.

As Ted rode up to the corral fence he looked through the bars, then started back in surprise with an exclamation.

"What is it?" asked Stella.

"A man tied to the back of the pony," replied Ted.

"Who?"

"I cannot tell. I cannot see his face."

"Open the gate, Kit, and let me in," said Stella, gathering up her reins.

"What are you going to do?" asked Ted.

"I'm going to catch that pony and bring him out. That man will be smashed to death in there by the other ponies if he isn't gotten out soon."

"Go ahead, but be careful."

Kit swung the gate open, and Stella dashed into the corral.

The ponies were running around the corral, following the line of the fence, and in the center of the bunch was the little bay pony with the inert, and probably dead, body of a man hanging head downward on the pony's flank, rolling horribly, and in constant danger of being hit by the flying heels of the other ponies, who were frantic at the smell of blood.

Stella rode among the ponies, following the circle with them, all the while edging in more and more until she was close to the little bay.

Then she was able to see the face of the man tied to its back.

"It's Farnsworth," she shouted to Ted, who was standing on the fence watching her movements.

"Get him out as soon as you can," Ted answered.

Stella rode to the pony's side, and managed to get hold of the bridle close to the bit.

Then she maneuvered for an opening by which she could lead the frightened animal out of the bunch.

"Get ready to open the gate," she called at last, and Kit stood with his hand on it.

As she came around again she began pushing the bay pony outward.

"Now!" she cried, swinging her own pony against the other with a prick of the spur, and breaking through the galloping bunch.

The next moment she and a half dozen of the frightened ponies swept through the gate, and as Kit closed it again Ted ran forward and caught the bay pony.

"Hurry him to the house," he said, running beside the bay.

His long yell brought the boys and the major to the veranda, and when they saw Ted running beside the bay pony, with Stella and Kit following, they rushed out to help.

"What is it?" asked the major, as Ted drew up to the veranda.

"Your brother," answered Ted gently, indicating the inert body tied to the pony's back.

"Get him off and into the house," said the major brusquely, his face white with apprehension.

Bud and Ben were working as for their lives at the rope by which the body of Frederic Caruthers was bound to the pony's back.

Soon they had him released, and between them bore the limp form into the living room and laid it on a lounge.

The clothes on the body were torn into strips, and the flesh was gashed in numerous places. This was the work of the wolf's teeth, which, during the chase, had repeatedly leaped at the unconscious man, trying to drag him from the pony's back.

"These wounds are not the worst," said Ted, looking down at Caruthers. "Off with his clothes, boys, and let us see where his real hurt is."

It did not take long for the boys to get Caruthers' rags stripped from his body, and Ted bent over him, examining him closely.

"Ah, here it is," he said, as he turned Caruthers over.

"What?" asked the major, crowding in.

"Here in the back," said Ted, pointing to a small, round, bluish hole just under Caruthers' right shoulder blade.

"By Jove, he's been shot through the body. That's what brought him to this."

"But how did it happen, I wonder, that he was tied to the back of the pony?" asked Ted.

"We'll never know until he tells us, probably," said the major. "If, indeed, he ever is able to do that," he continued, after a slight pause, looking sorrowfully at the young fellow, who seemed to have breathed his last.

But Ted's ear was pressed close to his heart, and his fingers sought the wounded man's pulse.

In a moment he straightened up.

"He's alive—only alive, and no more. But perhaps we can save him yet," he said. "Hustle, fellows! Stella, get me some hot water as soon as possible. Bud, arrange a cot in my room near the window. Major, if you have any brandy, let me have some. Kit, get the bandages ready and prepare some carbolated water. All alive now."

Ted's vigorous action was followed by the others, and in a few minutes Caruthers was stretched out on the cot in Ted's room.

At the movement the wound began to bleed, which was a good sign, and Ted proceeded to wash it with warm water, and began to probe for the ball, to ascertain, if possible, how deep it had gone.

As he was engaged in probing a slight groan came from between the blue lips of the victim.

"All right, I've found it," said Ted, in a low voice to the major, who was bending anxiously over the body of his brother.

"It's all right," continued Ted reassuringly. "It didn't go in very deep, and if he can hold out for a moment or two I think I can get it out. I've taken out worse ones than this."

Ted continued to work with the probe, and occasionally Caruthers stirred and groaned.

Then came a gentle tug, and the bullet rolled out of the

wound upon the sheet.

It was followed by a spurt of blood, which Ted looked at closely.

"No danger," he said. "It is not arterial blood. Give me the water, and then the bandages."

With deft and practiced fingers Ted bound up the wound as well as a surgeon might.

"Now for a sip of the brandy, and we'll have him around all right," said the young amateur surgeon.

He forced a teaspoonful of the ardent spirits between the pale lips of the wounded man, which was followed by a spluttering cough, then a long sigh, and Caruthers opened his eyes.

For a moment he glanced around, and with a faint smile closed his eyes again, and sank into a gentle sleep.

"Bully!" exclaimed Ted, with satisfaction. "He'll get well now, I think, but he had a close call. A little longer on the back of that pony, jostled and being tossed around, would have finished him in spite of his splendid physique."

"What shall we do now?" asked the major.

"There is nothing we can do except care for him faithfully, and nurse him. Some one will have to watch him, and give him his medicine, which I shall prepare from your medicine chest, major."

"Let me nurse him," exclaimed Stella, who had come into the room in time to hear this.

"The very thing, if you don't mind," said Ted.

"Mind! I should like to. And you know that I can nurse some," said Stella proudly.

"I know it from experience. Keep him quiet. Don't let him talk, and whenever he gets restless give him a spoonful of his medicine. He mustn't be allowed to toss around, for that would start internal bleeding. He is not out of the woods by a long shot. When he is well will be time enough for him to do his talking, and tell us what happened to him. Now, fellows, we'll clear out and give nurse and patient a fair show."

For several days Caruthers hung between life and death. Most of the time he was in a state of delirium, during which he continually muttered something about "joy." When Stella told Ted about this he was greatly puzzled. What had the poor chap to do with joy?

Then it suddenly occurred to him that Caruthers meant Ban Joy, Helen Mowbray's Japanese servant, who was called Joy for short.

"He wants to tell us about that Jap," said Ted. "Evidently he knows something about the murder of his sister, and wants us to find the Jap."

"Thar's nothin' doin' until he gets over his fever an' is strong ernough ter talk," said Bud, "So ther best thing ter do is not ter mind what he says, but ter git him over his fever."

Stella was well-nigh worn out, but she would not consent to leave the bedside of the sick man, except at short intervals, when Ted or Bud, who were the best nurses among the boys, took her place that she might get some much-needed sleep.

That night Caruthers awoke from a long sleep and looked up at Stella.

"Where am I?" he asked, in a low voice.

"You are with friends," she replied gently. "Hush, you are not strong enough to talk."

"Yes, I am. I am all right now. Whose house am I in?" he asked.

"You are in Major Caruthers' house."

"I am glad. Is Ted Strong here?"

"Yes."

"Send him to me. I must talk to him. How long have I been here?"

"About a week."

"Hurry. It may be too late."

Stella saw that Caruthers' head was clear, and that he had something important to communicate, and that it would not be well with him if he were permitted to worry, so she went out, and presently Ted entered the room.

"Well, old chap, you look fit," he said, giving Caruthers' hand a gentle pressure.

"I'll be all right in a day or two. But I must talk with you. Tell me, have the Gray Wolves been here yet, and have you driven them off?" said Caruthers excitedly.

Ted was sure now that the patient had relapsed back into his delirious talk, and tried to soothe him.

"I'm all right," said Caruthers impatiently. "I know what I'm saying. I don't mean the pack that chased me."

"No, we have not been attacked by wolves," Ted answered.

"Then you will be. Have you seen Joy—Ban Joy, the Jap, I mean?"

"No."

"That is strange. He should have been here if he got away."

"I'm up in the air as to what you mean. If you are strong enough, perhaps you'd better tell what you mean, beginning at the time you left us, and telling it as briefly as possible."

"All right. But first give me a dose of that medicine."

Ted administered the medicine, which was a mild stimulant, and Caruthers began:

"When I jumped through the window, I did so, not because I was afraid of the four men, but to save you from trouble. I knew that the fellows had been sent to get me, not by the authorities, but by my brother-in-law Mowbray. You know about him?"

Ted nodded, and Caruthers went on:

"I went directly to Sombrero Peak. I knew they would look for me in another place. I was right, but I had not foreseen another thing. When I was in hiding I was surprised by the sudden appearance of Ban Joy and his sister Itsu San, the servants of my sister. They, too, had fled from Mowbray and his gang of murderers.

"This was somewhat inconvenient for me, for I knew that Mowbray, while he would not probably get on my track until I could communicate with you, would easily track the Japanese, and I was not in any position to defend myself and them, for I was out of ammunition, having lost my cartridge belt. But I found a small cave and fortified it as well as possible, and awaited the coming of the Gray Wolves."

"The Gray Wolves?" said Ted, with interrogation in his voice.

"Yes, that is what Mowbray and his thieves and murderers call themselves. You will know why, I'm thinking, before long."

"But to proceed: We continued to live in the cave for a few days, Joy contriving to trap rabbits and birds, upon which we lived. Then, in a moment of foolhardiness, I determined to go out and see if I could find out whether we had been followed, and at the same time try to get to San Carlos and supply myself with a Winchester and some cartridges, for I knew that, if I was properly armed, I could stand off the gang.

"Well, I saddled the little pony and started out, after telling Joy to come here if I didn't return. I scouted cautiously among the hills, trying to find the pass on the other side of the peak which led out to San Carlos."

"To make a long story short, I rode right into the trap, and was caught by the Gray Wolves. I had six shells in my revolver, and as they surrounded me I fought for my life, and I am glad to say I got three of them before they got me. But I couldn't hit Mowbray, although I tried my best to do so. He seemed to bear a charmed life. As soon as I had fired my last shot I wheeled the pony and fled. Up to this time I had not been hit, but just as I was getting safely away, having jumped through the men surrounding me, clubbing them to the earth with the butt of my pistol, I turned to look back. I saw Mowbray bring down his rifle and take deliberate aim at me, and I shuddered, because Mowbray is one of the finest shots in the world. Then I heard the report of his weapon, and felt the sting of the bullet. He had aimed to strike my heart, but the turn of my body saved me."

"But how did you come to be tied to the pony's back?" asked Ted.

"When I was struck by the bullet I felt myself going. I knew that very soon I would lose consciousness, and in that event I would soon be captured, so it behooved me, while I still retained my senses, to save myself. There was a lariat hanging to the horn of the saddle, and I proceeded to tie myself to the pony's back as well as I could. You see, I knew that the pony would go home when he found himself free.

"I was no sooner well tied to the pony's back when I heard the howl of the wolves, and recognized the voice of White Fang."

"White Fang?"

"Yes, the master of the pack. Have you not heard of him. He is well known in this part of the country—a wolf with almost human intelligence, fierce, a perfect devil of an animal, to whose pack every ranch in this country has paid heavy tribute. You will know more about him if you stay here. He is the devil in the hide of an animal.

"Well, I resigned myself to my fate, with a prayer that the little pony would get me to the Bubbly Well Ranch before the wolves pulled me from his back. And he did."

"But you said something about the Gray Wolves visiting us?"

"Yes. They will be here. Prepare to defend your lives and the house. They know I am here, and they know that you have my sister's treasure. That is what they want."

"How do you know that?"

"Joy told me, and more, which you will learn later. But I feel faint, and can talk no more. 'Ware the Gray Wolves!"

CHAPTER XXII

THE WOLFSKIN

Frederic Caruthers' warning was received seriously.

Ted and the boys consulted about the defense of the house, for the news of the Gray Wolves was not much of a surprise to Ted, who had all along felt that they were sure to be attacked by Mowbray and his men when they found that Major Caruthers and the broncho boys had emptied the Mowbray house of all its valuables.

The fact that there was an organized body of murderers and thieves under Mowbray called the Gray Wolves was not inappropriate.

But if the Gray Wolves came to the attack, the boys were prepared to receive and deal with them as they would with any band of marauding animals.

"We'll establish a guard at once," said Ted, "and it will stand as organized until this thing is settled."

"It will have to be kept up night and day," said Ben Tremont. "If these chaps are as clever as I think they will probably seek to do us harm by day as well as night."

"Thar's sense in thet thar," said Bud. "Better make it two watches."

"All right," said Ted. "Ben will have charge of the day watch, and take six of the boys, whom he will detail for duty as he thinks best."

"How do you want to arrange the hours?" asked Ben.

"Suit yourself about that, but I would suggest that the day be divided from six o'clock to six o'clock, day and night."

"Suits me," said Ben. "That will give my six boys a stunt of two hours each, which will make it easy for every one, and insure a constant and careful watch."

"Bud, you will be captain of the night watch," said Ted. "How do you want to arrange it?"

"I would patrol ther house outside," said Bud. "And my fellers would work in pairs. I should think Ben's men could do their best work from the cupola on top o' ther house, usin' ther major's spyglass ter keep tabs on ther horizon in every direction. At night, we can only watch close to the house outside."

"That sounds all right. Get your first guard established at once. We don't know how close they may be to us right now."

Kit was sent into the cupola with the spyglass and a Winchester with its magazine full, to take the first watch.

It was not necessary to give Kit any instructions, for he was a most intelligent guard.

He had not been on watch more than an hour when he whistled to Ted, who was crossing the yard on his way to the corral.

"What is it?" said Ted, stopping and looking up.

"I wish you'd come up here a moment. I see something which puzzles me mightily. It's kind of uncanny," replied Kit.

Ted laughed at Kit's fancy, but went into the house and climbed into the cupola.

"What is it?" he asked, taking his place beside Kit.

"Take the glass and look along my arm to where my finger is pointing, and tell me what you see."

Ted did so, and, after looking for several moments, took down the glass and said:

"It looks to me like a wounded wolf. I never saw a wolf make such strange motions."

"Quick! Look again. What do you see?"

"By Jove!" said Ted slowly. "If I hadn't seen it, I wouldn't have believed it. That is a wolf all right, but it seems to be waving something white at us. It doesn't seem to be able to move along. I wonder what it is."

"Some trick, probably. Remember what Frederic Caruthers said about the Gray Wolves' visit, and the cleverness of the fellows?"

"Yes. What do you think of it?"

"I think it is a lure to excite our curiosity, and get us to go out there and fall into a trap."

"That sounds reasonable."

"You will notice that the wolf is just over the top of a rise on the prairie. The question is, What is beyond the rise, in the hollow?"

"I'm going out to find out."

"I wouldn't if I were you, Ted."

"Why?"

"I'm afraid it's a trap, and that you'll fall into it."

"We'll never find out what it is if we don't go out there."

"That's a cinch, and that's just what they want you to do."

"Well, I'm going."

Kit knew that when Ted said anything in the tone of voice he had just used he meant it, and that it was useless to argue with him.

"All right, go as far as you like," he said. "I'll keep my eye on you, and if anything happens I'll sound the warning."

Stella and the other members of the Moon Valley outfit were resting against the time when they would be called to duty, and only Kit was there to see Ted catch Sultan out of the corral, saddle him, and ride away.

Ted rode slowly across the prairie to where he had seen

the wolf.

But the wolf had disappeared from view just as Ted started from the corral, and Kit could see it no more. He took this for a bad omen. Evidently, the wolf had seen that he had lured a rider from the ranch house, and, having accomplished its purpose, it was no longer necessary to expose itself to attack.

As Ted drew nearer to the spot where he had seen the wolf he went more slowly, and carefully examined his revolvers, and swung his knife sheath loose, so that he could get at that weapon quickly, if it became necessary.

Although he looked carefully to the front, he could not see the wolf.

Kit saw that Ted had missed the place where the wolf had been seen, and that he was too far to the right. He observed, also, that Ted was going cautiously, and that he was preparing for an attack, and he was sure that Ted would be able to take care of himself against fair odds.

Now Ted went forward again and soon gained the top of the rise.

He went very cautiously, peering over the edge.

Suddenly he sprang back and whipped out his revolver, and slowly let himself out of his saddle.

"Ted's found him," muttered Kit in the cupola to Stella, who had climbed up to his side to learn how the watch was going.

"Let me have the glass, Kit," she said.

Kit handed it to her, and she trained it on the figure of Ted, who was creeping along the top of the hill.

"Oh, Kit, he sees the wolf," cried Stella, interpreting for Kit's benefit the little drama being enacted for their benefit on the far-away hilltop.

"What's he doing now?" asked Kit, who was growing impatient from seeing nothing except the changing expressions on Stella's face.

"Nothing!"

"Pshaw!"

"Ha!" Stella gave forth an excited little exclamation.

"What is it? Give me the glass."

"Go away!" Stella pushed off Kit's hand that was reaching out for the glass.

"Now he's gone. He's out of sight. No; I can see his head. It's going up and down."

A long pause.

"Well, what's doing?" said Kit eagerly, and somewhat impatiently.

"Can't see a thing."

"Oh, rats! Let me look."

"Keep quiet. I see his head now."

"Is that all? What's he doing?"

"Here he comes. I can see his shoulders all bent over."

"Is he hurt?"

"Of course not, silly."

"Then why is he bent over?"

"I believe he's carrying something. Yes. He has something in his arms. Goodness, gracious me!"

"What is it?"

"Why, he's carrying a wolf in his arms. But what a funny wolf."

"I insist upon having the glass. I'm the fellow on watch."

"Kit, you're very rude. Don't bother me. Don't you see through me? Am I not telling you everything that occurs?"

"Oh, what's the use?" Kit shrugged his shoulders in a disgusted way, as if he were expressing the futility of arguing with a woman, and wishing that she were a boy, so that he could punch her head and take back his glass again.

"What's the matter with the wolf?" Kit asked at last, in a sulky tone.

"If you get mad at me, Kit, I won't talk to you." Stella took down the glass for a moment and looked at Kit severely.

"All right, fire away, but tell me what's going on, for Heaven's sake. Don't break off in the middle that way."

"It's an awful big wolf, and its hide don't fit it. Its legs stick out of the skin, and I can see one of its feet. Gracious, it has a queer sort of a boot on it, and this wolf has human hands."

"Stella, quit your fooling. What is going on out there? This is serious. It's no time for nonsense."

"I'm not fooling. I'm quite in earnest. Now Ted's lifting the queer thing onto the saddle, and holding it there."

"Has he killed the wolf, or man, or wolf man, or woman, or whatever crazy thing it is? I knew there was something queer about it," exclaimed Kit.

"I'm sure I don't know whether he killed it or not. I couldn't see through the hill."

"What's he doing now?"

"He has started toward the house, leading the pony and holding the thing in the saddle. Here! Take your old glass! I'm going to ride out and see what it's all about."

She thrust the spyglass into Kit's hand, and, with a merry laugh at his look of disgust, disappeared through the scuttle, and a few minutes later he saw her riding like mad across the prairie toward Ted.

In the course of a half hour they were both back at the house, and Kit's curiosity led him to desert his post to find out what Ted's strange burden was.

Ted lifted something from his saddle and carried it into the house very tenderly.

Stella was very silent, and followed Ted closely, helping as well as she could to uphold his burden.

"What is it?" asked Kit.

"A girl," answered Stella curtly.

"A girl?"

Stella paid no attention to him, but rushed ahead of Ted, and led the way to her own room.

"This way, Ted," she cried. "She must be brought in here."

Ted did as he was told, and laid the strange thing he carried on Stella's bed, and stepped back to look at it.

It was the skin of an enormous gray wolf, which all but enveloped a human form. Between the opening in the head, where once had been the cruel jaws of the wolf, peeped a pretty, brown face. But the eyes were closed. And a little, brown hand swung inertly from the place where a wolf's paw once had been; while below was a dainty foot, incased in a Japanese stocking divided, like a mitten, for the big toe.

"Who, or what is it?" asked Kit, looking curiously down at the strange object.

"I think it must be Itsu San, the little Japanese girl who was Helen Mowbray's maid," answered Ted.

"Great Scott, how did she happen in this fix?"

"I don't know. We'll have to wait until she recovers."

"Is she hurt?"

"I don't think so. I think she is merely exhausted by fatigue, hunger, and fear."

Meanwhile, Stella was busy cutting away the wolfskin in which the Japanese girl was concealed and entangled.

The commotion had brought the boys into the room, and they gazed with wonder at the sight.

"Now, you chaps clear out," said Stella, pushing them gently toward the door. "Do you want to scare the poor thing into fits when she comes to? The sight of all you fellows will frighten her worse than ever."

The boys hastened to leave the room, and Stella had just closed the door upon them when Itsu San, for it was she, opened her eyes and gave a little scream of joy when she saw that she was safe, and in the presence of a very pretty and kind-looking American girl of her own age.

"Don't be frightened," said Stella.

"I not no fright now," said Itsu San, with a charming smile, that was like that of a happy baby.

"How in the world did you come to be in this horrid thing?" asked Stella, kicking the wolfskin, which she had thrown to the floor.

"I come to give warn," answered the Japanese girl.

"About what?"

"The Gray Wolves."

"Go ahead and tell me."

"The Gray Wolves catch my blother. I hide, and hear them talk and say they kill all evelybody here."

"When?"

"Mebbe so to-night. Mebbe so to-mollow."

"Who said that?"

"The devil man."

"Who is he?"

"Mistah Mowbray."

"Mowbray and his men found you and your brother in the place where you were hiding, and took your brother after you had succeeded in hiding. Is that it?"

Itsu San nodded for reply.

"You heard them talking among themselves, and Mowbray planned to attack this house, and kill us all?"

Again the Japanese girl nodded.

"When they had gone you found this wolfskin, and, thinking that it was the only way in which to escape, you crawled into it, and crept all the way here, playing wolf, to warn us?"

"Yes. I crawled to their camp, and heard them talk. I tried to get close to my blother, to cut him loose, but they saw me and drove me away, and shot at me."

"Mercy! But I don't see why they didn't see through your disguise. It wouldn't fool any one."

"It was the half dark."

"Oh, yes. But why didn't you get out of the skin when you came within sight of the house?"

"I not have the strength. I climb the hill and see the house. Then I fall down, and not can rise again. All what I can do is to wave my handkerchief. Then I faint."

"You are a brave and lovely girl, and I already love you like a sister," said Stella warmly. "You shall stay here, and need not be afraid. We will be ready for the Gray Wolves, and they will not kill either us or you. Your warning comes just in time."

CHAPTER XXIII

BAGGING THE GRAY WOLVES

That night Ted Strong went on watch himself in the cupola, while Bud and Clay Whipple marched around the house in opposite directions.

Until the threatened attack took place Ted determined that he would watch the house personally, in addition to the regular guard.

About midnight Ted heard a slight noise out on the prairie.

The night was bright and frosty, and the stars shone with a peculiarly brilliant radiance, seemingly larger, brighter, and nearer the earth than in more northern climes.

Instantly his acute senses located the place whence the noise had come.

It was merely a slight rustling, but as there was no wind Ted knew instantly that it had been made by some creature.

His eyes, fixed on the spot, soon became accustomed to the faint light, and he saw an indistinct form that was so near the color of the earth that a pair of eyes not so sharp as his would have failed to detect it.

So indistinct was it that it looked almost like a wraith of grayish-blue smoke by the starlight.

Presently, as he still stared closely at it, he saw another form much like it steal through the dead grass toward it.

Then, over the hills on the east, rose the moon in its first quarter, shedding a pale light over the prairie.

Ted was now able to see that there was a pack of wolves, instead of two, as he at first thought.

The boys on the ground could not see the wolves on account of the tufts of grass that scattered over the prairie, and, had they seen them, would not have been able to distinguish one from the other.

It seemed strange to Ted that the wolves had not yet given voice. It was unusual for wolves to come so near a ranch house in numbers without giving warning by howling.

Suddenly the reason why they did not dawned upon him.

They were not wolves, but men in wolves' clothing.

Ted chuckled at the thought.

The "wolves" did not know yet that they were discovered, for they could not see Ted in his cupola watch-house, although they could easily see Bud and Clay as they walked around the house, now in the full light of the moon.

Ted was suddenly startled by hearing a noise to the left, and at the same time he heard Bud stop in his march. Evidently he had been attracted by the sound also.

As Ted looked he saw the cause of the noise. It was a wolf, larger than the others, which had crept closer to the house.

As he was looking at it he was astonished to see it rise up.

Then he caught the glint of a revolver barrel in the moonlight.

In an instant he knew the meaning of it.

With the precision of a machine his own rifle rose to his shoulder, and, without a second's hesitation, a streak of flame belched from it, followed by the roar of the report.

Looking closely through the smoke, Ted saw the "wolf" straighten up to the full stature of a man, then fall to the ground, over which it went writhing and tossing, while at the same time the most human of yells expressing agony came from it.

This was the signal for the other "wolves" to howl, and the most unearthly noise come from all sides of the house.

These were followed by a perfect fusillade of rifle and revolver shots from everywhere, most of them aimed at the cupola.

But as soon as Ted had fired the shot that had brought down the man wolf he had jumped through the scuttle into the attic of the house, and the balls harmlessly riddled the cupola.

From a window on the second floor Ted saw a score or more of forms leap into prominence; the forms of men who cast aside their skins of wolf, and who had turned their wolfish howls into the scarcely less fiendish yells of men.

At the sight he rushed downstairs, and found the boys hastily gathering in the dark living room, arming themselves from the gun rack, and taking their places beside the windows.

In the middle of the room stood the major, supporting with one arm the unsteady form of his brother Frederic, who had risen at the first alarm in spite of his wound, and who insisted upon fighting with the rest.

"The Gray Wolves have come," he said. "They will be hard to drive off. But you must do it, or go yourselves."

Stella and the young Japanese girl were standing at one of the windows peering fearfully out.

"Come away from there, Stella," said Ted. "They might see you and fire."

"All right, Ted, but you can bet that I will be in this somewhere," said Stella. "It's my business to defend this girl, and I'm going to do it."

Ted smiled, but said nothing, and passed on around the room, seeing that the boys were properly placed to resist the attack when it came.

Outside all was quiet again. The howls had ceased, and not a man was in evidence anywhere. It was the calm before the storm.

"What's the plan?" said Bud, coming up to Ted, for he and Clay had run into the house at Ted's shot from the cupola.

"I hardly know," answered Ted. "My plan is somewhat

upset. I thought at first that they were going to attack us immediately in this room. But they seem to have changed their minds."

"I've got a hunch," said Bud, scratching his head in a meditative way.

"Let us have it. That's what we need now."

"They're creeping up on us. I see one o' them a minute ago. They're countin' on gettin' up ter ther house before we expect 'em, an' then pourin' a volley inter us, an' puttin' us out o' business quick."

"That would be like that brute Mowbray."

"I've got it figgered that way. Now, s'posin' we fool 'em by not bein' here. They sneak until they git so's they kin fire through ther windows without any danger ter themselves, an' run away. But we ain't here."

"Where will we be?"

"Comin' up on them from behind."

"That's the stuff. Notify the boys at once. We'll get behind the house and creep up on them through the grass. We'll fool them at their own game."

As silently as ghosts the broncho boys deserted the living room and went to the back door. After carefully reconnoitering the situation without, Ted softly opened the door, and led the boys into the shadow of the house, and they crept away through the tall grass.

Only Frederic Caruthers and Stella and the Japanese girl

remained in the house.

Skirting the house grounds, the boys were soon out on the prairie, giving their enemies a wide berth.

Raising his head slightly from behind a tuft of grass, Ted took stock of the position of the enemy.

In the shadow of the house beneath the windows of the living room he could see the still darker shadows of the Gray Wolves.

Leading the boys into a semicircle from which at a word of command they could rush the house, Ted passed this word along the line:

"If they enter the house, as they probably will, we will close in quietly, rush the house, and capture them inside. Let none of them escape, and make no noise."

They had not many minutes to wait before the Gray Wolves began to get uneasy.

Evidently they expected some movement within the house, and the continued silence puzzled them.

But suddenly, like the scream of a tempest, the still air was shattered with wild yells and pistol shots, followed by the crash of breaking glass.

The Gray Wolves had stormed the house, breaking in the windows, smashing in the front door, and making all the noise they could, with the object of frightening the inmates into a condition where they would be unable to defend themselves.

Stella, with young Caruthers and Itsu San, had locked themselves into a back room, which they could defend for a few minutes at least against all comers.

As the Gray Wolves attacked the house Ted gave the word to advance, and they moved forward as one man, crouching behind the grass tufts to be out of sight of any guard the Wolves might have set.

It took not more than a minute or two to reach the side of the house, and look through the windows.

Inside the living room men could be seen running back and forth, searching for the broncho boys and the treasure.

Finally a wild yell told Ted that the safe had been found.

"That's good," said Ted to Bud. "They're at the safe. It will take all their attention for a while. They don't know, poor fools, that the treasure has been carried out and buried elsewhere. There's where we'll bag most of them. When we get in, boys, look out for Mowbray. Don't let him escape."

At a signal the boys climbed into the living room, which was now deserted, for the Wolves had scattered all over the house. Most of them were in the major's room working on the safe.

They had tried to move it from the house, but it proved too heavy for them, and they were now trying to break it open with an ax which they had found in one of the lower rooms.

Ted had heard the blows as they beat upon the lock, and in the din it was not a difficult thing for the broncho boys to get into the house without being heard.

Several of the Wolves, in searching the lower part of the house, had discovered the locked room in which Stella and the other two were in hiding.

They had attempted to batter down the door, only to be driven from it by shots sent at them by Stella and Caruthers.

"Trouble back there, Bud," said Ted. "I guess some one is trying to get at Stella. Take a couple of the boys, and go back and stop it."

"What are you goin' ter do?" asked Bud, who was afraid the rescuing assignment would cut him out of the fight above stairs.

Just at that moment there was a tremendous explosion overhead, the crash of glass and the triumphant yells of the Gray Wolves.

"I'm going upstairs," yelled Ted. "When you've driven off or captured these fellows down here, come up."

At this he dashed away for the broad stairs that led to the upper story, followed by the broncho boys and Major Caruthers.

They had just reached the landing above when the yell of triumph turned to one of baffled rage, for the Wolves had found that the safe was empty.

Ted Strong, with a look such as a conquering warrior might wear, burst into the room where the Wolves were clustered around the empty safe.

Behind him followed the boys.

Edward C. Taylor

"Surrender!" shouted Ted.

The Gray Wolves wheeled to look into a perfect battery of rifles. Not to surrender meant death. To attempt to raise a hand would bring a shot, or a dozen.

The Gray Wolves realized that they were in a trap, and that if they made the least resistance they would be shot down.

"Throw your guns on the floor!" commanded Ted.

He was obeyed.

"Gather up those guns," said Ted. Bud and Clay stepped forward, and gathered in the rifles and revolvers.

Ted's eyes were running over the group of prisoners trying to pick out Mowbray, when suddenly there was a smashing of glass, and, as he turned in that direction, he saw a form taking a flying leap through the window to the ground, and, quick as a flash, he fired and rushed to the window.

But when he got there his only reward was the sight of a man on horseback headed for the hills, swaying dangerously in his saddle.

Mowbray had escaped, but he had taken with him an unpleasant reminder of Ted Strong.

CHAPTER XXIV

WHITE FANG LEADS HOME

Ted herded the Gray Wolves into one of the rooms and placed guards at the door and at the outside windows.

The desperadoes were thoroughly cowed. Burk was so frightened that he was willing to do anything Ted said, and cringed to the leader of the broncho boys like a thrashed cur.

"What are you goin' to do with us?" he asked Ted.

"I'm going to put you where you will no longer disgrace the office you held by the authority of the United States," said Ted promptly. "You will get all you deserve."

"Let me down easy," begged Burk.

"You don't deserve it. You will be in jail as soon as it gets light enough to march you to Rodeo."

The first thing for Ted to do was to get rid of his prisoners, then to go after Mowbray, the archcriminal, and bring him to justice, and to arrest Ban Joy, the Japanese thug, whom he was convinced was the murderer of Helen Mowbray.

Edward C. Taylor

There was one more thing that demanded his attention for the safety of the live stock as well as the people of the Bubbly Well Ranch, and that was the destruction of White Fang, the demon wolf that was as well known in that part of the country as a destructive agency as Mowbray, the thief and murderer, himself.

For years White Fang had preyed upon the ranchmen, exacting a heavy toll in cattle and sheep. Every huntsman in the country had taken to the chase for him, but the cunning old rascal had outwitted or out-footed them all.

The following afternoon the broncho boys, led by Ted Strong, marched up the main street of Rodeo to the jail with a score of desperadoes bound to their horses.

When they appeared a great many of the townspeople, friends of the prisoners, gathered and made a demonstration to take them away from the boys.

Ted immediately formed the boys in a circle about the prisoners.

With rifles trained upon the crowd the broncho boys held them off while Ted spoke to them quietly, but with a force that carried conviction. He told the people just what the prisoners had done, and what he expected to prove against them, hinting that there were other men in the town who would join them in jail if what he suspected proved to be true. Later in the day a strange thing happened: Several men in high office disappeared from the town, and were never seen there more.

Having turned his prisoners over to the sheriff, the boys rode back to the Bubbly Well Ranch, feeling safe from further depredations for a time at least.

On the lower part of the ranch the wolves had been playing havoc with the calves and the yearlings, and the major's cowboys were continually bringing in news of the depredations of the pack.

The pack was led by old White Fang, the cowboys said, and they could do nothing with him. Whatever traps they laid for him were upset by the cunning of the old rascal, and he made life miserable for the men responsible for the cattle.

"What are we going to do about him?" said the major one day to Ted. "I suppose we'd better organize a big hunt, and drive the wolves out of the country."

"No use," said Ted. "The old beggar would hide in the mountains until it was over, and then renew the attack on you."

"What do you propose, then?"

"I'm going out after him myself, and I'll not come back until I get him."

Stella, who was curled up in a big chair in the living room reading, looked up quickly when Ted said this, and smiled out of the corner of her mouth, for she scented sport in this.

"I think I'll go along," said the major.

"I'd like to have you, major, but it won't do this time. You are too heavy a rider. It will take a light rider to turn the trick with White Fang," answered Ted, and the major looked a bit taken back.

But Stella chuckled to herself. If it took a light rider, she was in that class.

Later in the day she saw Ted and Bud go toward the corral. Ted carried in his hand a new, strong Mexican lariat.

She watched them a few minutes before she realized their mission.

"I believe they're going on the wolf hunt," she said to herself, "and without me." Her eyes flashed. "We'll see about that."

She ran into her room, and soon emerged ready for a ride. But when she got on the veranda Ted and Bud were galloping away across the prairie.

Without hesitating she ran to the corral, caught her pony and saddled it, and was in pursuit.

Ted heard the clatter of her pony's feet and turned to see her coming at whirlwind speed, and slowed up to wait for her.

"Ha, ha!" she cried, as she came up with them, her face wreathed in smiles. "Thought you'd go without me, eh?"

"Didn't think you'd care about such a commonplace thing as chasing a wolf," said Ted.

"Well, I'm going," she answered, putting her pony into a gallop.

They rode for the lower pasture, which ran up into the foothills of Sombrero Peak, where the recent depredations of the wolves had been bothering the cow-punchers.

They passed small herds of cattle grazing here and there, attended by herders, who waved their hands to the trio as they swept past.

As they were entering the foothills Ted's keen eye caught sight of a slinking form on the rise of a hill running parallel with their path.

He reined in suddenly and looked long at it.

"By Jove, I believe that's our game over there," he said. "Take a look at it, Bud and Stella. Don't you think that is White Fang?"

"It shore is, er his twin brother," said Bud, to which Stella nodded acquiescence.

"Take it easy," said Ted. "We'll ride toward him, and when we get as close as we can without his bolting, put your spurs to it and chase him for all you're worth. He can run like a scared rabbit."

They rode easily toward the wolf, who looked up at them with a wise, sidewise twist of his hoary old head, but did not increase his speed any.

"He's tolling us into the hills where he can easily get lost," said Ted. "Don't let him do it! Head him off! Turn him back to the prairie."

Diverging, they rode parallel with White Fang again, and, before he suspected their maneuver, they were ahead of him, and began to close in.

But finally White Fang stopped and watched them for a moment, then deliberately turned and set off on the back trail at a smart lope along the ridge he had come.

"I wish we had a couple of Russian wolfhounds here," said Ted, as the three were breezing along in the trail of White

Fang. "That would make it something like a chase."

"I'm bettin' that ole galoot will give us somethin' ter do before we ketch up with him, at that," said Bud.

"Close up on him," said Ted. "He's having too good a time."

They let their horses out a notch or two, and closed up on White Fang, who was off the ridge by this time, and galloping across the prairie.

The old wolf did not seem to have as much steam in him as usual, and loped along in easy fashion, occasionally looking over his shoulder at them, apparently gauging the distance and their speed.

"The only way to get close to him is to spurt when he isn't thinking about it," said Ted. "Let 'em out!"

A prick of the spur sent their horses forward on the leap.

Ted was coiling his rope in his hand ready for a cast, and Stella and Bud followed his example.

"When we get close enough to throw, scatter out, and be ready to let your rope go if either of us misses. All ready now!"

Ted dashed forward, swinging his rope around his head, and when he was close enough he made a beautiful cast and the rope went through the air as true as a bullet, hovering in a sinuous loop above White Fang. But just as it was about to settle the wily old rascal dodged to one side, and the rope fell into the sand.

"He's a cute chap," shouted Ted, bringing in his rope without slackening his speed, while Bud's rope flew through the air and missed the wolf by about a foot.

Stella was in a bad position to throw, and withheld her rope.

Again they closed in upon the wolf, who had begun to grow more wary and had hit up his speed, dodging and turning on his trail, making some swift turns and nimble feats of horsemanship necessary to keep within roping distance of him.

In this manner a dozen or more unsuccessful casts were made.

At last Ted got tired of the hide-and-seek game, and determined to end it.

"I'm going to get him this time," he shouted, gathering his rope firmly. "Back me up!"

He dashed at White Fang, with Bud and Stella on either side of him. Swinging his rope about his head, Ted watched his opportunity.

Suddenly the loop left his hand and shot as unerringly toward the wolf as if it had left the muzzle of a rifle.

It soared through the air like a thing of life, twisting as gracefully and sinuously as a serpent. For an instant the wide loop hovered over the gray, swiftly running animal. Then it fell suddenly, and settled over and around the seemingly doomed animal.

But White Fang, king of the pack, was too old a villain to be caught so easily. He leaped through the loop of Ted's lariat like a circus performer through a hoop.

But Stella's rope whizzed through the air and caught the old fellow unawares.

Then it seemed as if all the forces of wild nature had been turned loose.

The wolf leaped into the air as he felt the rope tighten around his neck, and threw himself here and there with a violence inconceivable, snapping at the rope and trying to sever it. But Stella's lariat was of Mexican rawhide, and even White Fang's sharp teeth had no effect on it.

The rope tightened and slacked in the struggle, and, had it been of ordinary texture, it would never have stood the strain.

Ted had ridden up to the plunging beast, and began to belabor it with his quirt, to take the spirit out of it. The wolf had never felt the sting of a whip before. It was such a new experience to it that it stopped bucking in sheer amazement. But Ted did not discontinue, and the wolf slunk upon the ground, its wild nature thoroughly tamed for the time.

"Stop!" cried Stella. "Let us see what he will do now."

Ted rode away, and the wolf sat up on its haunches, and, lifting its head toward the mountains, gave a long, wailing, dismal howl.

"He knows he's done for," said Ted. "That's his death song."

"Let him do what he will," cried Stella.

Presently White Fang rose, tried to shake the rope from his neck, and when he found that he could not do so, got up and started on a trot toward the mountains.

"Follow him," cried Ted. "He's leading us home. Who can say what we will find there?"

They followed the wolf through coulees and over rocky ridges in the foothills, and through a canon at the base of Sombrero Peak.

They climbed rocky paths, higher and higher up the side of the peak. White Fang's captors followed him silently. No more did he try to escape from the rope. He seemed to have given up hope, and was going home to die.

At last they arrived at the wall of a precipice, along which ran a narrow ledge just wide enough for their ponies to travel.

The path was well worn, as if many animals, including men, had passed that way.

Suddenly it dawned upon Ted where the wolf was leading.

Where but to the rendezvous of the band of the Gray Wolves?

He straightened up and looked to his revolvers, and then the wolf slunk around a bend on the cliff's side and walked into a cave.

Ted followed him closely, and stopped in the entrance in amazement. Just within sat Mowbray propped against the side wall, his face drawn and haggard, his eyes half glazed with approaching death.

But he stirred as Ted appeared, and groped about for his revolver.

Edward C. Taylor

"Stop!" cried Ted. "The game's up!"

Mowbray's hand dropped weakly by his side, as the wolf slunk to him and licked his face, at which the dying man raised his arm and placed it around the neck of the king of the pack, the most savage wolf in Arizona.

Ted could not but respect this strange exhibition of animal affection, so unusual.

There was a moaning cry from the depths of the cave, and Ted dismounted and went in to see what had caused it.

Chained to a rock he found the emaciated body of the Jap, Ban Joy, whom he suspected of being the murderer of Helen Mowbray. Here was luck. The wolf had led him to the two men whom he most wanted to capture.

"Now, Joy, I want you to tell me the truth," said Ted, when he had released the Japanese. "Did you murder Miss Mowbray, and why did you do it?"

The Jap looked at him with growing intelligence in his eyes.

"Me no kill. Mistah Mowbray kill with cord. I see him, and he tly to kill me."

Ted looked at Mowbray, who had straightened up and was listening.

Then he nodded his head, and signaled to Ted to give him a drink of water. After he had drunk he seemed stronger.

"Come here," he said, in a hoarse whisper. Ted went to his side.

"I might as well confess," he said. "It will make the end easier. I will be dead in a few minutes, for I am mortally wounded. I would have released that poor devil of a Japanese, but I hadn't the strength to go to him."

"Take it easy," said Ted.

"I murdered Helen Mowbray by strangling her with a cord," he said, after a pause. "I did it because I had gambled away everything I had and needed money—and she wouldn't give it to me.

"I lived for many years in India, and there I became a member of the sect known as the Thugs, who use a cord to strangle their victims. She cast me off, and when she refused to help me I became enraged and killed her. I am sorry now, for she was a fine woman, but I needed money."

"Then Farnsworth had nothing to do with it?" asked Ted.

"Nothing."

"Tell me another thing. Did Farnsworth, so called, have anything to do with the murder of the Spooner family in Somber Pass?"

"No, I and my men did that. Farnsworth has led a pretty clean life. He has stood for the crimes I committed for the sake of his sister. Wherever and whenever I got into a scrape I used his name, and put the crimes I committed upon him, and he stood for them on account of his sister's name."

"Is he a bad man? Has he killed many men?"

"Only such as he had to, to defend his sister's name. I say it was I who was guilty of the crimes charged to him. I hate him, and always have done so, but I am dying, and it is only fair play to clear him."

"That is all I want to know," said Ted, trying to make the man more comfortable. But he was beyond help, and in less than a half hour he sighed, and his wicked spirit passed away.

Ted and Bud buried him on the mountainside, and, after releasing White Fang, watched it for a few moments.

It went to the edge of a peak overlooking a deep chasm, and there sat on its haunches howling dismally.

Then, to the amazement of all, it straightened up and leaped far out, turning over and over in its descent until it fell in the rocky bottom of the chasm, crushed and broken.

Ted and the broncho boys, together with Stella, remained at the Bubbly Well Ranch until well into the winter, when the entire party returned to the Moon Valley Ranch to spend several uneventful weeks.

CHAPTER XXV

TED'S INDEPENDENCE

"Is this the Moon Valley outfit?"

A young cavalry officer galloped up to the head of a beef trail that strung backward for the better part of a mile, the cattle plodding on wearily, guarded by a dozen or more tired and cross cow-punchers.

"It is, lieutenant," answered Ted Strong, eying the epaulets on the officer's tunic, and reading his rank.

The lieutenant was in anything but a pleasant frame of mind, and looked sneeringly at Ted, and at the tired cattle behind him.

"Well, another fifteen minutes' delay would have cost you the contract," he said. "It seems to me that you have been taking your time. Don't you know that a government contract means business, and that to-day doesn't mean to-morrow?"

This was said in such an uppish and unpleasant manner that Ted could scarce restrain an angry reply, for he was tired out with the long drive, which had been unusually full of dangers and vexatious delays.

Edward C. Taylor

But instead of making a sharp answer he merely smiled at the officer, and said:

"Yes, I understand all about government contracts and the penalties for not living up to them. But I am within the government reservation, and here are my cattle, and I have, as you say, fifteen minutes to spare."

"Well, we consider that you are overdue, as you should have been here in time to have the cattle inspected and formally accepted before the time allowance elapsed."

"Nothing in the contract that says so," said Ted, still pleasantly.

"Well, it's usage, and that goes in the army."

"I'm not in the army."

"I don't want any words with you on the matter. It is sufficient that you are late, and that you have been the cause of a great deal of worry and annoyance."

Ted was beginning to get angry at the officer's tone and looks.

He turned from the lieutenant to the herd, and shouted:

"Bud, round 'em up and bed 'em. This is as far as we go to-night."

"No, you don't," said the lieutenant. "You will drive into the quarantine pasture, where your stock will be inspected in the morning."

Ted paid no attention to him, and the rounding up of the herd began as he had ordered, while the lieutenant fumed and fussed and swore.

At last he could stand it no longer, and dashed away from Ted's side to where Bud was superintending the work of the cow-punchers.

"Here, none of that," he said brusquely to Bud, who looked even more disreputable than Ted.

"See here, who are you alludin' at?" asked Bud, wheeling around on him.

"I'm talking to you. I want those cattle driven in to the pasture, and I want no delay or nonsense about it," cried the officer angrily.

"Now, run along, little soldier boy, don't yer see I'm busy?" Bud looked at the officer with a tolerant pity.

Ted now rode up and interfered.

"I'm capable of giving all the orders necessary to my men," he said gently. "You will please not interfere."

"Who are you?" asked the lieutenant, with a sneer.

"My name is Ted Strong."

The lieutenant looked at him with some curiosity and respect.

"Oh," he said. "I thought perhaps you were some kind of a foreman. My name is Lieutenant Barrows."

Ted acknowledged it with a slight bow.

"I am in charge of this delivery of beef to the department, and as you are already late I wish you to send this herd further into the reservation."

"I am sorry I cannot comply with your wish," said Ted, "but it will be impossible to-night. The cattle made a forced march to-day, and are tired out, and, besides, they have just been watered, and have only time to graze a full feed before they bed. I am explaining all this to show you that my action in not doing what you wish was not through spite, but in the best interests of both the government and ourselves."

"It is my duty to inspect the animals, and—"

"I can't help that. The cattle do not go forward a foot farther to-night. I will get them into the pasture early in the morning."

"That will be too late," said the officer curtly. "I shall inform the commandant of the post, Colonel Croffut, that you are late and that you refuse to obey orders."

"Confound your impudence, who are you to give orders to me?" asked Ted, mad in a minute.

"As I told you, I am the inspector, and it seems to me that it would be good policy, to say the least, to cater to my wishes somewhat."

"What do I care for your wishes? Less than that, if I am doing the right thing and stand within my own rights;" and he snapped his fingers.

"Perhaps you may be sorry."

"That's my affair."

"Very well. I am to understand that you refuse to move the cattle on to-night."

"You've got it right."

The lieutenant bowed, and, turning, rode slowly away with an ugly scowl on his face.

"I reckon Little Bright Eyes has got it in fer you now," said Bud, who had ridden up in time to hear this part of the conversation. "He's aimin' ter do some dirty work, I reckon."

"Oh, bother him! He got me all worked up and angry, and that always makes me feel bad. I wish he had happened to be somewhere else. Forget him! We'll drive the herd in early in the morning. He couldn't have inspected the beeves this evening, anyway."

It took some little time to get the big herd in shape for the night, and Ted was washing himself and putting on some clean clothes when a soldier dashed up on a horse and asked for Mr. Strong.

"I am Strong," said Ted, rubbing his head and neck vigorously with a rough towel.

The soldier looked at Ted in some surprise, as the colonel had alluded to him as the "government beef contractor."

"Well?" said Ted.

"I guess it's your father I want," said the soldier.

"Guess again. There's no such person here."

"Are you the beef contractor?"

"Surest thing you know. What do you want?"

"Colonel's compliments, sir, and the colonel would like to have you call at his quarters at the first convenient moment."

"What about? These beef cattle?"

"I don't know, sir; I didn't hear him say."

"All right. Tell him I'll be there in a few minutes. Where is his house?"

"Last house on the right-hand side of the parade, as you go in."

Ted nodded, and went on dressing himself. He was as tired as a dog, but he supposed the commandant wanted to talk to him about the cattle, and he would have to go.

As he rode up to the commandant's quarters he saw a young man and a very pretty girl talking on the veranda, and when he had ascended the steps he saw that the man was none other than Lieutenant Barrows.

He was just about to ring the bell when the girl looked at him, and her eyes brightened because Ted Strong, straight and stalwart, with his fine, handsome head and straightforward, honest eyes, was a person very good to look at.

"Do you wish to see papa?" she asked, coming forward.

"Colonel Croffut expressed a desire to speak with me," answered Ted, lifting his hat.

"If you will wait a moment I will call him," said Miss Croffut, for, of course, Ted had guessed who she was from her question.

She tripped into the hall, and called to her father, and then entered a room, and was followed by the commandant himself.

"So you are Ted Strong, the beef contractor," said Colonel Croffut, looking Ted over.

The colonel was a big man with a pink face and a brusque manner.

"I am," said Ted coolly.

"Excuse me. Take a seat. You needn't go, Hallie. Keep your seat, Barrows." The colonel motioned Ted into a chair, and took one himself.

For several minutes he sat blowing clouds of smoke into the air from his cigar, but saying nothing.

Miss Croffut and Lieutenant Barrows continued their conversation about lawn tennis and riding, as if Ted were not there, but the lieutenant observed that Miss Croffut's eyes strayed often toward Ted, and it made him irritable.

"See here, young man," said the colonel, turning suddenly upon Ted in a manner that in another person would indicate that the commandant was very angry. "What do you mean by sending such a message to me?"

"I sent no message to you," said Ted quietly. "I didn't even know your name until your striker mentioned it to me a few minutes ago."

Had Ted looked at the young lady at the other end of the

veranda he would have seen an irrepressible smile flit across her features, as she looked at her father.

"That was a facer for dad," she whispered to Lieutenant Barrows, who frowned. "The idea of telling papa that he had never heard of him, the great warrior and Indian fighter, Colonel Croffut."

The colonel stared at Ted with a sort of amazement for a moment, and grunted:

"Well, you're likely to know a great deal more about me before we're through with one another."

"I hope so," said Ted pleasantly. "But what is your business with me?"

"I'll speak of it when I come to it," said the old soldier.

"Then you'll have to be quick about it, for I've been in the saddle continuously for six weeks, and I'm tired. Besides, I've got a day's work to do before I turn in to-night."

There was something crisp and business-like in Ted's speech, and not at all impertinent, that caused the colonel to look at him again.

"What's this I hear about your refusal to accede to our just demand that the cattle intended to fill your contract be turned into our pasture?" asked the colonel sharply.

"Only this," answered Ted: "I arrived here just in time, with my stock worn out from forced marches. I had just let them have all the water they could drink, and it was necessary that they should have a good feed in order to rest well to-night to be in condition to stand inspection to-morrow. I was well within my rights in deciding not to move them any farther to-night."

"I understand that you were impertinent to the officer who made this request to you," thundered the colonel.

Ted laughed softly to himself.

"If I was impertinent to him I was there and perfectly responsible, personally, for my conduct. It was wholly unofficial, and I cannot see why he should come to you with it."

Ted looked at the lieutenant, who had flushed angrily.

The girl looked from Ted to Barrows, and then at her father.

"That is not the question, sir. He represents the army in his person when he comes to you on the army's business."

"Well, I can't fight the whole army," said Ted, laughing, "but I can certainly take care of myself in all ordinary matters."

Barrows half rose in his chair as if he was going to resent Ted's remark.

"Sit down, Barrows," said the colonel explosively. "The young man is right as far as that is concerned. Now, sir, I've half a mind not to accept your beef at all. I consider that you have not properly filled the contract."

"I certainly have," said Ted stoutly. "The beef was on the government reservation fifteen minutes before the time limit according to the acknowledgment of Lieutenant Barrows himself."

"I said no such thing," almost shouted the lieutenant.

Edward C. Taylor

"Be careful," said Ted. "That is giving me the lie direct. Several of my men heard you say so."

"Mr. Barrows, please be quiet," said Miss Croffut. "I shall go in."

"I beg your pardon, Miss Croffut," said Ted, rising and bowing. "I had no intention of carrying on a quarrel in your presence. Colonel, I shall be glad to discuss this matter with you in your office if you wish, but not here. I have no quarrel with you, and I do not propose to, if I can avoid it."

"I presume you mean that you would quarrel with me," said Barrows, blustering up.

"I have no objection in the world, but not in a lady's presence," said Ted, turning from him carelessly.

"I don't like your attitude at all, Mr. Strong," said the colonel. "That is not my idea of army discipline, in fact, sir—"

"Excuse me, colonel," said an officer, bustling up, "don't forget that to-morrow is beef-issue day to the Indians, and that we must have three hundred head before noon to-morrow. There is not a hoof in the government pasture."

Barrows was trying to attract the other officer's attention with vigorous shakes of his head, which Ted, although his back was toward Barrows, saw reflected in the window.

What could the matter be? Were they so short of beef at the post and a beef issue coming off, and then attempt to bluff him with their army rulings? He saw through it all, and now he would stand pat, and take nobody's bluff.

The officer walked away at a signal from the colonel, who

turned to Ted.

"I want you to go back to your herd and drive it into the government pasture at once, do you hear, at once?" he said in a tone of great severity.

"I think not," said Ted. "The herd stays where it is until morning, or if it must be driven at all it will be over the way it came."

"What do you mean, sir?"

"I mean that I forfeit the contract. The cattle are mine to do with as I please. I shall immediately proceed to drive them off the reservation."

"But that will ruin you."

"That's my business. Good evening, sir."

"Wait a moment. Don't you know that we must have the beef; that there is an Indian beef issue to-morrow?"

"I didn't know it until a moment ago. Now I know a lot more than I did when I came here."

"Confound it, boy, there'll be an Indian uprising if we don't give them their beef to-morrow."

"That's for you to take care of. Good evening. The contract is declared off."

CHAPTER XXVI

A COMPROMISE

Ted hurried back to the cow camp.

"Stuff's off," he shouted, when he came within shouting distance. The boys, who were lounging around the fire, resting from their arduous drive, sprang to their feet.

"What's the row?" asked big Ben Tremont.

"They insist upon our driving the herd about five miles farther into the reservation to-night, so that that lazy lieutenant who is to do the inspecting in the morning will have as little trouble as possible. I refused to do it, and they tried to run a sandy on me, but I wouldn't stand for it. If they'd been white to me I would have had the cattle in there if it took me all night."

"That duck o' a lootenant wuz a trifle gay," said Bud. "He tried to run a blazer on yer Uncle Dudley, but I told him to run along, an' I reckon he'll have no Christmas present for me this year."

"Did you tell the boss there was nothing doing in the moving line?" asked Ben.

"You bet I did," answered Ted. "That gay lieutenant who was here ran at once to the boss with his tale of woe, and the boss threw his chest out at me and tried the little-boy game on me. He thought he had me bluffed when in comes another officer, who told him that a beef issue to the Indians was due to-morrow, and that there wasn't an animal in the post pasture."

"Wow!" exclaimed Bud. "That means trouble for some one, unless they can dig up something to take its place, for an Indian who has his mouth made up fer fresh meat is lierble ter become rantankerous if he don't get it."

"I guess that's why they were so anxious to get the beef up to the pasture to-night," said Kit.

"Of course. When I heard that all my nerve came back to me, and I decided that I would give those officers a lesson."

"What are you going to do?" asked Ben.

"Drive the herd off the reservation."

"Gee, that will put us in the hole bad."

"Oh, I don't know. We'll trail them a little farther north, keep them a few months on free range, then drive them to the railroad and slide them into Chicago on a rising market. I had the whole thing figured out in case we got here too late, which I expected to do on account of our being held back by dry weather and too much water, coming in streaks."

"I'd like to have been there when you were throwing your bluff into the colonel. I suppose he had the surprise of his life."

"He looked like it. By Jove, he has a mighty pretty daughter, if he is a grouch himself."

"Seem to have an eye for beauty yourself."

"Not as keen as yours." Ben blushed when Ted said this, for Ben was always having a new girl and talking about her.

"I noticed her because she was so pleasant, and so different from her father, and that fellow Barrows, who seems to be very soft on her."

"Well, we have no fight with the ladies of the post," said Ben.

"How did it end?" asked Kit, who always wanted results.

"I simply told them that they couldn't have the cattle now, and walked away."

"That must have been a facer."

"Seemed to be, for the colonel called after me to know if I was aware that if the beef issue didn't come off there would probably be an Indian uprising, and I told him it was up to him."

"Well, I suppose it's hike," said Bud, pulling on his boots.

"Yes, get the dogies up, and we'll trail them back until we are out of the reservation. It's not far."

The boys mounted, and rode among the cattle, getting them to their feet.

Soon the herd was moving slowly along the back trail, with

Ted and Bud pointing them out.

Suddenly, from the woods to the right rode a band of horsemen in the dark, for the sun had long since gone down.

"What's this? A holdup?" asked Bud.

"Can't tell yet. By Jove, I believe they are soldiers. I wonder if they are going to try to stop us."

"S'posing they try it?"

"We'll have to ride it out. I wouldn't be held up on the reservation now for anything. That would spoil it all. They would do anything they wanted with us if we stood for that, and throw out a lot of legitimate stock to get square with us."

"What do you mean?"

"If they're soldiers, and try to keep us in, you ride back and start the herd to stampeding. Let the soldiers take care of themselves. If they're regular cavalry, they will be able to ride well enough to get out of the way."

"Bully idea. O' course, we can't help it if the cattle get scared at them bright uniforms, an' git ter runnin'." Bud chuckled at the thought.

"Halt!"

The voice of Lieutenant Barrows rang out commandingly.

"Now's your chance, Bud," said Ted. "Mind you, get them started good and plenty. I don't care if they run five miles."

Presently, from the rear of the herd came a shout of warning,

　　　　　Edward C. Taylor

and the herd increased its speed from a lazy walk into a trot.

Back in the darkness the cowboys were riding through the herd hurrying up the cattle with their quirts.

From a trot they broke into a gallop, and this soon grew into a perfect rout, for cattle are easily frightened at night.

As soon as Ted saw that the cattle were going to run, sure enough, he dashed across the intervening space to where the dark forms were standing in the path of the oncoming cattle.

He saw at once that it was Lieutenant Barrows and a squad of cavalrymen, and that they were armed with carbines. He resented this, as the lieutenant had no business to arm his men in this way for such an errand.

As Ted rode up, he shouted:

"Get out of the way, if you don't want to be trampled to death."

"What do you mean, you scoundrel?" shouted Barrows. "Halt, when I give the command, or take the consequences."

"Out of the way, you fool!" shouted Ted, as he swept past. "Don't you see that the cattle are stampeding?"

If the lieutenant did not know it, being so recently out of West Point, the men did, for with a yell they turned and rode like mad for the side lines.

Then, for the first time, the young officer, hearing the sullen bellow of the cattle and the thunder of the hoofs, turned and followed Ted.

But the leaders were almost upon him, and, realizing that death was following him fast, he gave an agonizing cry.

Ted heard the cry, and understood its import.

While he disliked and despised the bullying officer, he had no desire to see harm come to him.

The lieutenant's horse, while a good-enough cavalry animal in times of peace, was not the match of the cow ponies, and was already badly winded, as well as frightened, and was losing ground steadily.

"Bear off to the right!" shouted Ted repeatedly. But the officer was evidently too frightened or rattled to understand, and kept blundering along.

Ted saw that disaster was sure to follow in a short while if Barrows didn't change his tactics.

The herd was going at regulation stampede speed now, but this did not cause Ted to think of his own danger when he deliberately turned Sultan and came galloping back upon the advancing sea of sharp horns.

In a moment he was beside Barrows, wheeled suddenly, and began to ride against the cavalry horse, forcing it to one side, and urging it on with lashes of his quirt.

At last he got the heavy brute going the way he wanted and soon it was out of danger, as the frantic herd swept by with a roar like that of a lightning express rushing over a culvert.

Barrows was sitting on his trembling horse, pale, and with beads of perspiration standing out on his forehead.

Edward C. Taylor

"You did that on purpose, curse you," snarled the lieutenant. "You made those cattle run."

Ted looked at him in astonishment. He thought at least that the soldier would murmur some few words of gratitude for having been saved from a horrible death.

"You're a grateful chap, I must say," said Ted. "You weren't far from kingdom come then, I can tell you."

"I'll see that you are punished for this," said Barrows, wheeling his horse and riding out of sight in the direction of the post.

It was two hours before the boys headed the cattle and got them to milling, and then broke them up and succeeded in getting them bedded down.

As they got a new camp fire made, and were lying around it, Bud said, with a laugh:

"That was a mighty slick trick o' yours, Ted. It certainly took ther herd off ther reservation in a hurry."

"I don't see yet why it was necessary to stampede them," said Ben, who was sore at having had to do so much work getting the herd together again.

"Can't, eh?" said Bud. "That's all er collidge eddication done fer yer? Why, if we hadn't got them cattle off'n thar pretty pronto, thet thar lootenant would hev bagged every animile on foot. But Ted, he foresee what they wuz up ter, an' ther simplest way wuz ter run 'em off in a fake stampede. It done ther work, too, fer we're out o' ther reservation whar they can't touch us."

Except for the night guard, the boys rolled themselves in their blankets and were soon sound asleep.

The next morning Ted began to drift the herd slowly into the north, where there was plenty of free range. They were still well within view of the fort.

It was almost time for the beef issue at the post, and Ted and Bud, walking their ponies slowly along in the lead of the herd, were talking about it.

"Wonder they ain't been out to head us off this morning?" said Bud.

"They know they cannot take forcible possession of our cattle when we are off the reservation," answered Ted. "Hello, what's that heading this way?"

Coming toward them from the direction of the fort, several riders were kicking up the dust in lively fashion.

As they got nearer the riders revealed themselves as four soldiers, accompanied by two ladies.

Suddenly Ted pulled in his pony, and grasped Bud's arm.

"If that don't look like Stella I'll eat my saddle blanket fried in butter," he said.

"Shore do look some like her," answered Bud, "an' that's ther same little ole red jacket what she wears."

In a few moments they heard Stella's hail, and answered it.

Then up galloped Stella and Miss Croffut, accompanied by the commandant of the post, Lieutenant Barrows, and two

Edward C. Taylor

other officers, a captain and a major.

After greeting the boys, and formally introducing Miss Croffut, Stella told them that from their last telegram she thought she might be able to catch them at Fort Felton, and had not hesitated in coming on, particularly as she happened to know Miss Croffut.

"What's this trouble you fellows have been getting into with the folks at the fort?" asked Stella.

"We're not having any trouble, but we had some in the night when the dogies stampeded us," replied Ted, with an almost imperceptible wink at her.

"None of my business, I suppose?"

"None in the least."

"See here, Mr. Strong," the colonel broke in, "I suppose I was somewhat hasty last night in talking with you, especially as you had arrived on time. I wish you'd turn back, and let us have those cattle."

"Like to if you'd said so a little earlier, but since morning, and the expiration of the contract, beef has gone up."

"What do you mean?"

"I mean that you haven't money enough to buy these cattle. What's the matter? Want a few head to feed to the Indians?"

"We want the whole herd, but as you have guessed the truth, we must have a few head to keep those crazy Indians from making trouble. They have heard that the cattle are gone, and I'm afraid that they will break loose and murder a lot of settlers to get even with Uncle Sam."

"What are the troops for?"

"We wouldn't dare go after them without orders from Washington."

"Well, you started it, and I would advise you to go on to the finish."

"If we don't get enough cattle to feed the Indians the post is ruined."

"You should have thought of that contingency when you sent your amiable young assistant out to me." He looked at Barrows.

"Well, I apologize for him. He was dead wrong, but so was I."

"Nothing doing! You would have given me the worst of it if I had been chump enough not to know the cow business as I do. But these cattle are due on the high range in a few days, and we must be moving on. Adios."

"Oh, Mr. Strong, please do let us have enough cattle for those poor Indians. The squaws and babies and growing children are actually starving, for the government has kept them on short allowance lately. Let a few head go to us."

Ted said nothing for several moments, during which they all looked at him anxiously.

"Come on, Ted, be a good fellow," said Stella, with a laugh.

"All right," said Ted. "How many do you want cut out?" Ted was looking at the colonel.

"I'd like to have the whole herd," answered the colonel.

"They're not for sale. They're going up to the high range for the rest of the summer, then to market, and I hope it will be a fairer one than this. But for the sake of the young ladies, who have more influence with this bunch in a minute than all the officers at Fort Felton have in a year, I'll cut out enough for the beef issue. How many head do you need for the Indians?"

"About five hundred," answered the colonel, in a very different voice from that he had used the night before.

"Bud, cut out, count, and deliver five hundred head at the post pasture. Stella, we're going on. Where's your aunt?"

"Up at the post. Say, Ted Strong, don't believe for a minute that I'm not going, too. I'll get a wagon for auntie, and we'll hit your trail in a couple of hours."

CHAPTER XXVII

THE BEEF ISSUE

When Bud and the boys rode into the herd to cut out the five hundred head of cattle, the four officers went away to inspect the animals as they came out, leaving Ted to talk to the two girls.

Nothing was said about the unpleasant interview on the colonel's veranda the evening before, but Stella laughingly told how she had decided at the last moment to follow the fortunes of the boys, and had dragged her aunt off to Montana without giving her time to think about it.

While they were chatting the colonel rode up.

"Mr. Strong, I wish you would come up to headquarters and get your voucher for these cattle before you go. I should like you to dine with us, also."

"Please do, Ted," said Stella. "Then you can ride back to camp with aunt and I. I have been trying to persuade Hallie to join our party for a week or two, and experience the joys and excitement of the cattle trail."

"I should like very much to go with you, but—"

Miss Croffut looked at her father with some apprehension.

"If Mrs. Graham will consent to add to her burdens as a chaperon I have no objections," said the colonel whose manner toward Ted had been simply reversed by the independence and manliness the broncho boys had exhibited.

"We should be very glad to have you with us, Miss Croffut," said Ted. "And if you have never been on the long drive I believe you would find much that would interest you."

"Then it's all settled," cried Stella. "I'm sure aunt would be delighted to have you, and you will like the boys. They are like a lot of brothers to me, only they are better than most brothers, for they let me do what I please, and are a help instead of a nuisance."

They all laughed at Stella's estimate of the usefulness of brothers, and rode away toward the fort, Ted leading the way with Miss Croffut, whom he found to be an exceedingly interesting companion, and who expressed her love for riding and other outdoor sports.

"We're going to see the beef issue," Stella called to Ted.

"All right," he answered. "It will be some time before the cattle are up to the pens, and, in the meantime, we'll leave you there, and ride over to headquarters and settle the business end of it."

The girls were left at the office of the Indian agent near the place where the cattle were to be issued to the Indians.

Scattered over the prairie near the agent's office were the members of the tribe, waiting patiently for their portion of the fresh meat, which, at certain times of the year, Uncle

Sam doled out to them.

It was a savage sight. Here and there were the smoke-browned tepees of the Indians, before which sat the squaws and papooses, and the old men and women.

The bucks, heads of families, strode back and forth majestically, with their rifles and old muskets in the hollow of their arms, while the young men and half-grown boys dashed here and there on their ponies.

It was an animated scene, and the two girls looked at it curiously, for neither of them had seen anything like it before.

While they were looking out of the window a shadow darkened the doorway, and they looked up to see a tall young buck Indian standing on the threshold.

He was very tall for a Northern Indian, and his broad, bronze-colored face, with its high cheek bones, and prominent, aquiline nose, with the black, beady eyes between, and the wide, loose-lipped mouth beneath, caused Miss Croffut to shudder unknowingly.

To her there was something repulsive about the fellow. But Stella looked at him boldly and inquiringly.

"How?" grunted the Indian.

"What you want?" asked Stella, in a business-like way.

"Me want agent," he answered, with a leer, which evidently he intended for a smile of fascination.

"Not here," said Stella sharply.

"Where go?"

"Get out."

The Indian stared at her with an expression of amazement, which gradually turned to one of admiration.

"Heap good-looking squaw," he grunted.

"Get out," said Stella again.

She was not frightened, only disgusted.

"Me Running Bear. Heap big chief. Heap rich. Heap brave. Running Bear want white squaw. Heap other wives cook for white squaw. Make plenty red dress."

When the Indian had first entered the room Stella thought that there was something decidedly familiar about the redskin, but when the name "Running Bear" fell from his lips, her worst fears were confirmed—this was the Indian with whom Ted had had trouble during the winter, when he had broken up the Whipple gang.

As he strode into the middle of the room, with his hand on the butt of the revolver that hung on his left hip, Miss Croffut uttered a faint scream.

Stella was not exactly frightened, but she felt that there might be some danger in being in the room with this Indian brute, with not a white man in hailing distance.

When he got nearer she smelled liquor. Running Bear had been drinking, and Stella knew that a drinking Indian is a crazy Indian who will do things he never would dream of doing when he is sober.

She unconsciously felt for her own revolver, but it was not at her side. Then she remembered that she had left it at the colonel's house when she had started out that morning.

She eyed the Indian closely as he advanced farther into the room, and saw that in the Indian's eyes there was a strange gleam. He reminded her of a snake about to devour its prey, as he moved toward her, almost imperceptibly, seeming not to move, and yet getting closer to her all the time.

Now he was quite close to her, and Hallie Croffut was sitting back in her chair gazing at the Indian with an expression of frozen horror on her face.

"White squaw give Running Bear a kiss," gurgled the brute.

Stella tried to scream, but her throat refused to give forth a sound. It was like the nightmare when one tries to scream for terror of the awful shape that is about to menace, but cannot utter a sound.

Somewhere outside she heard her name. It was Ted calling to her, but she could not answer.

Now the Indian was only a step away, and had reached out his arms to grasp her.

Suddenly the door flew open, and there stood Ted Strong. But only for an instant.

With one leap he was into the room, and as the Indian turned, with that beastly leer still on his face, Ted was upon him.

Catching the Indian by the collar, he swung him around, while at the same time his left arm flew forward, and his fist

Edward C. Taylor

struck the Indian's jaw with a smash that sent his head back, and wrung a groan from him. Again and again the fist encountered the Indian's face, rocking his head horribly, until it hung upon his shoulder, and then, with an exclamation of disgust, Ted flung the brute from him, and the inert body rolled into a corner, where it lay still.

"Oh, Ted," exclaimed Stella, "that Indian is Running Bear, with whom you had trouble when putting the Whipple gang out of business."

"I know it, but I don't think he'll bother us any more. Come, girls," said Ted, "it's time to go out and see the beef issue. They're reading the names now, and the bucks are assembling."

Outside a strange scene was being enacted. A clerk from the Indian agent's office was sitting on top of the fence of the cattle corral reading the names of the Indians from a large book.

"Na-to-no-mah, John Fisher!" called the clerk, and a middle-aged Indian stepped forward listlessly and stood aside.

"The first name is his Indian or tribe name," explained Ted. "The name John Fisher is the name given him in Washington, so that the clerks will not get him mixed with an Indian whose name is similar."

So the reading went on, and after each name the clerk said "one" or "two," meaning that the owner of the name was entitled to one or two cows, according to the number of members of his family.

"Running Bear!" called the clerk.

There was no answer.

"Running Bear! Where is Running Bear?" The clerk looked around anxiously, for Running Bear was a prominent Indian, and was entitled to three cows, or as many as he could graft, and was never known to miss a beef issue. There were murmurs of wonder among the Indians at the absence of Running Bear, and the clerk was about to mark off his name, when he staggered out of the agent's house, groggy from the punishment he had received, with one eye a vivid green, and holding on to his jaw as if he was afraid of losing it.

"Ah, there you are, Running Bear," said the clerk. "You look as if you had collided with a streak of lightning. What's the matter?"

But the Indian only shook his head and pressed his jaw harder.

"Reckon you've got the toothache, eh? Well, when you get your teeth fastened into a piece of fresh bull meat you'll be all right."

Running Bear gave one look, in which all the concentrated hatred of a lifetime was to be seen. Then he turned away and went out to his tepee, where one of his squaws bound his jaw in a wet cloth.

But the roll had been called, and the Indians stood expectant close to the gate of the corral.

While the clerk stood up on the fence with his list he repeated the names and the number of cattle to which each Indian was entitled, and men inside the corral opened the gate and drove them out.

Edward C. Taylor

As a frightened cow or angry steer was loosed from the corral it was met with shouts, wild and blood-curdling, from all the Indians, and its owner sprang upon his pony and took after the poor beast, driving it into the open beyond, and away from the house and corral.

"Now begins the chase," said Ted. "We'll get out here where we will have a good view, but I don't think you will care to see much of it. It gets to be pretty—well, pretty raw after a while."

"Why don't they kill their beef in a slaughterhouse and give them the meat, instead of turning the animals over to them alive?" asked Stella.

"The Indians wouldn't stand for that," answered Ted. "This is the only sport they have in a year's time. You see, they are not permitted to leave the reservations to go far away to hunt big game, and they take it out in hunting, or playing they are hunting, these miserable cows."

"I don't see any fun in that," said Miss Croffut.

"You haven't the imagination of an Indian. You see, they make believe they are hunting buffalo again, and the chase is quite as exciting to them as if they were doing the real thing."

By this time the prairie was covered with steers and cows, lumbering along in front of the Indians, who were pursuing them with shrill cries, shooting at them with bows and arrows or with rifles, striving always to wound them, but not to kill them too soon, for if they killed them right away they would miss the fun of the chase.

This made the beef issue a carnival of brutality, and Ted

soon saw that the girls were getting tired of it.

In the center of the great circle in which there were several dozen cattle running around aimlessly, pursued by a yelling, exultant, bloodthirsty band of Indians, were several wounded steers and cows, which had gone down and were unable to rise. Several groups of Indians, squatting on the rim of the circle, were shooting at them.

This was dangerous business, and the white spectators moved back out of range.

The shooting was very reckless at times, and the Indian agent had to protest to the soldiers, who, under Lieutenant Barrows, had the issue in charge.

Ted and the two girls were sitting on their ponies, watching the show from a position of safety, as they were out of line of any of the shooting parties.

Without warning a ball sang through the air, clipped through the mane of Ted's pony, and pierced the sleeve of Ted's jacket, passing out between him and Miss Croffut, who was by his side.

As Ted looked up hastily he caught a gleam of blue across the circle as it dodged behind the group of yelling and shooting Indians.

Ted glanced at Stella, and saw a look in her eyes which plainly said:

"Did you see it, too?" And Ted nodded.

Miss Croffut had screamed as the ball went past, and Ted's pony, burned by it, reared.

"Let's get out of this," said Ted quietly. "Those Indians are beginning to shoot wildly, and some one is going to get accidentally hit. I wonder that the soldiers don't regulate it better."

"They are afraid of getting the Indians angry," explained Miss Croffut. "The war department allows them to do as they please at this function, to keep them quiet at other times."

But most of the poor dumb brutes had succumbed to this slow method of butchering, and the squaws, with horrible cries, rushed into the field, every one to the steer which her lord and master had killed, and the hideous rites of skinning and cutting up the animals was begun by the women, who were even more bloodthirsty than the men.

"Come, we don't want to see this," said Ted, and led the way from the field.

"It is time for dinner," said Miss Croffut. "Then we must get ready for the trail. We will get a wagon from the store-keeper—a regular camp wagon with beds and a tent. Papa will arrange it all, and he will detail an orderly to drive it for us, and care for our things."

"That will be fine for you and aunt, but for me—the saddle and the camp fire," said Stella.

CHAPTER XXVIII

A SLAP ON THE FACE

As they were riding toward the post they were joined by Ben, Bud, Kit, Clay, and Carl, who came riding up like Cossacks, and were presented to Miss Croffut, on either side of whom they fell into place, and began to talk animatedly and enthusiastically about the coming trail.

Ben expanded mightily in the presence of a new girl, while quiet Kit contented himself by slipping in a witty remark that was pointed enough to puncture Ben's gas bag of grand talk once in a while, to the great amusement of the army girl, who had never before met such fine, free, and easy, yet gentlemanly, fellows.

Ted and Stella were riding together behind them.

"Did you see him?" asked Stella at last, looking up at Ted.

"See who?" asked Ted.

"The man who shot at you, trying to murder you, and cast the blame on the Indians," she replied directly.

"Oh, that was an accident," said Ted. "I saw a flash of a blue coat over where the shot came from, but it was probably an Indian with a blue shirt on."

"And you didn't see who it was?" she asked again wonderingly.

"No."

"Don't you even suspect?"

"Hadn't thought of it."

"Suppose it was not an accident, who do you think would be most likely to try to shoot you from ambush, and make it appear an accident?"

Ted thought a moment. Could it be possible that it was not an accident? For a few minutes after the ball had plowed its way through their little party he had thought perhaps it might have been sent at them accidentally, as the Indians were doing some pretty wild shooting, and then again he almost believed it to be an intentional shot. It could not have come closer to him from such a distance, and yet so narrowly missed his heart, unless it was intended for him.

"Let me see," he mused. "Why, of course," he said, with a smile. "I didn't think of it before. It must have been that Indian, Running Bear, who was trying to get square for the punching I gave him."

"Ted, you're as blind as a rat," said Stella.

"Did you see the fellow who shot at me?"

"I did. Got a good, square, sure-enough look."

"Who was it?"

For a moment Stella did not reply.

"You'll hardly believe it," she answered, at last.

"I'll believe you. I don't know that you ever told me anything that was not the truth."

"But it seems so incredible, that I would hardly believe it if I had not seen it with my own eyes."

"Well, out with it."

"It was Lieutenant Barrows."

"Stella! You can't mean it."

Ted stopped his pony, and stood staring at the girl.

"It was he who fired the shot. I am positive of it. I saw him do it, and was just about to cry out a warning when the bullet struck your pony and passed through your coat sleeve, and he dodged out of sight."

"The hideous cur!" exclaimed Ted, who was the apostle of fair play, and who always felt bitterly when he saw another practice false, and especially an officer, who was supposed to uphold all the best standards for a gentleman. In fact, "an officer and a gentleman" were synonymous to him.

"It seems incredible," he said, at last. "I didn't think he was much of a chap, he has not had much experience, and I thought he would grow out of his bad habits."

"He's horrible," exclaimed Stella impatiently. "But that is not

Edward C. Taylor

the worst of it. Hallie is engaged to marry him some day. Think of it!"

"Too bad. Of course she must know nothing of this. She must believe that it was an accident."

"Of course. Unless she mentions it we will say nothing about it, and I'll tell her that you do not care to have anything said about it."

"That's the thing. Pretty bad outlook for her."

"Yes, and the worst of it is, she's crazy about him, and the colonel, her father, is very much in favor of the marriage, and is doing everything he can to bring it about. You see, Barrows is very rich."

"Is he the son of Barrows, the railroad multi-millionaire, do you know?"

"Yes, Hallie told me all about it. She says his father is going to have him promoted through his influence in Washington to be military attache to one of our embassies in Europe. He has completely dazzled her with his wealth, and the prospects ahead of her."

"Too bad."

"And she is such a sweet and sensible girl, but she has no mother, and the other ladies at the post, especially Mrs. Calhoun, the major's wife, have put a lot of nonsense into her head."

"Well, if she comes with us, we'll try to get some of it out."

"It looks as if Ben was trying to do that now," said Stella, pointing to where Ben was talking to the girl, who was laughing happily.

"Yes, or putting a lot of another brand into it."

"Don't they make a handsome couple. Ben is such a fine-looking chap in the saddle. I wish he would do something to cut out Barrows."

"Look out. Don't you go to meddling in this affair," laughed Ted. "Well, here we are at the colonel's. I reckon he didn't count on this addition to his table."

As they rode up to the others, Hallie Croffut was insisting that the other boys remain for dinner, and the colonel, hearing the contention from his chair on the veranda, came down to add his invitation to that of his daughter.

So it was that they all stayed, and just before dinner was announced Lieutenant Barrows rode up and joined the group.

He was hot and dusty, and in a bad temper. He acknowledged the introductions to the boys superciliously, and barely nodded to Ted.

Hallie looked at him with a puzzled frown, but said nothing, and entered the house with Stella.

During dinner Ben sat at the left hand of Hallie, with Barrows opposite.

Ben was in his usual good spirits, and was so easy and gentlemanly in his deportment, in spite of his rough clothes, that Stella was quite proud of him.

While he kept Hallie in a constant gale of laughter by his

witty remarks, Barrows did nothing but scowl at him, when he was not casting sinister glances at Ted, who, however, never looked at him.

After dinner the girls rushed away to get ready for the trip, and the boys went out on the veranda to wait for them, while the colonel and Barrows went into the library, ostensibly to talk over business of the post, as Barrows was officer of the day.

But presently Ted heard the voices of the two men rising above the normal pitch.

"I seriously object to Hallie going with such people."

The voice was Barrows', and it was angry.

"But they are all right," said the colonel. "I know Strong well by reputation, and the Grahams are old friends of mine. Knew them for years when I was in New Mexico. Hallie and Stella went to school together. There can be no objection on that score."

"But this cad Strong is nothing but a common cow-puncher, and his companions are even worse."

"They're worth more than you are financially," said the colonel. "That is, they have made more individually than you have made. I'm not saying what your father gives, or will give you. And that counts for something."

"Well, there is no use saying anything more about it if you are willing to give your consent to Hallie traveling in the company of, and camping with, such a low blackguard as that fellow Strong."

"You dare not call him that to his face," came an indignant voice. Evidently Stella had entered the library in time to hear Barrows' speech.

"I am surprised to hear you speak in that manner of one of my guests," came the voice of Hallie Croffut. "Papa, I'm going with Stella. At first I hesitated to leave you and Clarence here alone, but now I am decided. You will not be very lonely, and I shall be very safe and happy with Stella and dear Mrs. Graham, who is like an own aunt to me, and with those gentlemen, the broncho boys. Good-by, daddy. We'll be back soon."

"So his name's Clarence, eh?" said Bud Morgan, on the veranda. "Well, wouldn't that jar yer?"

In the library Hallie was kissing her father good-by, and then offered her hand to Barrows.

"Good-by, Clarence," she said. "I hope you'll be in a better frame of mind when I get back."

"I want to talk to you privately before you go," said Barrows, in a sulky voice.

"It is not necessary," answered the girl.

"But I insist upon it. It is my right."

"You have no rights I do not give you. This is good-by."

"I'll make you regret this yet. I'll—"

"Hold hard, Barrows. Remember, you are in my house, and that you are talking to my daughter. Threats to a girl do not come gracefully from a gentleman." The colonel evidently had sprung to his feet, and his voice was cold and harsh.

"Very well, I will not threaten. I will execute."

The young officer strode from the room and through the hall, pausing to pick up his cap.

At the door he came face to face with Ted Strong, who was standing there quietly, waiting for the moment when he should think his presence would be necessary in the library.

As the two came face to face, Barrows stopped and looked into Ted's eyes with a look of intense hatred. He was as white as a sheet, and his lips trembled.

"So you have been acting the eavesdropper, eh?" Barrows said, with a sneer. "I hope you heard all I said about you, and that is not all I think, either. Would you like to hear some more."

"I don't care what you think about me. That will do me no harm. But if you desire to retain your beauty I would advise you to keep it to yourself. You probably know what I think of you, you cowardly assassin." Ted spoke these words in a tone intended only for the ears of Barrows himself.

"What do you mean?" stammered the young officer, pale as death.

"You know. You missed my heart at the beef issue by an inch or two, but you were seen, you cur, and you can't lie out of it. If I were to tell it, you would be drummed out of the army, and every place else where there are square men. Keep away from me and mine in every way, and especially with your filthy tongue. If you do not, I'll break you."

Barrows uttered an unspeakable epithet to Ted under his breath.

A loud crack sounded far enough to reach the ears of those in the library, and bring the broncho boys to their feet. Across the white face of Lieutenant Barrows were the crimson finger marks left by Ted Strong.

Without a word the lieutenant swung on his heel, and walked down the steps, mounted his horse, and rode away.

In the doorway stood a young girl who looked at his going with wide eyes. She was very pale, but as Barrows rode away without a word or a glance backward, a flush slowly mounted to her forehead.

She turned and threw her arms around the neck of Stella, for it was Hallie Croffut who had seen the blow delivered.

"He didn't even offer to resent the blow," sobbed Hallie. "Is it possible that he is a coward?"

"There, dear, I wouldn't worry about him," said Stella soothingly. "It was very wrong for Ted to do so."

Ted, who was standing near, also watching the departing lieutenant with some surprise, heard these words and turned to look at the girls.

He smiled, however, when he heard Stella trying to comfort Hallie by blaming him, for over the shoulder of the crying girl his girl pard winked at him with a smile that assured him that, no matter what she said, she thought that whatever happened he was all right.

"Say," drawled Bud to the other boys, "Ted put ther bloom o' youth on Clarence's cheek, didn't he?"

"He certainly did," said Ben, "and probably saved Clarence from getting a good, stout punch on the nose from me."

Ben held up for inspection a fist as big as a picnic ham, and worked it around as if it was fitted to a toggle joint.

"He didn't get all that was coming to him, either," said Kit. "If ever there was a cad he's got the job."

"And seems to be swelled up over it, too," said Clay.

"Ach, yes, dot iss der vay mit dem army offichers," sighed Carl. "Dey vas so conspicuousness in deir uniforms dot dey vos ridiculousness."

"Say, Dutch, you want ter look out or you'll blow out all o' yer teeth some o' these days sayin' them words," warned Bud.

"Well, it isn't such a good joke as it seems," said Kit reflectively. "A young fellow in the army, and with the backing he has, can make it pretty disagreeable for fellows like us living and doing business in a country where an army post is part of the civil government. Have you thought of that?"

"Kit's right," said Ted. "I guess we've made an enemy. But I'll be mighty glad of it if it serves to accomplish one thing."

"What's that?" asked Ben.

"If it will keep him away from Hallie Croffut," was the answer.

"I reckon there's others who will help attend to that," said Ben sturdily, whereat several of the boys smiled. Ben was forever coming to the rescue of maidens in distress, especially if they were more than merely pretty.

"We've all got to do our share at cheering the poor girl up," said Kit, with a sly glance at Ted, who grinned.

"Oh, I guess I'm large and strong enough to carry my own burdens," said Ben. "I've managed to pack a good many of them' so far without getting round-shouldered."

"Yes, and without losing your appetite."

"Hush, boys," cautioned Ted. "Here come the girls."

Stella came out of the house, bearing in her arms a lot of shawls and bundles, followed by Mrs. Graham and Hallie Croffut.

"When you see me coming at this stage of the game loaded down like this you'd know for sure that Auntie Graham was going on a roughing trip."

"That's all right," said Kit. "Mrs. Graham can take whatever she likes on the trips, if she'll only go along."

"You're a nice boy, Kit, to say such nice things," said Mrs. Graham, smiling. "But you're all nice boys to take an old lady like me with you, and stand for all my laziness and tantrums."

"That's right, auntie, you keep on with that line of talk, and you'll get these fellows so spoiled that I'll have to begin training them all over again. I just had them so that they were going along all right. But you mustn't let them know they're nice, or they'll quit being nice right there. Come, fellows, help carry Auntie Graham's things down to the wagon. We've got to get started pretty pronto."

They were all ready to start when an orderly dashed up on horseback, and handed Hallie a letter, saluted, and rode off.

The girl tore open the envelope, and read its contents.

"What shall I do?" she asked, handing the letter to Ted.

Ted's eyes ran over it rapidly.

"Forget it," he answered, crumpling the note in his hand and throwing it away.

CHAPTER XXIX

RUNNING BEAR'S SQUAW

As they rode away to join the herd, which had been moving slowly northward, Hallie and Stella rode together, and Hallie was telling her friend what she felt, and what she thought about her break with Lieutenant Barrows.

"That note was the most impertinent thing I ever read," Hallie was saying.

"What was it all about? Ted did not think it was of much importance," said Stella.

"And yet it was all about him."

"You don't say so. What was it?"

Stella was not very curious about the letter, for she was too free and independent to care what an enemy said of her or her friends. She had that intense loyalty of character that put tried and chosen friends before all the world, and she believed and stuck to her friends through all and above all. But this was a characteristic of all the broncho boys.

She didn't believe that anything any one could write about

Ted Strong could hurt him, at least it could not with her.

"It forbade me going with you on this trip, and said some awful things about Mr. Strong," said Hallie.

"Is that all?"

"It said that Ted was a scoundrel, and that he felt it his duty to expose him, and that, moreover, Ted had declared himself his enemy, and he was going to get the bitterest sort of revenge for the insult Ted had offered him. And—and a lot more."

"If he wanted revenge, why didn't he take it while he had the chance? Anyway, Ted doesn't seem to be very much afraid, so I'm not going to worry."

Ted realized that he had made a bitter and dangerous enemy.

Barrows would be dangerous because he would not fight in the open, but would stab him in the back. The way in which he had taken the slap on the face proved that he was an open coward, but secretly was brave enough in his blows. The shot fired by him at the beef issue was proof enough for that.

But Ted, while he determined to keep his eyes open, was not borrowing trouble, and soon put Barrows and his enmity out of his mind.

They caught up with the herd in the middle of the afternoon, and Hallie, who had never seen so many cattle before in her life, was delighted with the experience she was about to undergo.

The weather was splendid, and Stella rode up and down with her along the line, introducing such of the boys as had not met her, and teaching her the points of the cattle business.

Finally, Hallie got hold of Bud, who volunteered to teach her how to shoot and throw a lariat, and she was perfectly happy, and soon forgot the unpleasant occurrences at her home before she left.

Stella was just spoiling for a good, hard gallop, and tried to get Ted to go with her in a race across the prairie, but he politely but firmly declined the honor, on account, as he explained, that he was responsible for the safety of several thousand head of cattle, and as he had been up against one failure with them so far he did not propose to face another because of neglect.

"All right, Smarty," said Stella. "You don't have to go. But you'll be sorry if anything happens to me."

"Stay with the herd, Stella," he said. "What's the use of tearing off alone across the prairie?"

"Not very much, as a matter of fact, but if you'd been shut up in a poky old hotel for a couple of weeks, and only going out with your aunt to shop around in stuffy dry-goods stores, you'd like to get out for a breezer yourself," she said.

"I reckon I would, but don't go far, and get back before dark."

She waved her hand to him gayly, gave Magpie a flick with her whip, and went flying across the country.

"Hi, Stella!" shouted Kit. "Where you goin'?"

But she was already out of hearing.

Edward C. Taylor

"Let her go," said Ted. "She's got one of her crazy riding spells on, and she'll just have to ride it out of her."

In a few minutes she was a speck on the horizon.

"That girl can ride some," said Kit, looking regretfully after her. Kit could "ride some" himself, and this afternoon he just felt like a good breeze across the turf, and no one suited him for a riding companion like Stella, for she was so fearless and bold, and never balked at a chance.

But Stella was gone, and the drive settled down to a steady thing.

We will leave the herd for the present to follow the fortunes of Stella, whose ride that afternoon had so much to do with fashioning the immediate fortunes of Ted Strong and the broncho boys.

As Stella was borne exultingly along through the clear, sharp air of the Montana uplands, she was singing in a high, sweet voice the cowboy song, "The Wolf Hunt."

"Over the hills on a winter's morn,
In the rosy glow of a day just born,
With the eager hounds so fleet and strong,
On the gray wolf's track we jog along."

As she paused at the end of the first verse she thought she heard an echo of it. It seemed that off to the north some-where she had heard an eerie "Ai-i-e!" But she listened attentively, bringing Magpie to a stop, and hearing it no more, concluded that she had been mistaken.

Then she galloped on, still singing at the top of her voice from sheer happiness and good spirits, the other verses of the wolf song, and, although she paused frequently for the repetition of the cry, she did not hear it until she had sung the refrain for the last time:

> "The race is o'er, the battle won,
> The wolf lies dying in the sun;
> His midnight raids are of the past,
> He's met the conquering foe at last.
> Well done, brave hounds! Thy savage prey
> Was shrewdly caught and killed to-day."

As she stopped and looked around her at the brown, rocky hills, once more she heard that shrill and heart-searching wail.

"What can it be?" muttered Stella, reining in her horse. "Is it a woman, or is it a beast trying to lure me on? It sounds like a woman in distress, and yet cougars can cry like that, also."

She meditated a moment, and then decided to take a chance.

She would search out the creature that had sent forth that desolate cry.

"Ai-i-e!" cried Stella, imitating the other.

"Ai-i-e!" came the reply.

It came from the north, and seemed only a short distance away.

Slowly Stella crept forward up the rocky hillside, pausing now and then to listen.

Once more she heard the wail. This time it seemed to be under her very feet, and, guarding against treachery, she drew her revolver, and walked softly on.

Suddenly she stopped in amazement. At her feet lay a young Indian girl.

She was lying on a blanket, and the yellow front of her deerskin tunic was stained with blood.

Without an instant's hesitation Stella was on her knees beside the girl, working with swift and gentle fingers to unfasten the tunic.

As she did so the girl opened her eyes, and, seeing Stella, smiled.

Then her Indian stoicism failed her, and she uttered a groan and fainted.

"Poor thing," muttered Stella. "Poor, wounded, wild thing. Here lies the wild wolf 'dying in the sun,' as the song says. I wonder if she knew the song."

But by this time she had opened the tunic and saw a bullet wound on the brown skin, through which the blood was oozing steadily.

She stood up and looked around for a water sign, and not far away discovered a little clump of willows, which advertised a spring.

She hurried to it and filled her hat to the brim with the cool fluid and rushed back to the wounded Indian girl, who had not yet recovered from her fainting fit.

Stella bathed her head, washed her wound, and then poured some of the water between her lips.

At that the girl opened her eyes, and, with another smile, opened her lips as if to speak.

"Rest now, dear," said Stella, with so much pity and love in her voice that the girl could only smile once more, and gratefully close her eyes.

It did not take Stella long to improvise bandages from some of her own garments, which she tore into strips, and bound up the wound so that it stopped bleeding at last.

Another drink of water so refreshed the Indian girl that she tried to rise, but Stella gently forced her back, and told her to rest.

Stella never rode away from camp without taking food in a small bag, which was attached to the cantle of her saddle.

She now bethought herself of it, and hurried away for it.

The Indian girl was ravenously hungry, and her faintness was as much due to her abstinence from food as from the loss of blood.

But when she had eaten she appeared much stronger.

"What is your name?" asked Stella.

The girl looked up at her and smiled.

"I am Singing Bird, daughter of Cloud Chief," she answered.

"You can speak English well," said Stella, at which the girl looked pleased.

"Yes, I went to the Indian school, and learned to speak and to sing hymns."

"How do you come to be here?"

"My man shot me."

"What?" cried Stella, in a horrified tone. "Your man shot you? What do you mean by that?"

"I am Running Bear's squaw."

"You are married to Running Bear?"

The girl nodded her head.

"And did Running Bear shoot you?"

"Yes. He shot me and left me to die."

"The horrible brute. What did he shoot you for?"

"He said he had too many squaws, and wanted a white squaw."

"Couldn't he have sent you away without trying to kill you?"

"I wouldn't tell him something."

"Oh, that was the reason, eh?"

"Yes, he married me at the school for my secret, and when I wouldn't tell him he began to hate me."

"Tell me about it. How long have you been married to him?"

"Five months."

"I thought you were rather young to be a wife. How old are you?"

"I am seventeen."

"Where is your home; where does your father live?"

"My father is in the Far North. I cannot go to him any more now. My man has turned me out and tried to kill me, but yet I live. But there is nothing for me now but to die."

"Indeed, you are not going to die. You are going to live with me until you are well, then you can say what you are going to do."

"The white lady is too good to an Indian girl."

"No, that is only right. How do you feel now? Do you think you could travel if I was to help you into my saddle?"

"I will do what my sister wishes," said the Indian girl simply, trying to rise. But the effort was too much for her, and she sank back, the blood spurting freshly from the wound.

"That won't do," said Stella, easing the girl back, and rolling up her jacket and placing it under her head. "You are not able to leave here yet. At least, you cannot ride."

The Indian girl was perfectly passive under Stella's guidance, and did not think of having a will of her own.

"I wish one of the boys had come with me," Stella said to herself. "Something always happens when I go away alone. I must get word to them somehow."

"I am going to fire my revolver to bring help," said she to

Singing Bird. "You will not be frightened."

The other girl shook her head.

Stella fired her revolver three times, and waited for an answer, but none came.

After waiting a while longer, she fired three more shots.

"No shoot again. Need bullets for wolves. Come around soon," said Singing Bird.

The day was going fast, and soon it would be dark. She could not leave the girl to go for help, for with the dark the wolves would come.

Singing Bird had fallen into a feverish doze, and Stella arose and gathered up some dry wood from about the spring, and carried it to where the girl was lying.

Stella had some matches in her outfit, and when it got dark she intended lighting the fire, hoping that the boys would see it when they came to look for her when she did not return at dark.

Again she brought water from the spring, and sat down beside her new-found friend to bathe her head and reduce her fever.

As darkness fell she heard vague rustlings in the tall grass, and looked carefully about. In the dim light she saw pale-green lights moving about, and knew that the wolves had smelled blood, and were gathering. But she was not afraid. She knew that she could keep them away with the fire and her revolver.

One of the wolves came quite close to the little camp and set up a howl, and the Indian girl awoke.

"White girl go to her friends," she said to Stella. "Leave Singing Bird to die as the Great Manitou intended."

"Indeed, I will not. I will stay with you until my friends come to me, and then we will take you with us and nurse you."

Stella thought it was time to light the fire, and as its flames leaped high, she felt more at ease.

When the wolves came close to the camp she fired her revolver at them, and drove them away.

The hours passed silently, Stella rising occasionally to replenish the fire and look at Singing Bird, who seemed to be sleeping. As a matter of fact, the young Indian, who had been reared out-of-doors, and was perfectly healthy, was recovering rapidly from her wound, although had it not been for Stella she would probably not have survived the night, for what the chill night air would not have done the wolves would have finished.

It was long past midnight when out of the west rose a clear, welcome shout that sounded as the sweetest music to her ear, the Moon Valley yell, and she answered it, while the Indian girl sat up and smiled at her.

They had been found at last.

Edward C. Taylor

CHAPTER XXX

"THE WOOFER" APPEARS

Presently Stella heard the clatter of many pony hoofs on the turf, then a succession of yells, and Ted, Ben, and Bud galloped into the circle of light made by her fire.

"Hello, what have we here?" asked Ted, riding up and flinging himself from the saddle.

"I found this Indian girl, Singing Bird, daughter of Cloud Chief, lying here with a wound in her breast that would have killed an ordinary mortal, but I think she is getting better."

"We got worried about you when you did not return for supper, and started out to find you. If we hadn't seen the reflection of your fire against the sky we would have passed you by. How did this happen?"

"She tells me she is the squaw of Running Bear, with whom you had an argument at the beef issue."

"Yes, I remember him. What about him? Why is he not here to take care of his wife?"

"He shot her and left her here to die, because he was tired of her, and, she says, because she would not reveal to him a secret."

"He certainly is a precious scoundrel, and deserves worse than I gave him, and if I ever meet him again I won't do a thing to him."

"But we must get this girl to a camp where she can be cared for, Ted. It is cruel to leave her here on the cold ground when she can have a cot and plenty of blankets."

"I don't know how we are going to manage it to-night."

"One of you can ride back to camp, and get the wagon and a lantern, and come back for her. She ought to have better attention than I can give her here."

"That's all right. Bud, ride back to camp and get the wagon out, and fill it with blankets and my medicine chest, and get back here as soon as your team will bring you."

Ben had sauntered down to where the willows were seen, and soon returned with a big armful of wood, which he tossed upon the fire, then sat just outside the blaze and popped away with his revolver at the little balls of pale-green light, the wolves' eyes, which he saw floating among the tall grass, and he always knew when he had made a bull's-eye by the howl, and the thrashing around that followed it.

Ted sat with Stella, watching the Indian girl, who had again fallen into a deep sleep.

"Did she say what her secret is?" asked Ted.

"No, I didn't ask her, and I don't intend to. If she wants to confide in me, well and good, but I am not a sharer of other peoples' troubles or secrets. I have as many of my own as I can take care of."

It was almost dawn when they heard the rumble of wagon wheels, and Bud drove over the top of the hill, and came toward them.

"By my Aunt Hester's black cat's tail, I never had sech a time gittin' a team hitched up as this one. It took me an hour to ketch 'em out o' ther pony herd, and yer talks about drivers, I'd jest as soon try ter drive two bolts o' red-hot chain lightning. But I've got all ther ginger worked outer 'em now, an' I reckon that nigh bay will not never buck no more."

"Now we'll see if she can be moved," said Ted. "I think we can lift her right on the blanket on which she is lying, and into the wagon, if you will lend a hand, Stella."

Each of the four took a corner of the blanket, and with some difficulty, for Singing Bird suffered excruciating pain with every motion, they got her into the wagon and started for the camp, driving slowly over the rough ground.

It was almost daylight when they reached camp, where willing hands helped to make the girl comfortable in a tent which Ted rigged up.

Then Ted and Stella went to work with all their surgical skill, and soon had Singing Bird's wound properly dressed. Stella stood guard over her, and nursed her as tenderly as if the Indian had been a sister of her blood.

Ted had stayed the herd until Singing Bird should be well enough to get up. The pasturage was fine, and after their arduous drive Ted thought that it would do the cattle no harm to have a long rest.

He was undecided what to do with the Indian girl. It was not altogether practicable to take her with them, and it did not seem to be the humane thing to leave her behind to again fall into the hands of her brutal Indian husband.

At last one morning Stella announced that Singing Bird was almost well. On account of her health and generally fine physical condition she had made rapid progress toward recovery.

"What are we going to do with her?" asked Ted, when Stella announced that Singing Bird was well enough to travel.

"I don't know what she wants to do," said Stella. "One thing I am sure of, I am not going to see her come to any harm. I have grown very fond of her, for she is a sweet, good girl."

"Let us ask her what she wants to do. I suppose we shall have to abide by her decision, for we cannot turn her adrift."

Singing Bird was sitting in front of her tent in the sun, watching the cowboys sitting around their camp, weaving horsehair bridles, cleaning their guns, mending their clothes, and doing other things that fall to the leisure of a cow camp.

"Singing Bird, you are well now, and able to travel," said Stella, sitting down on the grass.

The girl looked at her and then at Ted with an expression of alarm in her face. They both saw that she feared what was coming.

"What do you want to do, Singing Bird? We must be on the trail again, for we have a long way to go to the big pasture to the north," Stella continued.

"I want to stay with you, sister," said the Indian girl simply. "I will die if you send me away. I will slave for you if you will only let me stay near you. I have no one else on earth. My husband has cast me out; my father will not have me back; the white man does not want the Indian. I am alone in the world. You have saved my life. I am your slave."

"That settles it," said Stella, with the hint of tears in her eyes. "You shall stay with me, dear. Ted, get ready to move the herd whenever you are ready. Singing Bird goes with me."

"All right," said Ted, glad that the matter was so easily disposed of. "You can do whatever you want to with this outfit. If you say she goes, why, she goes."

He went out to where the boys were to give orders for getting the herd on the move again.

"We'll hit the trail in the morning," he said. "It will take some time to break camp, and we might as well stay around here the rest of to-day and get an early start in the morning."

Far out on the prairie they heard a cheery shout, and saw coming toward them a horseman, driving before him a bunch of six steers.

"Git on to ther new herd crossin' our trail," said Bud derisively. "Jumpin' sand, hills, but thet feller hez a big bunch o' cattle."

"Wonder where he got them all. He's surely a big drover," said Kit.

But the stranger hustled the six steers into the camp, and pulled up a scrawny little cayuse, and, taking off his hat with a flourish to Stella and Hallie, who had joined the boys, said:

"Your pardon, ladies an' gents, but what may be ther brand that is burned inter ther hides o' yer esteemed cattle?"

Ted looked at him questioningly, and saw a tall, thin, bronzed individual, dressed in a most unusual costume for a cow-puncher, for such he evidently was from the manner in which he had driven the cattle, and the way in which he sat and handled his horse.

He had a strange face, half humorous and half sinister. One moment he would be merry and gay, but in an instant, and for an instant only, it would change to suspicion and caution. He was lean of frame, but very muscular, and his eyes were of a keen, piercing blue.

"Any particular reason for wanting to know?" asked Ted quizzically, smiling up at the tatterdemalion of a cowboy.

"Well, I reckon," was the drawling reply. "I picked up six strays out here a ways, an' they don't belong ter no brand in this yere part o' ther country, so I suspicions they belong ter some pilgrims' road brand. Now, yours is ther only bunch o' trail cattle what's passed this way recently, an' me, bein' wise ter ther ways o' ther plains, hez ther hunch thet they might be yours. Right cute o' me, wa'n't it?"

Ted laughed at the chap's half-humorous, half-serious manner.

"Our brand is the Lazy Z," he replied.

"Then them critters aire yourn. Look 'em over, an' if they don't belong ter you, hand 'em back, an' I'll make 'em ther noocleus o' a herd o' my own."

Ted rode up to the six strays, which were peacefully grazing not far away, and examined the brand. They belonged to the herd, all right, and he said so.

"Well, stranger, much obliged to you for picking them up and bringing them in," said Ted. "Now, what can I do for you? Those critters are worth a hundred dollars or more to this outfit. I'll split with you."

"No, you won't, stranger, seein' it's all ther same ter you. I may be a measly, fleabitten, hongry, lone maverick o' ther plains, but thar's one thing I ain't, an' that's a 'lost and found' department, 'suitable reward offered, an' no questions asked.' When I picks up a man's strays I hands 'em in if I can find him, or if I was so blame' hongry I couldn't resist ther temptation I might butcher one fer ther sake o' sinkin' my molars inter a tenderloin steak. But thet's ther wust a feller could say fer me. If ther critters aire yours, take 'em, an' welcome."

"All right, pardner," said Ted, who had taken a fancy to the fellow. "At least, you'll eat with us."

"Shore I'll break bread. I'm as hongry ez a shipwrecked sailor. When does ther tocsin sound?"

"The dinner bell will ring in about half an hour. Get down and turn your cayuse out to graze, and join us about the fire."

"Which means ter open ther mouth o' my war bag, an' give up my pedigree."

"Something like that," said Ted, with a laugh.

The ungainly cow-puncher slid out of his saddle like an eel, and slipped the saddle and bridle off his pony, and, giving it a slap on the haunch, sent it out to eat.

Throwing his horse furniture on the ground near the fire, he squatted in the ring of boys about, and proceeded to roll a cigarette in a leisurely way.

"Say, hombre," he said, looking at Ted. "You've got a mighty tidy outfit yere."

Ted nodded, and continued to watch the stranger's face.

"Which outfit mought it be?" asked the cow-puncher, picking a live coal out of the fire and placing the end of his cigarette against it.

"Moon Valley, Black Hills," said Ted.

"An' your name mought be—"

"Ted Strong."

The stranger paused with his cigarette halfway to his lips, and lifted his eyebrows.

"Sho! Yer don't say?"

"But I do."

"Well, I'm right proud ter meet up with yer, an' be able ter do yer a small service. My handle is numerous, not because I've ever had any serious reason ter change ther one my daddy give me, but because ther cow-punchers has a most humorous way o' hitchin' whatever label they thinks fits onter a man."

"What's your present label?" asked Ted.

"Ther cognomen what I packs with me now is sure fantastical.

Edward C. Taylor

I'm known on ther Western free range as 'The Woofer.'"

"'The Woofer'? That's a strange name."

"It ain't my real name, which is 'Tennessee Al.'"

"How did you come to be named 'The Woofer'?"

"Well, it's jest a piece o' foolishness," said the cow-puncher, laughing at the recollection of it.

"Tell us about it."

"Well, it was this away: About two year ago last Chrismus I wuz punchin' cows over on Coburn's ranch. Chrismus Eve ther boys got some cagy, an' we all decided ter go inter Cut Bank, ther tradin' town some ten mile away, an' cellybrate. It wuz a bad night, with ther wind blowin' out o' ther nor'west, an' ther promise o' a bliz."

"Wallace Coburn balks some at ther boys leavin' ther cattle, fer he sees thet thar's some danger o' their driftin' in ther night. But yer don't can up a lot o' cow-punchers Chrismus Eve when they wants ter go, so finally he grunts out that we kin go, an' off we starts."

"'Fleshy' Wheeler, so called because he wa'n't no bigger round nor a lemonade straw, kep' a saloon in Cut Bank, an' thar wuz ter be a day. Well, we-all went ter ther dance, which progressed beautiful, when one o' ther boys come in an' announces that a big herd o' cattle had drifted through ther town while we wuz trippin' ther light fantastic toe, and that one o' ther critters had fallen inter ther town well."

"Naturally, ther town people objected ter havin' range cow mixed in with their drinkin' water, an' hinted strong that it wuz up ter us cow-punchers ter git it out, at ther same time emphasizin' their invitation with a lot o' shiny six-shooters."

"Well, we goes inter caucus, an' decided thet ther cow belongs ter ther Coburn outfit, an' that we're too humane ter let a pore critter stay in a well Chrismus Eve, when joy an' peace an' merriment is reignin' everywhere."

"Now, as you-all knows, when a cow is hauled out o' a bog or a well she don't feel no gratitood, she jest gits mad plumb through an' h'ists her tail, an' runs fer ther fust thing she sees afoot, with her horns ready fer immediate business."

"Before we goes out ter git ther cow outer ther well, we tells Fleshy ter stand guard at the door, an' when ther cow charges, ter let us in, then slam ther door in ther cow's face. He agrees."

"We ropes ther cow, an' altogether pulls her out an' puts her on terry firmy. Then we hits it up fer ther house, with ther cow as mad as a woman scorned, an' only two jumps behind me, what is ther last man ter git under way."

"Ther boys hits ther house, an' Fleshy lets 'em in, but me, bein' some feet behind, he doesn't see, at least, that's ther way he explains ter me later, an' he slams ther door in my face jest ez ther cow arrives."

"My only chance is ter keep runnin', an' I starts around ther house, hopin' that when I gits ter ther door ag'in Fleshy will have discovered his mistake, an' have it open hospitablelike fer me, but cold feet fer ther cow."

"But, no, ther door is closed an' bolted, an' I start on another lap around ther house with Mrs. Cow a-snortin' an' a-blowin' in my immediate vicinity, an' comin' fast. Every time I hit ther ground with my hoofs I grunted 'woof.' I wuz gittin' winded, what with runnin' an' yellin', so thet I wuz gruntin' 'woof' most all ther time."

"Inside, all wuz merriment, an' me runnin' fer my life, fer ther cow wuz most industrious, an' didn't know what it wuz ter git tired."

"Well, ter make a long tale short, I kept runnin' an' gruntin' 'woof' at every jump, ther sweat runnin' down an' freezin' on my clothes, until mornin', when ther cow gits tired an' goes away. Then ther boys comes out an' finds me, an' says they're mighty surprised ter see me, havin' conclooded that I'd gone home."

"'We hear somethin' goin' "woof" all night, an' thought it wuz ther cow,' says Fleshy, 'an' we didn't dast open ther door fer fear she'd want ter come in, an' as there wuz ladies there, it wouldn't do. Wuz that you what was woofin' all night?'"

"After that I wuzn't nothin' ter them boys but 'The Woofer.'"

CHAPTER XXXI

SINGING BIRD'S SECRET

The boys laughed at the story, for Woofer, as they began to call him immediately, told it in a most comical manner. They all took to him immensely, and regarded him as quite an acquisition to the camp.

Dinner was announced by McCall, the cook, and Woofer certainly did justice to it, being, as Bud remarked in an aside to Hallie, "holler all the way down to his toes." He confessed that he had had nothing to eat but a little mud, which he had absorbed when he got a drink at a water hole, since the noon of the day before.

Ted had been thinking about the man. It would do no harm to have another puncher in the outfit, and would relieve the night guard, which at times was a little overworked.

"Say, Woofer, you won't take a reward for bringing in our strays, how would you like a job with this outfit?" he said.

"I don't want you to think I'm workin' ther grub line," said the cow-puncher quickly.

When a cow-puncher is said to be working the grub line, he

is known as a thriftless cowman who cannot hold a job long anywhere, and who travels from ranch to ranch, staying only long enough at each to get fed up, then passing on with a few dollars in his pocket, to repeat the operation elsewhere.

"Certainly not," answered Ted. "If I believed that I wouldn't offer you the job."

"All right," said Woofer. "This outfit looks good to me, an' I'll jine, an' go ter work instanter."

"You're on the pay roll, then."

Woofer proved quickly that he knew the business thoroughly, and when, the next morning, the herd got under way, he took the left point, with Bud on the right, and headed the herd into the north.

For several days life on the trail was monotonous. Whenever Ted could be spared from the herd he and Stella and Hallie Croffut, and sometimes Ben or Kit, took long rides off the trail with their rifles, after a pronghorn or black-tail deer, and frequently they had venison for supper.

The life was most fascinating to Hallie, who enjoyed every minute of it, and had seemingly forgotten the unpleasant features of her start with the party.

Singing Bird rode in the wagon, with Mrs. Graham, waiting on that lady in the capacity of maid. Stella had undertaken to teach her the duty of maid, and the girl soon did for Mrs. Graham what had taken a great deal of Stella's time.

The Indian girl was devoted to Stella, and whenever she was near, followed the pretty white girl with eyes in which shone devotion and affection.

She had made herself so useful, and was so self-effacing that every one wondered how they had ever been able to get along without her.

Stella had conceived a real affection for her, she was so gentle and sweet of manner.

They had long talks together in the evenings, sitting away from the fire, the Indian girl telling her white friend all about the life led by the Indians, their wrongs at the hands of the white men, their religious beliefs, their songs, and their folklore.

And, more important than all, she taught Stella the language of the Blackfeet and the Sioux. Stella was a good scholar, and it was surprising how rapidly she picked up the Indian tongues. Later she was to feel gratitude to the Indian girl for this knowledge.

For several days Stella had noticed that Singing Bird was uneasy and apparently unhappy, and it worried her.

She spoke to Ted about it, and he was of the opinion that the Indian girl was getting homesick, that her wild nature was asserting itself, and that she was experiencing a longing to be among her own people again, and free from the conventions of civilized life.

Stella did not think so, and determined to speak to Singing Bird about it at the first good opportunity.

One day the chance came as they were walking together in a wood near which they had camped.

"What is the matter with you, sister?" asked Stella kindly. "Is it that you are not satisfied with our ways, and that you want to leave us?"

Singing Bird looked at her with troubled eyes, in which the tears soon began to well up.

"My sister knows that I love her," she said, "and that I would not leave her unless she wishes me to."

She looked at Stella inquiringly.

"No, I want you to stay. But if you are troubled, you must tell me as one sister would tell another."

"I will tell you," said the Indian girl simply, "and I would have told you long ago, only that I did not want to trouble you, nor make trouble for any one else in the camp."

"What do you mean by making trouble for any one else in the camp?"

"I mean that the new man who drives the cows is a bad man. Beware of him."

"You mean the man called Woofer?"

"Yes, it is he whom I mean. He is the traitor, and he doesn't like the master, Ted Strong."

"How do you know that?"

"From what he has said to me. He is the bad man."

"But tell me all about it. I didn't know that he had talked to you, even. Why did you not tell me this before?"

"The white man threatened to kill me if I told."

"Now you must tell me all."

"We will sit down here, for there is much to tell."

Singing Bird took a seat upon a fallen tree, and Stella sat down beside her.

"Proceed," said Stella, "and leave nothing out."

"When he first came to the camp, I wished he would not stay," began Singing Bird, "but every one seemed to think he was the good man, and who am I to say anything against the wishes of my friends who saved my life and made me a home?"

"Did you know him then?"

"Yes. I have seen him at the white soldiers' fort. He is the friend of Running Bear. He is a bad man, who steals other men's cattle."

"But he brought ours back to us."

"That was a trick to get into your camp. He is as cunning as a bad Indian. One day he came to me when no one was about, and told me that he had seen my husband, Running Bear, and that I must go back to him. I was frightened, but told him I would not do so. Then he begged me to tell him the secret I have. I told him I could not do it."

"You have never told me that secret."

"But I will. Always I have intended to do so."

"When you are ready. But go on."

"Then he told me that if I would tell him the secret he would marry me himself." The Indian girl flushed. "You know, sister, that it is a great thing for an Indian girl to marry a white man."

"But you are already the wife of Running Bear," said Stella, who was puzzled.

"That is the Indian marriage, and soon broken. But when I told him I didn't want to marry him, he got very angry. I told him I was going to stay with you, and he said that if I did I would be killed with all the rest of you; that it was coming, and that Mr. Strong had many enemies who were stronger than all of you."

"Did he hint when this was going to take place?"

"Yes, when we get to the Far North."

"Did he say anything else?"

"He told me that if I didn't go with him to-night he would kill me when I slept."

"We shall see about that," said Stella spiritedly. "But why is all this fuss being made about you and your secret? It must be something very important."

"Yes, to the white man, but not to the Indian."

"Then why did Running Bear shoot you because you would not tell him?"

"He wanted to sell the secret to a white man for whisky."

"Who is the white man? Do you know?"

"Yes. But I do not like to tell."

"You have told me so much, you must tell me the rest."

"The white man is a soldier at the fort."

"A common soldier?"

"No, a chief, who carries a sword."

"Oh, an officer. What is his name?"

"He is called Barrows."

"Oh! And he offered Running Bear whisky for your secret? That is bad."

"Yes. Chief Barrows wants the secret, and he has sent the man who drives cows here to make me tell it."

"Singing Bird, you must tell me the secret."

"I will."

Stella settled herself to hear the Indian girl's story.

"It began when I was a little child," said Singing Bird. "One time when my father's tribe was hunting, we came to a place where a lot of white men were digging in the sands of the big, muddy river."

"Was that the Missouri?"

"The white men call it so. We camped beside them, and one day I saw them washing out of the sand little grains of yellow metal, which they thought much of, although the

Indians would rather have iron, the black metal."

"They were hunting for gold."

"Yes. In their talk with my father they said that somewhere up the river was the mother of the gold, where all this came from. They asked my father if he knew where it was."

"Now, my father had found where there was plenty of the yellow metal. But he, too, was shrewd, and, seeing that the white men prized it so highly, he thought he would go back and get the gold, and sell it to the white men for iron and shot and powder and blankets."

"The white men guessed that he knew where the mother of gold was, and asked him. But he refused to tell them, and went away."

"The white men followed us for days. One evening I was with my mother, and heard my father tell her where the yellow metal was on the opposite side of the river, pointing to a great sycamore tree that grew on the river bank. 'Beneath that tree lies much of the yellow metal,' he said to her, and I saw the tree, and knew what he said was true.

"That night the white men came to our camp and had a long talk with my father, trying to make him tell where the mother gold was, and, when he would not, suddenly they fell upon the camp, and, after killing some of the young men, drove my father and the others away. At the first shot my mother ran away into the woods with me."

"That was horrible," interjected Stella.

"As my mother ran, she was shot in the back, but she kept on running until she was out of sight before she fell."

"Then the white men went away, and I lay there with my mother until she breathed no more and was cold."

"I cried for a long time because it was dark and cold, and I could hear the wild animals in the woods all about me."

"This frightened me, and I began to call 'Ai-i-e!' which is the Indian way of lamentation, and I cried louder all the time to keep the wild animals from me."

"And did no one hear you?"

"Yes. In the night I heard a noise in the wood, and it was the noise of a man walking, an Indian man, for it was soft, made by moccasins. Then I cried louder, and soon my father came and picked both me and my mother up in his arms and carried us away into the woods, where he buried my mother, and went away into the North again.

"But as I grew up, I thought often about the mother gold and the place where it was hidden by the Great Spirit, for so I had heard my father say. Once when I spoke of it to my father he told me never to speak of it to him again, for it was cursed, having taken away from him his son, who was killed by the white men, and my mother.

"So never did I talk of it. But when Running Bear heard of it from some of the old men who had been with my father, and heard that I was the only one of all the tribe who knew where it was, he began to court me, and then bought me of my father for twenty ponies.

"We had not been married long when he asked me to take him to the place of gold, but my father told me not to do so, and I did not. Then he began to beat me, and tried to kill me, but the secret is still mine."

Edward C. Taylor

"In time others heard that I possessed the great secret of the hiding place of the mother gold, for when Running Bear was drunk he would boast that his squaw was the richest woman in the world, because of her secret, and many men have tried to get it from me. Then the army chief, who carries the sword, got hungry for the gold, and gave Running Bear plenty of whisky to make me tell where it was, and now he has sent Woofer to make me tell, or to kill me."

"Will you tell Ted Strong where the mother gold is hidden?" asked Stella.

"I will, if you wish me to. But it is accursed."

"Nonsense. That is only a superstition. Now that you have told me, all will be well. Be careful, and do not let Woofer see you alone, and if he lays his hand on you, scream for me. We will now go back to the camp."

As the two girls walked away with their arms around one another's waists, a tall, gaunt man rose from behind a dead tree not far away, and over his face spread a shrewd smile.

It was Woofer.

CHAPTER XXXII

A NIGHT CHASE

The tent occupied by Singing Bird was pitched some distance from that occupied by Mrs. Graham and the two girls, Stella and Hallie, and when she had attended to the wants of Mrs. Graham, she retired to it.

It was early in the evening, and when she saw that her friend had retired, Stella sought out Ted, and told him the story she had heard that afternoon.

At first Ted was inclined to be somewhat incredulous about Woofer's share in it as told by the Indian girl, but when he thought it over and put together certain facts which had come to his attention, and recalled questions, apparently innocent at the time they were asked, which Woofer had put to him from time to time, he began to suspect that the merry cowpuncher was, after all, merely acting a part.

Ted took Bud into consultation, and the three went over the matter carefully.

If it were true that Barrows was after the gold, he had a double cause to do injury to the broncho boys.

There could be no doubt that Barrows, by virtue of his position, was capable of being a very dangerous foe, especially in this part of the country where the boys were virtually alone, and where they had no friends, and were compelled to rely absolutely upon themselves.

That their doings were probably known to Barrows by means of a system of espionage conducted by Woofer, who, Ted now recalled, was in the habit of leaving the camp for long, solitary rides at intervals. What could be easier than when Woofer heard them talking about their plans to ride out and meet a courier sent by Barrows to get the information?

Ted resolved not only to fight Barrows with his own weapons, and to a finish, but to interfere with his plans to get the gold in the mine to which Singing Bird only could guide them.

It was necessary, therefore, to guard the Indian girl closely, and this he proposed to do, and when he had rid the camp of Woofer, and scoured the country for Barrows' spies and sent them off, he would proceed to the mine.

As it was, they were headed in the direction of the Missouri River, and it would not be at all out of their way, or interfere with their business.

Woofer was sitting with the boys around the camp fire, regaling them with stories of cow-punching in various parts of the country, and making of himself a most agreeable companion, and Ted, watching him carefully, could see nothing guilty or suspicious about him.

But that didn't prevent him from keeping his eyes open.

Gradually the camp settled down for the night.

Stella went to bed after she had peeped into the tent occupied by Singing Bird, and satisfied herself that she was sleeping quietly and safely.

One by one the boys rolled themselves in their blankets beside the fire, and dropped into deep slumber.

Woofer had said good night among the first, saying that he was very tired, and would "crawl into the wool," as he expressed it.

Only the night guard was awake, as they rode around and around the sleeping herd, their voices breaking out softly into song as a restless steer arose and sniffed the air and began to walk around.

Ted was lying in his blankets, breathing softly and deeply, evidently sound asleep.

Overhead the stars sparkled brightly, casting a radiance upon the earth that made things several feet distant perfectly observable.

Woofer's blankets had been spread at the edge of the circle farthest from the fire. Ted also slept on the outer rim, and not more than ten feet from Woofer.

It was past midnight, as Ted could tell by the stars, for he was not asleep, although feigning to be.

He lay facing the place where Woofer was circled up in his blankets, when he saw the cow-puncher raise his head cautiously, not more than an inch or two, and look around.

Ted closed his eyelids to a mere crack, for the light from the

Edward C. Taylor

fire shone on his face, and in that position watched Woofer's movements.

Woofer was very sly and cautious. Ted had observed that he had ostentatiously pulled off his boots when he lay down. Now he could see by the movements of the blankets that he was pulling them on again out of sight.

"That fellow is going to get up in a minute," thought Ted, "and I think I know just what he is going to do."

He had not long to wait, for presently Woofer crawled out of his blankets on the far side, and began to wriggle away on his belly, like a snake.

Ted still kept his eyes upon him.

Once Woofer stopped and looked back to see if his escape from camp had been observed, or if any one was stirring.

Ted had not moved, and apparently was as sound asleep as ever.

Reassured that no one had seen him leave his blankets, Woofer proceeded until he was without the radius of the camp fire's glow, when he rose to an upright position.

But Ted could still follow him by the starlight.

Evidently believing himself safe, Woofer did not again look around, but walked slowly and silently toward the tents, which were plainly to be seen about fifty feet distant from the fire.

The tent in which the Indian girl was sleeping was farther from the fire than that occupied by Mrs. Graham and her two charges.

Ted had slipped from his blankets at the moment when Woofer rose to his feet, and was creeping along, close to the ground paralleling Woofer's progress, but about twenty feet to the left.

Woofer arrived at the Indian girl's shelter and stopped, and seemed to be listening.

This gave Ted time to creep nearer.

He saw the cow-puncher lift the flap of the tent and look within, still listening carefully for anything that would tell him that Singing Bird was awake.

Ted was not more than ten feet away when Woofer disappeared.

He had entered the tent.

Suddenly from within it there came a muffled cry, then the tent began to pitch and toss. Evidently a savage struggle was going on within.

But it was all so silent that had Ted not been within striking distance of it, he would not have heard anything of it.

Suddenly the tent flew apart, and Woofer appeared, carrying in his arms the insensible form of the Indian girl.

Woofer was a very powerful man, and he ran swiftly from the tent bearing the girl in his arms as if she were a child.

Ted dashed after him. It did not occur to him to raise an alarm.

Edward C. Taylor

But as swiftly as he ran, Woofer had the better of him, for a few strides took him out of Ted's sight.

Ted stopped and listened, blaming himself for not closing with Woofer sooner.

Not a sound of Woofer's retreat came to his ears.

Suddenly he heard a nicker at his elbow almost, and looked around. It was Sultan, who had smelled him, and had come to him, and was now rubbing his velvety nose against Ted's sleeve.

In an inspiration Ted leaped upon his back, and caught the headstall, which he always left on Sultan when he turned him loose in the night so that he could get him in a hurry should there be a night alarm of any sort.

An idea came to him as soon as he felt Sultan under him.

Woofer undoubtedly had thought to have a horse saddled and ready waiting for him somewhere near the camp. If he could only get Sultan to call to it and get an answer, he would soon find him.

He had no sooner conceived the thought when Sultan whinneyed like a trumpet call.

From a distance came an answering cry. It was the voice of Magpie, and Ted knew it well. Stella's little black-and-white mare and Sultan were the greatest friends, and when she heard him call, she replied.

Woofer was about to steal the most valuable and swiftest of the animals, except Sultan. That was another reason why Ted was now so keen on the chase. He turned Sultan's head in the direction of Magpie's call, and the little stallion galloped away like the wind.

Ted had no bridle, but that was not necessary, for he and Sultan understood one another so well that a slight pressure of the rider's knees was all the guidance the horse needed.

Again came Magpie's shrill call, and this time Sultan nickered and fairly flew. Somewhere ahead, in the darkness, Ted heard for the first time the hoofbeats of the pony, and knew that Woofer had reached it and was away.

"Follow her; catch her, Sultan," called Ted, and Sultan seemed to understand, and let himself out to his full stride, although he missed the firm, guiding hand on the bridle.

Magpie was put to her utmost, but she was heavily handi-capped by carrying double for a race against Sultan, who was not even burdened by the heavy saddle he usually bore.

So it was that Sultan steadily gained on the little mare, who was not disposed to do her utmost even under whip and spur, which Woofer did not spare.

They were now racing in the dark along the ridge of a deep coulee, the wall on the right of which went down steeply to a depth of thirty or more feet.

Ted could not see the way, but he knew that they were riding a perilous path, and that a slip of the foot or a rolling rock might cost them their lives.

But he knew Sultan's feet were sure, and that unless an accident which could not be avoided took place, they were safe.

He had so gained on Woofer that he could now see him dimly outlined against the sky in advance of him.

If it were only level ground on which he could urge Sultan, it would not be a matter of more than a few minutes before he would be up with him.

But evidently Woofer saw him, also, for there was the flash of a revolver, and a ball sang past Ted's head.

He dared not fire in return for fear of hitting Singing Bird.

But the race must end soon, for Ted was steadily gaining.

At length they swept down from the ridge and into the coulee, along the level bottom of which they galloped, Sultan always edging up, closer and closer to Magpie, who evidently was slowing down.

Now Ted spoke to Sultan and urged him for the first time, and the gallant little beast spurted forward, and in an instant's time was abreast of the other horse.

Ted's eyes were almost put out by a blinding flash, and there was a deafening roar.

Woofer had placed his forty-five close to his head, leaning far out of his saddle, and fired.

By same interposition of Providence, however, the ball went past his head, singeing his hair, and he bent forward and struck Woofer on the head with the butt of his own weapon.

Woofer seemed to shrink in the saddle, like a wet rag, and the Indian girl was slipping from his arms to the ground when Ted seized her and transferred her to his own saddle.

At the same moment the insensible form of Woofer slipped to the ground.

Feeling herself free of her burden, Magpie came to a stop, and trotted back to where Ted was waiting for her, and rubbed noses with Sultan.

The Indian girl had been rendered unconscious by a blow on the head in the tent, and was just recovering as Ted rescued her from a fall to the ground.

Presently she opened her eyes, and, not knowing what had taken place within the last few minutes, she tried to struggle out of Ted's arms, at the same time uttering shrill screams, and trying to use her finger nails on his face. She was fighting like a wild cat, and it was all Ted could do to prevent her from injuring him, while he was trying to get her quiet enough to realize the change in her fortunes.

Finally she recognized his voice and ceased to struggle, but sat up and looked at him in amazement.

"It is I, Singing Bird," said he. "I followed you and took you away from Woofer. You are safe."

Then she saw it was so, and remained quiet.

He let her slip to the ground, and then assisted her to mount Magpie, and thus they rode slowly back to camp.

Before going Ted got down from Sultan's back and found Woofer, who was lying where he fell. He was not in a serious condition, but Ted knew that he would suffer from a severe headache when he awoke. Then he would have to take care of himself, alone on the vast prairie without a horse. But it was his own lookout, and perhaps it would teach him a much-needed lesson.

When they reached camp the night guard was changing, and, seeing Ted and the Indian girl come riding in together, the boys aroused the whole camp with their eager questions.

Ted told them briefly all that had happened during the attempted abduction of Singing Bird, but the time was not ripe to divulge the burden of the Indian girl's story of the gold in the mother lode.

CHAPTER XXXIII

THE LOCOED STEER

The daring attempt to abduct the Indian girl made a strong impression on every one of the Moon Valley outfit, and they resolved that they would not be caught napping in that manner again.

The herd continued to move forward slowly toward the north, with nothing to vary the monotony.

The long, grassy slopes of Montana furnished the best of feed, and the country was plentifully watered with clear, flashing mountain streams, and, all in all, it was an ideal cow country.

The herd was now well up toward the northeast corner of Montana, and not far away was the Missouri, near the banks of which Ted intended to hold the cattle until they were in fine condition, and then drive them by easy stages to the railroad.

One day Bud rode up to Ted with a very serious face, so unusual a thing that Ted looked at him with a grin.

"What's the grouch about now, Bud?" he asked.

Edward C. Taylor

"I ain't got no grouch," answered Bud.

"No? You look as if some one had handed you a lemon."

"No lemons in mine, but I jest got a hunch that this yere outfit is being follered, an' that thar's some dirty work doin'."

"What makes you think that?"

"I found a couple o' dead steers back a bit with our brand on them."

"Great Scott! What seemed the matter with them?"

"All swelled up."

"Poison?"

"That's what makes them swell up. There's no disease in ther herd, what I kin diskiver. All healthy enough. But some o' them is showin' signs o' loco, an' thar ain't no loco weed on this range."

"That's mighty strange. I hadn't noticed it. What do you think of it?"

"I believe that dog Woofer is follerin' us, an' has been spreadin' poison o' some kind on ther range what either kills or makes ther steers crazy."

"If that is true, it is the most serious thing that has come our way in a long time. It wouldn't take much of that sort of work to put the whole bunch out of business and leave us with not enough cattle to pay to drive back to the road."

"That's right. We'd be in a pretty fix with the best o' our herd rottin' out here on the prairie. And about all we've got is tied up in it, too."

"What do you think is behind it?"

"Barrows, the dirty little coward of an officer back there at Fort Felton, striking back-hand blows at us through his money, by hirin' crooks and murderers to do his dirty work. There's more than one man at work at this."

"I've no doubt you're right. By Jove! I'm going to take a look at the situation myself."

"Be careful about goin' too far away from the herd alone."

"I will; and, say, warn Stella and Miss Croffut about going out of sight of the herd, and to always fire a signal if strange men approach them when away from camp."

"I'll put everybody on, and warn them to be on their guard."

As Ted rode on, he turned the matter over in his mind.

Not knowing exactly if poison had been given the cattle, or if they had eaten of a poisonous weed, of which he had no knowledge, Ted was in a quandary. But it was questions like this that came before cowmen on the range, and it was the successful ones who solved them.

Ted felt, therefore, that it was up to him to get at the cause of the trouble which had unexpectedly come to him.

If he was being followed by a band of cattle poisoners who worked in the night, the sooner he knew it the better, for he could then lay plans to put them out of their nefarious business.

As he rode, he came across three swollen bodies of steers, and examined them. Clearly they had been poisoned, as Bud had said.

Far out on the range he saw a lone steer. Thinking that it was a stray, he rode toward it, with the intention of driving it back toward the herd.

For a herd steer, it was acting in an unaccountable manner. At times it galloped away in a frantic sort of way, throwing its head from side to side, then as suddenly stopping, and, with drooping head, standing quietly. Then away it would go again, charging at some unseen foe, only to become stupid once more.

"Something wrong with that brute," said Ted to himself. "Either it has got into a nest of rattlesnakes and has been bitten and is charging them, or it is locoed. We'll soon see."

He kept on fearlessly toward the steer, which continued its strange conduct.

When he was still several feet away the steer noticed him for the first time, apparently. It lowered its head and looked at him in a dazed sort of way.

This steer was known as Blue Eyes, on account of the curious bluish patch of hair that grew around one of its eyes. It had always been known as a particularly intelligent and tractable beast.

But now it was a very demon, with gleaming, blood-shot eyes and pawing hoofs, uttering deep, guttural bellows, and throwing the sand up over its back to the accompaniment of its thrashing tail.

"You look pretty dangerous, old fellow," muttered Ted, stopping his pony and gazing at it from a safe distance.

"No signs of rattlesnakes around here, or I'd smell them," soliloquized Ted. "Wonder what's the matter with you."

For answer, the steer gave an extra flip to its tail, and, without further warning, charged upon Ted with head down and wicked horns gleaming like bayonets. Ted's horse gave a snort of fear, and trembled in every muscle.

Ted at once realized his danger, and wheeled his horse like a bullfighter as Blue Eyes dashed past him, its horn scraping his leg.

"It's fight or run," thought Ted, "with a poor chance to get away from the brute. When they're in that condition they can run like an automobile."

Again the steer, having recovered itself, turned to the attack.

"I'll have to put a few bullets into that brute, if this thing keeps up much longer. It's just crazy enough not to be afraid of a man on horseback, besides, it's a good deal more active than usual." Ted's thoughts were keeping time with the swift actions of the brute, which was wheeling and charging like mad, so that it took all his agility and superb horsemanship to keep clear of it.

Now the horse was getting tired, and was almost useless because it was losing whatever sense it had had, and was becoming awkward and unmanageable.

The steer stood off for several minutes looking at Ted in a lowering way, but when Ted tried to run from it, it was close to his heels in a minute, and he had to simply throw the horse to one side, bringing it to its knees, to avoid the brute.

"That settles it," said Ted, taking his forty-five from its holster and advancing slowly upon the frantic steer.

As it started to charge again he fired directly at the middle of its forehead.

But the animal was hardly staggered, as the missile flattened on its skull and fell harmlessly to the ground.

"This won't do," said Ted. "I've got to get into this game myself. No more peek-a-boo goes with Blue Eyes. I'll do the tackling for a while."

He wheeled out of the way, then turned suddenly and rode after the steer, firing four balls in rapid succession into its body.

But this did not seem to affect the animal's spirits at all, and Ted rode off a short distance and reloaded.

When he turned again toward the beast it was charging, and was so close to him that he hardly had time to get out of its way.

He might have made it had not the horse caught the smell of blood, which was running from the steer in several places.

This rattled him so that he lost his footing, and the next instant he was struck on the withers by the steer's horns and went rolling over and over on the prairie, while Ted Strong flew from his back, and landed heavily on the sod, with his revolver knocked from his hand.

The locoed steer stood a few feet away pawing the earth and

looking at him with dim eyes, all blood-shot and crazy, not making a move toward him, yet always seeming about to do so.

Stealthily, inch by inch, Ted crawled toward where his forty-five lay on the ground.

It was six feet from where he lay to that gun, and he prayed silently that he could reach it before the steer changed its mind and rushed him.

He knew it would do no good for him to rise and go toward the weapon. If he did, the steer would immediately rush him, and that would be the end of things for him, for he would stand no chance whatever against that terrible beast, crazed, and powerful beyond its ordinary strength.

As long as he crept gently the steer seemed not to notice him.

Now he was within five feet of the revolver with his arm stretched out at full length. It was only four feet now, and still the steer did not make any move to attack him.

He was trying to think where he would shoot it. In the throat, ranging so that the bullet would pierce its heart; or through the eye, and so reach its brain.

Now his fingers closed around the weapon, and he clutched it convulsively, leaping to his feet like an acrobat.

At the same moment the steer, bellowing like an insane thing, charged upon him, and he fired into its blue eye.

The ball pierced the brain and killed the brute instantly, but did not stop the headlong flight of it, and before Ted could step out of its way, it struck him with the force of a locomotive. As he went to the ground, the dead steer fell on top of him.

Ted's fight with the steer had been seen, and across the prairie two flying figures simply split the air. When they reached the side of the prostrate steer, they flung themselves to the earth and flew to the rescue of Ted. One was Stella and the other was Bud.

"Is he dead?" asked Stella breathlessly.

"I reckon not," answered the cow-puncher, who, secretly, was very much afraid he was; he didn't see how Ted could help being dead, having been charged by a steer, and having gone down beneath its weight.

He was struggling like a demon to lift the heavy animal from Ted's body.

The bulk of the steer was lying across Ted's chest, whose face was black from the congestion, so that Stella dared not look at him.

"Pump yer gun fer all it's worth," commanded Bud, in a rough voice. "Keep shootin' till yer bring 'em on ther run. We've got ter get him from under this steer soon, er he'll be all in."

Stella had snatched her Winchester from the boot of her saddle, and fired it in rapid succession into the air until the magazine was empty. Then she refilled it, and began shooting again.

Presently she heard answering shots from the direction of the camp, and in a few minutes several horsemen came tearing over the top of a distant hill, to disappear into a valley and come into sight again on a nearer hill. Soon, with a shout that fairly split the air, six of the boys, led by Ben and Kit, threw themselves from their saddles in front of her.

"What's the matter?" they yelled in unison.

"Throw that steer off Ted," she commanded.

Then they saw what the matter was, and altogether they hoisted the steer, and Ted was freed of the terrible weight.

He was scarcely breathing, for the wind had been completely knocked out of him. Ben laid him flat on his back, and, straddling him, with his knees on the ground, began to work Ted's arms with an upward, backward, and outward motion, as if he was restoring the breath to a half-drowned person. Soon a flush came into Ted's face, and he gave a gasp, and his breath came in short, painful inhalations. As Ben continued the exercise, his breathing became regular, and he opened his eyes with surprise, to see so many of his friends about him, and particularly big Ben straddling him and apparently holding him down. He thought at first that Ben was responsible for his prostrate condition, or that he had struck him.

"What are you doing?" Ted said angrily. "Let me up, dog-gone you."

But when he saw the dead steer on the ground beside him he remembered what had happened, and sat up and laughed with the others.

It did not take him long to recover after this.

"I'm going to try to find out what caused this beast to go mad," said Ted. "There's certainly something wrong about it."

"How are you going to find that out?" asked Ben.

"I don't know yet, but I will," Ted answered. "Come on, two or three of you fellows. The rest of you ride back to the camp. You may be needed there. We can't guard things too closely these days."

The party separated, and Ted, with Bud, Ben, and Kit, rode away, but they had gone only a little ways when they heard a noise behind them. It was Stella galloping toward them.

"I'm going, too," she said, and go she did.

Riding about half a mile west they came to a deep coulee, into which they descended and followed its course for a short distance, when suddenly Ted held up his hand as a signal to halt.

"I smell burning paper," he said, and, getting down from his saddle, went forward alone on foot, as silently as an Indian.

Suddenly he bent forward, examining something on the ground, and motioned the others forward. They rode to his side, and saw him looking at a small, dead camp fire.

"Some one camped here last night," he said, thrusting his hand into the warm ashes. "And whoever it was burned papers in it before he went away this morning; the smell of them is still in the air." But no nose in the party was keen-scented enough to detect it except Ted's.

Ted was still pawing among the ashes, when a change in expression swept over his face, and soon he pulled out several small pieces of charred paper. They were only burned on their curled-up edges, and Ted saw that they were covered with writing, evidently part of a letter.

"What's this?" he exclaimed, after he had spread them out, and studied them attentively. "Here are some words. There is not very much sense in them, though."

"What do they read?" asked Stella.

"This is all I can make out of it: 'I *end you *** **nds of ***is **een. ***tter it on *** *rass. nce rr ws,'. Sounds as crazy as the steer, doesn't it?"

"That's as easy as living on a farm," said Stella, who had been looking over Ted's shoulder.

"All right, Miss Smarty, what is it?" said Ted laughingly.

"See, it's part of instructions to some one, and the way I read it is like this: 'I send you so many pounds'—I don't know just how many, but from the spaces the weight is expressed in three letters or three figures. The next is presumably a poison, although I wouldn't have thought of it if you hadn't spoken of it. What does two words, the first ending in 'is' and the other in 'een' mean, I wonder?"

They all scratched their heads for an answer.

"Why, sure, I have it," said Ted. "It is Paris green."

"That's it. Clever boy. Then there's 'tter,' which simply shouts 'scatter' at you. After that 'rass.' That's not hard. It reads so far: 'I send you, say six, pounds of Paris green,' although it must have been more than that. 'Scatter it on the grass.'"

"But the rest of it. That will stump you," said Ben.

"That's what caused me to get next to it first. It's Clarence Barrows, as sure as you're born!"

"Stella, you're right, by jinks!" shouted Bud. "Ther sweet-scented Lieutenant Barrows has sent men out yere ter poison our critters, and we've caught him with ther goods on."

CHAPTER XXXIV

THE BOBWHITE'S CALL

The discovery that Lieutenant Barrows had lent himself to such an enormous crime in the sight of all cowmen as to attempt to poison a herd of cattle, served to keep them all silent as they rode homeward, but around the fire that night their tongues loosened as they discussed it.

They told Hallie Croffut nothing about it, as they wished to save her pain, for as far as any of them knew she was still betrothed to Lieutenant Barrows, who was proving himself an enemy indeed.

"I see how it is, and how easy," said Ted. "They have been following us ever since we have been on the trail, but from a secure distance, generally riding parallel with us, out of sight in coulees, watching us continually."

"But how could they poison our cattle, without our seeing some of them sometimes?" asked Kit.

"Easy enough. Probably there are only two of them, for more would be in the way, and run more risk of being seen."

"But about the poisoning part of it? I don't understand how

they could do it."

"That's easy, too. They are probably a day ahead of us all the time, guessing at our probable direction of march. If they guess it wrong, they try it over again, for they are never more than a mile or so away. When they pick out a place where they think we will graze, they scatter the Paris green on the grass for the cattle to lick up. It takes a good-sized dose of the poison to affect so large an animal as a steer, and that is probably why we have not lost more of our stock by that means. They could never get quite enough, that is, the most of them, to kill them. Such as are dead did get enough to make them loco first, and kill them afterward."

"Another thing," said Kit: "We have had several heavy rains in the early morning lately, and that has served to run the poison off."

"I wouldn't wonder, also, if they haven't missed our route several times, and left the Paris green to poison some other herd," said Stella.

"Their salvation, I am convinced, is also due to the peculiar quality of the water they have found to drink. Who knows but that it is a perfect antidote for the Paris green?" said Ben wisely.

"Oh, slush!" interposed Bud. "I reckon ther truth is they haven't begun ter poison in right earnest yet. From ther letter, I would think that they had just received the stuff and were trying it out before they begin the big poisoning stunt. I'll bet Woofer is the chief actor, and that he's just met ther feller what brought ther poison out with him. Having found that it worked on a few o' ther cattle, they'll spread it on thick ahead o' us. An' ther wust part o' it is, thar don't seem no way ter circumvent 'em, onless we go hunt fer 'em, an' put 'em out er business quick."

"Well said, Bud," was Ted's comment. "There's no way of discovering the confounded stuff. We can't go ahead with a microscope and a chemical laboratory to analyze every blade of grass along the route for Paris green. The best we can do is to take our chances and keep going north. But I think we'd better establish outside picket lines which will stay well in advance, and off to the flanks. If it can be done, this system will succeed in at least frightening them off for a while. Everybody prepare to stand extra hours in the saddle."

A line of outriders was established at once, and the herd pushed on, and for several days there were no evidences that any more of the cattle had been poisoned.

They were nearing the river, as they could tell by the gradual sloping of the land to the east, and the flatness of the country.

One afternoon about four o'clock Brock, one of the hired cow-punchers, came riding into camp as fast as his horse would run, and fell out of the saddle. He had been shot through the leg, and was almost insensible from loss of blood when he succeeded in getting in.

When he was able to speak, he said to Ted:

"I was riding picket about two miles off to the west. As I topped a hill I saw a body of men about a quarter of a mile away. With my glasses I saw that they were soldiers, and wondered what they were doing so far from a post, as there isn't one nearer here than Fort Felton."

"Soldiers, eh?" asked Ted. "Cavalry or infantry?"

"Cavalry."

"How many of them were there?"

"I should say about fifty."

"Did they see you?"

"They must have seen me, for I saw them brought to a halt, and remain that way for several minutes, while the officer was looking at me through his binoculars. After they had satisfied themselves as to what I was, they galloped to the north, and I soon lost sight of them behind the hills."

"I wonder what troops are doing out here. I haven't heard of any trouble with the Indians, and there is no gang of outlaws this far north that it would take troops to subdue."

Stella looked at Ted significantly, and he read her thoughts.

Could it be that Lieutenant Barrows had been able to use his influence, or his cunning, to bring a detachment of troops so far away from the post to attend to his own personal affairs, while ostensibly on the government's business?

He dismissed the thought, however, as soon as it was conceived. It appeared to be too ridiculous.

However, they were all on their guard now. They realized that there were others on the range, and they were aware that a powerful and vindictive enemy was close at hand.

"How did you come to receive the shot in the leg?" asked Ted, breaking the silence.

"As I turned to ride to camp to report what I had seen,

something moved down in the coulee. At first I thought it might be a wolf or coyote, but as I drove the pony into it a shot was fired, and it got me in the leg. I didn't wait for any more, as I did not know how many men there might be, and I deemed it wise to get to camp alive with the news."

"The poisoners!" was Ted's brief comment.

"They've got us pretty well hemmed in," said Ben. "They mean business."

"Yes, but we'll break through, and beat them yet," said Ted, with conviction.

But they were a long ways from being out of danger yet as they were soon to know.

That evening Ted, accompanied by Stella and Hallie, rode out of camp. Ted wanted to spy out the land in advance to see if there were any signs of the troops and the poisoners.

They were riding along out of sight of the camp, talking cheerfully and feeling perfectly safe, when they were brought to a sudden stop by a command, "Halt!" given in a gruff tone.

They stared in amazement when they saw that they were surrounded by a detachment of soldiers, and that the command had been given by a sergeant. A dozen carbines were leveled at them.

"What's the meaning of this?" asked Ted, with a smile.

"Orders for your arrest," answered the sergeant gruffly. "Disarm the man."

Several soldiers stepped to Ted's side, and the one who attempted to take Ted's rifle from its boot on the saddle received a kick on the chest that sent him sprawling on his back.

But as the kick was delivered, and before he could do anything further in his defense, Ted was struck a ringing blow on the head with the butt of a carbine, and was dragged from the saddle.

As he went down he heard a shout of alarm.

"Don't shoot!" he heard the sergeant cry. "Let her go. We don't want her, anyway."

Then Ted knew that Stella had escaped, to carry the news back to the boys, and to bring assistance.

"I wish the Indian girl had been along," the sergeant said to one of the men. "We'd have all we wanted, then."

"Oh, we'll get her later," was the reply.

Ted was hoisted to his feet in no gentle manner, and then he discovered that his arms had been bound. Sitting on her pony was Hallie Croffut, pale but calm, regarding the scene with an expression of contempt.

"What is the meaning of this, Brown?" she asked, addressing the sergeant

"Orders from a s'perior officer, miss," said the sergeant apologetically, saluting respectfully.

"Well, you and your superior officer will be sorry for this day's work when the colonel hears of it," was all she said.

The sergeant saluted again, and ordered the men to march.

Ted was lifted into his saddle, and, in the center of the detachment, was marched away.

They rode thus for several miles, when, in the gathering dusk, Ted saw ahead of him a small cabin.

In a few moments they were in front of it, and Ted and Hallie were assisted to the ground and bade to enter.

In the center of the room, seated at a table, was Lieutenant Barrows, who scowled at Ted, but hadn't the courage, apparently, to look at his fiancee.

Hallie Croffut did not address him, but he felt the glance of scorn she gave him, for he winced under it.

"For what am I arrested?" asked Ted coolly.

"You will discover when your trial comes," was the cold reply.

"And why have you dared to detain me?" asked Hallie.

"Your father's orders, Miss Croffut," he said almost inaudibly.

"I believe that you are lying. If you are, Heaven help you, for there is not a decent man in all the army who will not hound you to disgrace. To think that you would countenance this outrage against your colonel's daughter is almost past belief. But now I know you for what you are, you cur."

Barrows went white as a sheet as she said this, and his lip curled back from his teeth, like those of an angry dog, as he

Edward C. Taylor

half rose to his feet with a gesture as if he would strike her. But he thought better of it, and sank back.

"Brown, take them away," he said to the sergeant. "I will hold you personally responsible for them."

The sergeant saluted, and, catching Ted by the elbow, marched him into the next room.

Hallie Croffut started to follow him, when she was stayed by Barrows.

"Hallie, won't you come back with me?" he pleaded. "If you will, I will release Strong and let the rest of it go."

"I wouldn't trust you out of my sight," said the girl. "Oh, how happy I am that I have found you out in time. You are the most miserable specimen of a man I ever heard of, and to think that you have called yourself an officer and a gentleman. But this is the last for you. If you were brave enough you ought to kill yourself to save the army from the disgrace of having had you in it."

"Curse you!" he cried, in impotent rage. "If you were not a woman I would knock you down."

"If you feel like it, don't let so small a matter that I am a girl and your colonel's daughter interfere with your pleasure. Strike me!"

But Barrows only stared at her with a white face, and with a muttered curse left the room.

"This way, miss," said the sergeant. She entered the room into which Ted had been taken, but he was not there.

In the middle of the floor was an open trapdoor.

"I must ask you to go down there," said the sergeant. "You will find a ladder. You will be safe, and it is not for long. We start for the post soon, I am told."

Hallie made no reply, but did as she was bid.

The cellar was as dark as a pocket, and she could see absolutely nothing as her feet touched the earth floor.

But she found a box, and sat down upon it. The trap was closed, a bolt shot in it, and she was in Stygian darkness.

She was terribly frightened at first, but there were no rats in the cellar, which she had at first feared, and she fell to thinking what it all meant. Surely the army must have gone entirely mad that she, Hallie Croffut, its pet, should be under arrest in a dark and musty cellar.

But presently her heart stopped beating. In a far corner she heard a faint noise.

Something else was in the place with her. What could it be? Where was Ted? What did it all mean?

Then she heard a groan, and an uneasy movement.

"Who is it?" Hallie asked, in a trembling voice.

"Is that you, Hallie?" It was Ted's voice.

"Yes, it is I. Where are you?"

"Over here in the corner. Those brutes threw me down the ladder, and it stunned me. Come here. Perhaps you can untie my hands. Then we will see what chance there is for escape."

Ted was soon released, and, climbing the ladder, tried the trapdoor, but found it securely fastened.

There had been no sound above them for some time, and Ted came to the conclusion that the soldiers were gone.

He was right. When the prisoners had been thrust into the cellar, Barrows and his men rode away, leaving them alone.

Hours dragged along in the dark, and they scarcely spoke to one another, both lost in their thoughts.

Suddenly Ted started up. Outside he heard a whistle, and he listened for it to be repeated. It was the whistle of the bobwhite. He knew that there were no quail in this region at this time of the year. He knew, too, that it was an Indian signal which Stella and Singing Bird had used between them. Could it be that Stella was outside, and that she was signaling the house, and thinking it occupied, did not dare come to it? He answered it as well as he could, knowing, however, that the sound would not get beyond the cellar.

For several minutes the whistling continued, then stopped. What if they had gone away?

After a long time, it seemed, he heard a stealthy noise overhead. Some one was crawling through the window. Then there was a light step overhead.

"Ted! Hallie! Where are you?" It was Stella calling to them, and they both raised their voices in a joyous shout. Then the bolt slipped, and the trap was raised.

"Come up out of there," cried Stella, "unless you like it.

Singing Bird and I started out after you. I met her on the way, and she trailed you here. She has just started back for the boys."

Edward C. Taylor

CHAPTER XXXV

A DUEL WITH LARIATS

Outside it was night, and beyond the clearing the woods were dark. Both Ted's and Hallie's horses were gone, and it would be impossible for them to start back toward the camp without them.

"We'd better hide in the woods until morning," said Stella. "Singing Bird will guide the boys here. Besides, we do not know when that brave warrior Barrows will return with his soldiers."

"That is a good idea," said Ted, and they crossed the clearing to the woods, and found a place of concealment from which they could see all that took place at the house.

The night was far advanced, and the girls were sleeping on a couch of dried pine needles, which Ted had gathered for them.

Ted was on watch to shield them from harm, and to drive away the animals of the night.

He was half asleep himself, sitting with his back to a tree with his head on his arms, which were crossed on his knees.

An unusual sound brought him to his senses instantly, and he was listening intently.

He heard the sound of horses' feet, and the subdued rumble of men talking.

There were only two horses, and they were coming on uncertainly.

Evidently their riders did not know their way, and were feeling along in the dark, which was intense.

"It ought to be along here somewhere."

It was the voice of Woofer.

"Well, I hope it is," said another voice, "I'm tired of this night riding. When did the boss say he'd be here?"

"Early in ther mornin'. He's goin' ter make an attack on ther cow camp ter-night, an' what he don't kill he's goin' ter bring here, an' stampede ther cattle an' scatter them all over ther range."

Woofer laughed as he said it.

"I don't care much what he does," he continued, "if he'll only turn over ther Injun gal ter me. That'll be ernuff fer you an' me, I reckon."

"Then what's he goin' ter do?"

"He's goin' ter take that Croffut gal, he's jest crazy about her, an' hike her off ter ther coast, an' put her aboard a private yacht he's got there, an' that'll be ther last o' her in this community."

"What's goin' ter happen ter ther rest o' them?"

"He's got er nice little deal fixed up fer Ted Strong. He wuz tellin' me thet if I wanted it, ther job was mine. I reckon I'll take it," and Woofer laughed heartily.

"You're ter be ther executioner, eh?"

"That's about ther size o' it."

"An' yer hate yer job, eh?" This was greeted with uproarious laughter.

"Like a kid hates candy."

"What's it goin' ter be?"

"A little rope play, I reckon."

"That's yer long suit. Hello, what's this? Here we are at the cabin."

Ted heard the men dismount and enter the cabin, and then their voices roaring with rage.

"They've escaped, darn 'em!" they heard Woofer shout. "Hey, there, turn out an' hunt 'em! Ther boss will be wild when he finds this out."

"Hunt fer 'em nothin', in this dark? Yer wouldn't find 'em in a blue moon. Why, it was all we could do ter find ther cabin."

"Well, they can't git far away. We'll find 'em in ther mornin'."

They retired to the cabin again, and slammed the door.

"Did you hear that?"

Stella's hand was on Ted's arm, and she whispered to him in an awed sort of voice.

"You awake?" he said. "Yes, I heard it, but don't let it worry you. They won't get us very soon."

They heard Hallie sobbing quietly.

"What's the matter, dear?" asked Stella. "Don't be frightened."

"Suppose he does," sobbed Hallie.

"Suppose who does what?" asked Stella, throwing her arms around her friend.

"Suppose Lieutenant Barrows does get me and takes me away on a boat. Oh, I shall kill myself!"

"Never fear," said Ted. "He won't do that. Why, the whole army would be up in arms and after him before he got fifty miles."

Hallie took comfort in this, and slept again, while Ted and Stella remained on guard.

As the night wore on, they both became very sleepy, and they must have dropped into a doze, for when they awoke at the sound of a loud laugh, the sun was shining brightly, and they were surrounded by soldiers, and Woofer was looking down at them with a sneering laugh.

"Jest like ther babes in ther woods," he shouted, and the soldiers laughed with him.

Ted was on his feet in an instant, feeling for his revolver, but it was not in its accustomed place, and he suddenly remembered that it had been taken from him by the soldiers the night before.

"Whar's ther lootenant?" asked Woofer. "He'd be glad ter see this tablow."

"He's gone out inter ther woods ter walk his mad off. When he got within strikin' distance o' ther cow camp last night his sand run out, and he started back. Then when he found that his birds had flown that was ther last kick what sent him down."

"What's he goin' ter do now."

"I reckon he'll make ther best o' what he's got now. Come, git up." Woofer spoke roughly to the two girls, and they arose. "Come along back to the cabin. Ther lootenant will be mighty glad ter see yer. One o' you sour doughs hunt up ther lootenant an' tell him ther lost is found."

Ted saw that resistance was useless, and, taking the girls by the hand, he crossed the wide clearing between the woods and the cabin; at the door of which they arrived just as Barrows strode up.

One of the soldiers was busy preparing breakfast, and the others were grouped around jesting about their night's work.

The two girls were sent into the room in which Ted and Hallie had been taken the night before, but Ted was not confined, and was allowed to walk up and down in front of the cabin.

Barrows did not attempt to hold conversation with any of

them, but sat at his table with his head in his hand, thinking moodily.

Evidently Barrows was an arrant coward. He had set out with the intention of ruining the Moon Valley herd, and killing all who attempted to resist him, but his courage had failed him.

Ted saw hope in this, if the boys would only arrive on time.

He thought over the conversation he had heard the night before on the arrival of Woofer and his companion at the cabin, with regard to his own fate. Evidently it meant something out of the ordinary, for it seemed to have given extreme pleasure to Woofer, for it was evidently the intention that all the advantage was to be with the cow-puncher. Well, it didn't matter much, so long as he had the ghost of a show himself. He was willing to take a long chance.

Breakfast was announced, and, as the soldiers sat down to eat, the cook came out with three tin plates on which there were bacon and bread, and tin cups of coffee for the prisoners, and they sat down together in the shade of the cabin and ate their food gratefully, for they were very hungry.

The meal was soon over, and Woofer began to strut up and down in front of the cabin.

"I reckon here's where I get my revenge, ain't it, lootenant?" he said, stopping in front of Barrows.

"Do what you please with him," said Barrows crossly, "but leave the girls alone."

"I don't want but one gal, an' she's copper colored," laughed Woofer insultingly, walking to his horse, which was already saddled.

"Now, young feller," he said to Ted, "I'm goin' ter give yer a chance fer yer white alley. I'm goin' ter try ter rope yer while yer dodges me. If I get yer, why—I'll drag yer, see?"

Ted saw that he was to have no chance for his life whatever.

He was to be afoot, while the other man was to ride and try to rope him, and, if he succeeded, drag him to death over the rough ground.

"Do you call that a chance for my life?" asked Ted.

"As much as you'll get," answered Woofer, with a canine grin. "Get out an' take a fightin' chance, or I'll rope yer an' drag yer without it."

Ted looked around the circle of grinning faces about him, and saw that there was no mercy for him. He must make the best fight he could.

Woofer had ridden out into the open and was coiling his rope in his hand ready for a cast.

As Ted walked out he saw in the grove the horses of the soldiers, and among them Sultan bridled and saddled, and a thought flashed through his mind that before the duel was ended he might find use for his beautiful stallion.

As soon as Ted was in the open, Woofer began to circle around him on a lope, steadily increasing the pony's speed, at the same time keeping the rope swinging about his head.

Ted wheeled on his heels, always keeping his face to the horseman, the pivot, as it were, of this little spectacle. Near the cabin stood the soldiers, watching the play with interest. Stella and Hallie were at one side, their eyes fastened on the scene with a sort of fascinated horror. Stella knew well the danger of the bout. In the doorway of the cabin Lieutenant Barrows leaned indifferently, smoking a cigarette, and watching the uneven contest with slight interest in its outcome, and with no regard whatever for the thing which all gentlemen hold sacred, that is, fair play.

Around and around rode Woofer, waiting for a good chance for a cast, but always finding Ted alert. But suddenly the rope flew from his hand with unerring accuracy, and Ted had just time to dodge it. It had been as swift and almost as deadly as the strike of a rattlesnake.

With a confident smile, Woofer drew in his rope again, coiling it, and making ready for another cast.

Again he circled and cast, and this time the rope settled over Ted's shoulders, and a great shout went up from the soldiers.

But before Woofer could tighten it Ted managed to wriggle out of it, and again Woofer drew it in.

Ted realized the danger in which he would stand if ever Woofer succeeded in getting him fast.

Suddenly his hand came in contact with something hard in his pocket. It was his knife, and he surreptitiously inserted his hand, and opened it, then drew it out concealed in his palm. He felt sure that if it was discovered that even this chance would be taken from him.

Again and again Woofer cast and Ted dodged, and the soldiers were getting tired of the monotony of it, and began to deride Woofer for not being able to get Ted.

This aroused the man to anger, and the next time he sent the rope over Ted's shoulders, and drew it taut. A wild cry went up as Ted was being dragged along as fast as he could run, and Stella turned white and gave a cry of fear.

But Ted reached up, just as he was about to be carried off his feet, and cut the rope in two.

At this a yell of protest rose from Woofer, but the men had at last turned with sympathy to Ted.

"Let him have the knife," they cried. "You have the horse and the rope."

Woofer was forced to be content, and he slowly dragged the rope back again, and made a new noose.

He was getting rattled, while Ted was gaining courage, and the rope did not come as accurately as when Woofer had not begun to grow weary.

The soldiers were now addressing rough pleasantries at Woofer, who was growing angry and trying harder than ever to rope Ted and drag him to death.

Then, quite unexpectedly, the rope settled over Ted's arms, for he had grown a little careless, and his eyes had been directed toward the top of the hill behind the cabin, where he had seen something that caused his eyes to open with wonder.

But when he felt himself being dragged along on a run he came to his senses. Stooping his head, he managed to get the knife between his teeth. Then he went along the rope, gathering it in his hands as he went, as if he were climbing it hand over hand.

A shout of joy went up from the two girls at this, for they saw his purpose.

On he went, the rope coming into his hand and being coiled on his arm. Woofer all the while was urging on his pony, trying to throw Ted off his feet.

Ted had now gathered in about thirty feet of the rope, or about half of it.

Woofer saw his game, and swore horribly, as he tried in vain to throw Ted.

When he thought he had enough rope, Ted bent his head once more, and his fingers grasped the knife with which he cut the rope and was free.

Suddenly a shrill whistle left his lips, and there was a nickering answer as Sultan left the other horses and came galloping to his side.

Stella threw up her hat and shouted, and the soldiers followed her example.

As Sultan galloped on, Ted leaped into the saddle, and began to make a noose in his lariat, for he now was equally armed with his enemy.

But Woofer was game, and came galloping back. He didn't know how good a roper Ted was, but he felt confidence in himself.

Around they went, circling like horsemen in a circus ring, with watchful eyes and whirling lariats.

But suddenly Ted's rope left his hand before Woofer could

divine his meaning, and pinioned the cow-puncher.

At the same moment Ted gave Sultan a prick with the spur, and the little stallion leaped into the air.

Woofer left his saddle and struck the ground with a bump that knocked the wind out of him.

This was not to the liking of the soldiers, who ran howling toward Ted.

"Drag him from his horse," they shouted.

"No, yer don't. Fair play fer all!" a clear voice rang out above the din, and the soldiers turned toward the hill behind the cabin.

On the summit stood Bud Morgan, his long, fair hair floating in the breeze, and on either side of him ten cow-punchers with their Winchesters trained upon the unarmed soldiers, whose carbines were stacked in the house.

"Three cheers for the broncho boys!" yelled Stella shrilly. "You can't beat 'em anyway you try."

CHAPTER XXXVI

THE MOTHER LODE

As the boys swarmed down the hill to where Ted and the girls were standing apart from the soldiers, who stood staring at them in amazement, they let out the Moon Valley yell, and acted as though they were a victorious army taking possession of a conquered city.

Lieutenant Barrows stood in the doorway in open-mouthed amazement at the change of scene, in which he and his men were not the captors, but the captured.

He started to bluster by ordering Hallie to get ready to accompany him back to her father.

"I shall not go," she said positively. "I don't believe that my father sent for me."

"I know he didn't," said Ted firmly.

"What do you know about it?" asked Barrows, with a sneer.

"I know that it was your intention to kidnap Miss Croffut and take her to the coast, where you would board a yacht and carry her out of the country."

"That's a—" began Barrows.

"Don't let the word lie pass your lips as applied to me, or I'll jam it down your throat," said Ted, advancing toward the officer, who turned pale and retreated.

"You shouldn't tell your intentions to such irresponsible persons as the Woofer, here. He told all about it early this morning so loud that the whole of Montana might have heard it if they had been awake. I heard it, and if Woofer denies saying that you did say so, then he's a liar, and I'm personally responsible for everything I say."

"I did say so, and I heard the lieutenant say so," said Woofer defiantly.

"Another thing, I have in my pocketbook scraps of a letter written by you in which you say you have sent Paris green out to poison our cattle, and you did succeed in a way, but not as you wished. Barrows, your game is played. You are at the end. I shall see that the proper authorities get all the details of this, and you know what will happen then. You will be chased out of the army like a mad dog, and all the influence you can bring to bear will not serve you."

Barrows was looking at Ted with terror in his eyes.

"My advice to you is to skip before the army gets on to you," continued Ted. "Disappear. Obliterate yourself. It will be easier for you to be thought a deserter than what will be thought of you if what we know about you goes back to the post."

Barrows stepped back into the cabin, and Ted walked to where he could keep his eye on the soldier.

Suddenly he jumped into the cabin and wrenched a pistol out of Barrows' hand.

"No, you don't," he cried angrily. "You can't pay for this by self-murder. You've got to live to pay for your meanness."

Barrows submitted to be disarmed by Ted. He stood looking for a moment at Hallie, and for a moment it seemed as if he would speak to her. Then, with a cry of agony, he rushed across the open, leaped upon his horse, and, plunging into the grove, was lost to sight.

"Sergeant, now you know what to do," said Ted. "There's only one thing for you to do. Hike for the post and tell the commandant anything you like to explain the absence of Barrows. But be sure to say to the colonel that his daughter is safe and well and prefers to stay with Miss Fosdick and her friends. I don't know how deeply you are mixed up in this cattle-poisoning, girl-abducting scheme of Barrows, but I give you the benefit of the doubt."

"Sure, sir, I didn't know anything about the cattle poisoning, nor do any of the men, and as for abducting the young lady, all I knew about it was that we were sent by the colonel to bring her back, that is, the lieutenant said so. We was to arrest you for stealin' cattle from the gover'ment. But I don't see as we can do anything, now that the officer in charge is gone. All right, sir, I'll tell the colonel all what you said, an' somethin' that's been layin' hard on my stomach ever since I got wise to the officer what's not in charge no more. Men, get ready to march."

The soldiers saddled their horses, and got ready to start on the march back to Fort Felton.

When they were ready to start, Ted walked up to Woofer and

Edward C. Taylor

the man who had come in with him in the night.

"Woofer," said he, "strike the back trail, and don't look around. You are not wanted in this part of the country. Remember, we are all deputy United States marshals, and not in the least afraid to use our authority. Hike!"

"All right, pardner, if you say you don't like our sassiety we won't force it on you. We'd like good company back to Felton, anyhow, an' the sojers has plenty o' grub. Adios!"

With a wave of the hand, the sergeant led his column out of the clearing, and, climbing the hill, struck into the southwest, where lay the fort.

When they were gone Singing Bird came out of the woods in which she had been hiding, for she was in mortal terror of Woofer.

When she knew that Woofer was in the vicinity she had run into the woods and immediately climbed into a tall pine tree that grew on the hill, where she was sure he would not be able to find her.

Now, when she came forth, she ran to Stella, in a very much excited state.

"Sister," she cried. "I have found it!"

"Found what?" asked Stella, in surprise at the girl's emotion, for usually she had the stoicism of her Indian blood.

"I have found the place of the secret, the place of the mother gold," cried Singing Bird, trembling with excitement.

"I have seen it, the place where my mother lay," she

continued, when her excitement had somewhat passed away.

"How?" asked the puzzled Stella.

"When I climbed the tree I saw the big, muddy river lying over there. I looked about. It seemed that I had seen it the same before. Then I remembered the night the white men killed my mother, and it all came back to me. Woofer was one of the men. He knew that we were coming near to it."

"How did you recognize it as the place?" asked Stella.

"By the tree across the river, and by the bluffs, and the turn of the river. Oh, I know it. You can't fool Indian on signs like that."

The boys were standing around listening eagerly, for this was the first time they had heard of the "mother gold." Briefly Ted related the story told by Singing Bird about the gold in the river, and how her father found the mother lode.

"I'm fer gettin' thar as soon as we kin," said Bud Morgan. "Whenever I smell gold I git tired o' ther smell o' cows."

"Looks good to me," said Ben.

"Me, too," said Kit, and the other boys raised a shout for the mother lode and the excitement of finding gold.

"But the cattle?" asked Ted.

"We'll drive them down into this valley, where part of the force can easily watch them, while the other part is engaged in the fascinating sport of gold hunting. Me for the gold." Thus Stella delivered herself, and that seemed to settle it.

Accordingly the cattle were driven down from the plain and into the beautiful grassy valley, with the Missouri flowing at the foot of it. Then they pitched their camp.

Singing Bird had gone into the woods on an exploring mission to find, if she could, the grave in which her father had buried her mother the day after the fight with the white miners, and had been gone an hour or more, when she came hurrying back, trembling like an aspen.

Rushing up to Ted, she fell at his feet.

"What's the matter now?" he asked, in a kindly way.

"I have seen him," she cried. "Save me! Save me!"

"Whom have you seen?" asked Ted.

"Running Bear. I go into the woods, and I see moccasin tracks; fresh ones. They are large and new, made this day. I run away from them. Then I see an Indian hiding behind the trees, always following me, and I turned and ran for the camp. He followed me until he saw the camp, when he turned and ran the other way."

"Are you sure it was Running Bear?"

"Oh, yes, I am sure. I know Running Bear. He was my husband."

"Well, do not be afraid. Running Bear will not hurt you. But don't go away from the camp."

Ted told the boys that the Indian was on their trail, looking for the mine himself, but that he would probably track them until they found it, and then try to take it from them by pressing to his service a band of Indians, which he could very well do.

When Stella went to look for Singing Bird that evening she could not be found. The alarm was passed to the boys, and a thorough search of the camp was begun, but the girl could not be found.

"She has done what I told her not to do," said Ted. "She has left camp, and that precious rascal has captured her. But he will not wring her secret from her. I am convinced that she would die first."

"But what are we going to do about her?" asked Stella. "We can't let her remain where she is."

"Where is she?" he asked whimsically.

"Where is she?" Stella repeated the question excitedly. "Do you suppose that I would be here if I knew. I don't know where she is, but I'm going to find out."

"Not to-night, Stella, surely."

"Yes, to-night. Right now."

"But—"

"There's no buts in this at all. Who wants to help me find Singing Bird?"

Every fellow in the outfit stepped forward.

"Well, I guess that's enough," she said, laughing. "But, I want you and Kit. The others can stay behind and 'tend the herd. We'll be back when we return." She waved a merry hand to the others, and the three strode into the woods, Bud bending eagerly forward to find the trail.

Presently Bud struck a moccasin trail, and they followed it until it mingled with another.

The first was undoubtedly that of Singing Bird. The other was that of a big man, or of a man with a big foot.

"I reckon she come out here ter find her mother's grave, an' met up with ther bully, her husband. Here they seem ter hev had a struggle, and then thar is only one track, but deeper, showin' that he was carryin' weight. I reckon he put his hand over her mouth an' carried her off by main strength."

"Poor Singing Bird," murmured Stella. "If she has really fallen into the hands of that brute, it's a sure thing that she'll be killed this time, and now we're bound to follow her and get her."

"That's interfering between a man and his wife," said Kit.

"I don't care. She's mine now, for I saved her life. She said so."

"All right, Stella, we'll find her if we swaller our chewin' gum. Forward!" Bud led the way, always with his eyes on the ground.

After traversing a few hundred yards he stopped.

"Here they're walkin' side by side again," he said, "and they're going toward the river."

They hastened on to the bank of the river, and there all trace of them was lost at the water's edge.

"They've crossed over, but not in a boat," said Bud. "I don't see how they could do it if they didn't swim. There isn't the sign o' a boat around here."

"Then over the river we go," said Stella. "But the question is, how?"

"I'll swim it," said Bud. "And if I find any trace of them over there, I'll holler."

Bud threw his guns on the bank and plunged into the water, and in a few minutes was across, for so near the headwaters it was not wide.

They saw him scouting along the shore, and presently he waved his hand at them, and pointed to the ground.

"He's found them," said Kit. "But how are we to get over?"

Kit ran up and down the shore, and soon found several logs, which he towed to where Stella was waiting, and fastened them together into a raft.

"There you are," he said. "Climb aboard, and I'll ferry you across."

Stella did so, and in a few minutes they were on the other side.

Bud showed them the tracks of Singing Bird, and they followed them into the woods.

Close beside the track was a huge stump of a sycamore tree, and Stella elected to sit down beside it and wait until they returned, as she was pretty tired. The boys passed on with the warning to fire her revolver three times if anything should alarm her.

As she sat beside the stump, she picked up a stick, and began poking in the earth at her feet. As she did so, there was a rumbling sound beneath her, and the world seemed to be slipping from her. This was followed by a rush of earth and a clatter of stones, and Stella went down with it.

She did not fall more than ten feet, however, before she stopped, a little shaken but unhurt.

When she had recovered somewhat, she looked about her.

Then she gave a little shriek of joy. It seemed as if she had fallen into a regular nest of pure gold, for the glittering grains were everywhere about her, on her clothes and in her hair.

Suddenly she recalled everything. She had found the mother lode that the Indian girl had told of.

Drawing her revolver, she fired three shots, the danger signal, and immediately it was answered by three shots, but from the side of the river she had just quitted.

This surprised her, but in a moment she heard a shout. It was Ted. Evidently thinking that something might befall her, he had followed, and in a few moments she heard him splashing in the water.

"Hello!" he cried.

"Here I am, Ted," cried Stella, and in a moment she saw his face outlined above her in the opening of the hole.

"How the deuce did you get there?" he asked.

"Oh, I just dropped in to take a look around, and what do you think I found? I've found gold by the bushel. Ted, this is the mother lode."

Ben, Carl, and Clay were with Ted, and soon Bud and Kit, who had heard the shots, came hurrying back.

When they heard what had happened they were much surprised.

"But this cannot be the place. Where is the sycamore tree Singing Bird said was a landmark?" said Ted.

They had pulled Stella out of the hole, and now she pointed to the big, old stump.

"That is what's left of it," she said. "If I hadn't that hunch to sit down here, we wouldn't have found the mother lode in a blue moon."

As they were speaking they heard a sound behind them, and turned to see Running Bear. He had crept up to them so silently that not one of them had heard him until he was a step away.

"Ugh!" he grunted. "White boy go away. This my country."

"Go to your grandmother," said Ted. "Where is Singing Bird?"

"She in Running Bear wigwam. Mebbe so you like Singing Bird. You can have same go away."

"What, and leave you in possession of all this gold? Not likely."

Edward C. Taylor

"Then Running Bear make you. Hate white boy. Not make play this time."

Before Ted was aware of his intention, the Indian had sprung upon him from the side. He was immensely powerful, and forced Ted backward toward the edge of the pit, evidently with the intention of breaking his neck by the fall.

But Ted managed to get a good hold at last, and forced him back gradually.

Then Running Bear came at him with greater strength, and again they wrestled perilously near the edge of the pit.

Running Bear took advantage of Ted's trip over the loose tree roots, and slowly forced him backward, in spite of his herculean efforts, to the pit's edge.

He had bent Ted's head back until his neck cracked, and if he threw him into the pit, it likely would kill him.

From where they stood, on the opposite side of the pit, none of the boys could get a shot at Running Bear without endangering the life of Ted.

It was a pretty tight situation, and the boys were really alarmed for Ted's safety, when out of the woods ran an apparition—a woman so covered with blood as to be unrecognizable. But Stella uttered a scream. She had seen that it was Singing Bird, who had been terribly injured by her brute of a husband, who had evidently tortured her to get from her the information she possessed about the mother lode.

Before any one could divine what she was about to do, the Indian girl had sprung toward Running Bear and plunged a long, keen knife into his back to the hilt.

It was an Indian's revenge. She had given him blood for blood.

Running Bear staggered backward, then suddenly wheeled, caught the knife from the girl's hand, and was about to plunge it into her, when he fell forward on his face and lay quite still.

Singing Bird weaved back and forth for a moment, then she, too, sank to the ground.

When the horror of the sudden tragedy passed from them sufficiently, the boys rushed to the side of the unhappy couple, but they both were dead.

That was the tragedy of the "Mother Lode Mine" on the upper Missouri, which became the property of the Moon Valley Company, and which paid enormously until it worked out, for it was only a pocket, thus putting an end to the placer mining on the islands farther down the river.

The rest is soon told. Barrows was never heard of again, for he knew that if he returned to take a court-martial for his misconduct, he would have fared badly.

That fall the officers at the post sent word to Ted that if his cattle were for sale they would be glad to buy them at his own figure, so that his independence in repudiating the first contract was a good thing after all, for, besides the profits which came from Stella's gold mine, the herd paid handsomely. But Stella never forgot Singing Bird, whose gentle life paid the penalty for the greed for gold. Not far from the mine she was buried, and a stone carved with the story of her death still marks the place where she was laid to rest.

Edward C. Taylor

Choose from Thousands of 1stWorldLibrary Classics By

A. M. Barnard
Ada Leverson
Adolphus William Ward
Aesop
Agatha Christie
Alexander Aaronsohn
Alexander Kielland
Alexandre Dumas
Alfred Gatty
Alfred Ollivant
Alice Duer Miller
Alice Turner Curtis
Alice Dunbar
Allen Chapman
Alleyne Ireland
Ambrose Bierce
Amelia E. Barr
Amory H. Bradford
Andrew Lang
Andrew McFarland Davis
Andy Adams
Angela Brazil
Anna Alice Chapin
Anna Sewell
Annie Besant
Annie Hamilton Donnell
Annie Payson Call
Annie Roe Carr
Annonaymous
Anton Chekhov
Archibald Lee Fletcher
Arnold Bennett
Arthur C. Benson
Arthur Conan Doyle
Arthur M. Winfield
Arthur Ransome
Arthur Schnitzler
Arthur Train
Atticus
B.H. Baden-Powell
B. M. Bower
B. C. Chatterjee
Baroness Emmuska Orczy
Baroness Orczy
Basil King
Bayard Taylor
Ben Macomber
Bertha Muzzy Bower
Bjornstjerne Bjornson

Booth Tarkington
Boyd Cable
Bram Stoker
C. Collodi
C. E. Orr
C. M. Ingleby
Carolyn Wells
Catherine Parr Traill
Charles A. Eastman
Charles Amory Beach
Charles Dickens
Charles Dudley Warner
Charles Farrar Browne
Charles Ives
Charles Kingsley
Charles Klein
Charles Hanson Towne
Charles Lathrop Pack
Charles Romyn Dake
Charles Whibley
Charles Willing Beale
Charlotte M. Braeme
Charlotte M. Yonge
Charlotte Perkins Stetson
Clair W. Hayes
Clarence Day Jr.
Clarence E. Mulford
Clemence Housman
Confucius
Coningsby Dawson
Cornelis DeWitt Wilcox
Cyril Burleigh
D. H. Lawrence
Daniel Defoe
David Garnett
Dinah Craik
Don Carlos Janes
Donald Keyhoe
Dorothy Kilner
Dougan Clark
Douglas Fairbanks
E. Nesbit
E. P. Roe
E. Phillips Oppenheim
E. S. Brooks
Earl Barnes
Edgar Rice Burroughs
Edith Van Dyne
Edith Wharton

Edward Everett Hale
Edward J. O'Biren
Edward S. Ellis
Edwin L. Arnold
Eleanor Atkins
Eleanor Hallowell Abbott
Eliot Gregory
Elizabeth Gaskell
Elizabeth McCracken
Elizabeth Von Arnim
Ellem Key
Emerson Hough
Emilie F. Carlen
Emily Bronte
Emily Dickinson
Enid Bagnold
Enilor Macartney Lane
Erasmus W. Jones
Ernie Howard Pie
Ethel May Dell
Ethel Turner
Ethel Watts Mumford
Eugene Sue
Eugenie Foa
Eugene Wood
Eustace Hale Ball
Evelyn Everett-green
Everard Cotes
F. H. Cheley
F. J. Cross
F. Marion Crawford
Fannie E. Newberry
Federick Austin Ogg
Ferdinand Ossendowski
Fergus Hume
Florence A. Kilpatrick
Fremont B. Deering
Francis Bacon
Francis Darwin
Frances Hodgson Burnett
Frances Parkinson Keyes
Frank Gee Patchin
Frank Harris
Frank Jewett Mather
Frank L. Packard
Frank V. Webster
Frederic Stewart Isham
Frederick Trevor Hill
Frederick Winslow Taylor

Friedrich Kerst
Friedrich Nietzsche
Fyodor Dostoyevsky
G.A. Henty
G.K. Chesterton
Gabrielle E. Jackson
Garrett P. Serviss
Gaston Leroux
George A. Warren
George Ade
Geroge Bernard Shaw
George Cary Eggleston
George Durston
George Ebers
George Eliot
George Gissing
George MacDonald
George Meredith
George Orwell
George Sylvester Viereck
George Tucker
George W. Cable
George Wharton James
Gertrude Atherton
Gordon Casserly
Grace E. King
Grace Gallatin
Grace Greenwood
Grant Allen
Guillermo A. Sherwell
Gulielma Zollinger
Gustav Flaubert
H. A. Cody
H. B. Irving
H. C. Bailey
H. G. Wells
H. H. Munro
H. Irving Hancock
H. R. Naylor
H. Rider Haggard
H. W. C. Davis
Haldeman Julius
Hall Caine
Hamilton Wright Mabie
Hans Christian Andersen
Harold Avery
Harold McGrath
Harriet Beecher Stowe
Harry Castlemon
Harry Coghill
Harry Houidini

Hayden Carruth
Helent Hunt Jackson
Helen Nicolay
Hendrik Conscience
Hendy David Thoreau
Henri Barbusse
Henrik Ibsen
Henry Adams
Henry Ford
Henry Frost
Henry James
Henry Jones Ford
Henry Seton Merriman
Henry W Longfellow
Herbert A. Giles
Herbert Carter
Herbert N. Casson
Herman Hesse
Hildegard G. Frey
Homer
Honore De Balzac
Horace B. Day
Horace Walpole
Horatio Alger Jr.
Howard Pyle
Howard R. Garis
Hugh Lofting
Hugh Walpole
Humphry Ward
Ian Maclaren
Inez Haynes Gillmore
Irving Bacheller
Isabel Cecilia Williams
Isabel Hornibrook
Israel Abrahams
Ivan Turgenev
J. G.Austin
J. Henri Fabre
J. M. Barrie
J. M. Walsh
J. Macdonald Oxley
J. R. Miller
J. S. Fletcher
J. S. Knowles
J. Storer Clouston
J. W. Duffield
Jack London
Jacob Abbott
James Allen
James Andrews
James Baldwin

James Branch Cabell
James DeMille
James Joyce
James Lane Allen
James Lane Allen
James Oliver Curwood
James Oppenheim
James Otis
James R. Driscoll
Jane Abbott
Jane Austen
Jane L. Stewart
Janet Aldridge
Jens Peter Jacobsen
Jerome K. Jerome
Jessie Graham Flower
John Buchan
John Burroughs
John Cournos
John F. Kennedy
John Gay
John Glasworthy
John Habberton
John Joy Bell
John Kendrick Bangs
John Milton
John Philip Sousa
John Taintor Foote
Jonas Lauritz Idemil Lie
Jonathan Swift
Joseph A. Altsheler
Joseph Carey
Joseph Conrad
Joseph E. Badger Jr
Joseph Hergesheimer
Joseph Jacobs
Jules Vernes
Julian Hawthrone
Julie A Lippmann
Justin Huntly McCarthy
Kakuzo Okakura
Karle Wilson Baker
Kate Chopin
Kenneth Grahame
Kenneth McGaffey
Kate Langley Bosher
Kate Langley Bosher
Katherine Cecil Thurston
Katherine Stokes
L. A. Abbot
L. T. Meade

L. Frank Baum	Paul G. Tomlinson	T. S. Arthur
Latta Griswold	Paul Severing	The Princess Der Ling
Laura Dent Crane	Percy Brebner	Thomas A. Janvier
Laura Lee Hope	Percy Keese Fitzhugh	Thomas A Kempis
Laurence Housman	Peter B. Kyne	Thomas Anderton
Lawrence Beasley	Plato	Thomas Bailey Aldrich
Leo Tolstoy	Quincy Allen	Thomas Bulfinch
Leonid Andreyev	R. Derby Holmes	Thomas De Quincey
Lewis Carroll	R. L. Stevenson	Thomas Dixon
Lewis Sperry Chafer	R. S. Ball	Thomas H. Huxley
Lilian Bell	Rabindranath Tagore	Thomas Hardy
Lloyd Osbourne	Rahul Alvares	Thomas More
Louis Hughes	Ralph Bonehill	Thornton W. Burgess
Louis Joseph Vance	Ralph Henry Barbour	U. S. Grant
Louis Tracy	Ralph Victor	Upton Sinclair
Louisa May Alcott	Ralph Waldo Emmerson	Valentine Williams
Lucy Fitch Perkins	Rene Descartes	Various Authors
Lucy Maud Montgomery	Ray Cummings	Vaughan Kester
Luther Benson	Rex Beach	Victor Appleton
Lydia Miller Middleton	Rex E. Beach	Victor G. Durham
Lyndon Orr	Richard Harding Davis	Victoria Cross
M. Corvus	Richard Jefferies	Virginia Woolf
M. H. Adams	Richard Le Gallienne	Wadsworth Camp
Margaret E. Sangster	Robert Barr	Walter Camp
Margret Howth	Robert Frost	Walter Scott
Margaret Vandercook	Robert Gordon Anderson	Washington Irving
Margaret W. Hungerford	Robert L. Drake	Wilbur Lawton
Margret Penrose	Robert Lansing	Wilkie Collins
Maria Edgeworth	Robert Lynd	Willa Cather
Maria Thompson Daviess	Robert Michael Ballantyne	Willard F. Baker
Mariano Azuela	Robert W. Chambers	William Dean Howells
Marion Polk Angellotti	Rosa Nouchette Carey	William le Queux
Mark Overton	Rudyard Kipling	W. Makepeace Thackeray
Mark Twain	Saint Augustine	William W. Walter
Mary Austin	Samuel B. Allison	William Shakespeare
Mary Catherine Crowley	Samuel Hopkins Adams	Winston Churchill
Mary Cole	Sarah Bernhardt	Yei Theodora Ozaki
Mary Hastings Bradley	Sarah C. Hallowell	Yogi Ramacharaka
Mary Roberts Rinehart	Selma Lagerlof	Young E. Allison
Mary Rowlandson	Sherwood Anderson	Zane Grey
M. Wollstonecraft Shelley	Sigmund Freud	
Maud Lindsay	Standish O'Grady	
Max Beerbohm	Stanley Weyman	
Myra Kelly	Stella Benson	
Nathaniel Hawthrone	Stella M. Francis	
Nicolo Machiavelli	Stephen Crane	
O. F. Walton	Stewart Edward White	
Oscar Wilde	Stijn Streuvels	
Owen Johnson	Swami Abhedananda	
P.G. Wodehouse	Swami Parmananda	
Paul and Mabel Thorne	T. S. Ackland	

www.ingramcontent.com/pod-product-compliance
Lightning Source LLC
Chambersburg PA
CBHW030802260626
47169CB00001B/162